The LEAPS Strategist:

108 Proven Strategies
for Increasing
Investment & Trading Profits

Michael C. Thomsett

MARKETPLACE B
Columbia, Maryl

Also Available from Traders' Library
(www.traderslibrary.com)

LEAPS Trading Strategies: Powerful Techniques for Options Trading Success with Marty Kearney

Learn powerful, proven LEAPS trading strategies from one of The Options Industry Council's popular instructor, Marty Kearney of the Chicago Board Options Exchange, as he presents an in-depth LEAPS trading workshop that covers it all, from the basics to more advanced techniques for incorporating LEAPS into your overall investment strategy. With a detailed online companion manual, you'll learn everything from the key elements for determining LEAPS prices, to methods for using LEAPS to produce monthly income and more!

Item # T197X-982460   Price: $99.00

Understanding Leaps: Using the Most Effective Option Strategies for Maximum Advantage
Marty Kearney and Marc Allaire

In tune with every nuance and unique aspect of LEAPS investing, Marty Kearney and Marc Allaire have written a thorough, "technique-oriented guidebook to the what, when were, why and how" of LEAPS trading. You'll discover not only what they are and how to use them to enhance the performance of your portfolio, but exactly which strategies and equity positions are best suited to LEAPS. Their insight and experience allows you to sail over some of the speed bumps others have hit along the investing road, and hone directly in on the best strategies for success using LEAPS.

Item # T197X-621421   Price: $49.95

LEAPS (Long-Term Equity Anticipation Securities) : What They Are and How to Use Them for Profit and Protection
Harrison Roth

LEAPS continue to grow in popularity and this is the most comprehensive and useful work on the topic. You'll find the latest, most successful strategies for trading LEAPS and reducing risk. Conservative, moderate and aggressive methods are all covered. Plus everything from buying LEAP calls to bear spreads with LEAP calls, trading LEAPS, LEAPS and taxes, and even a worksheet on discipline and LEAPS.

Item # T197X-2497   Price: $60.00

These books and thousands of others are available at:
www.traderslibrary.com
Go there today and experience savings of up to
70% off on all books, videos, DVDs, and more!
Or call us at
1 (800) 272-2855 ext. T197

This book, along with other books, is available at discounts that make it realistic to provide them as gifts to your customers, clients, and staff. For more information on these long lasting, cost effective premiums, please call John Boyer at (800) 272-2855 or you may email him at John@traderslibrary.com

ISBN 1-59280-102-1

Printed in the United States of America.

1 2 3 4 5 6 7 8 9 0

Contents

Introduction

Exploring a New World of Possibilities

Uncertainty—that one factor every investor lives with—is a constant in the market. The chaos we have to accept in short-term price volatility, coupled with the ever-changing market itself, makes investing today far more risky than ever before.

The scandals that came to light in recent years have demonstrated just how much market risk we face every day. The problems associated with corporate management, boards of directors, analysts, and independent auditing firms make stock investing far less safe than we believed in the past. A study of Wall Street also shows that in periods following scandal and price decline, the public has tended to shy away from the market for several years-at least until the memory of the latest scandal faded away. The most recent problems are somewhat different than scandals of the past, because strong new legislation and stock exchange policies have changed the way that corporations, auditing firms, and management can act now and in the future.

What does this mean for you as an investor? While new laws and policies may prevent a repeat of past abuses, they cannot completely protect you; even so, the volatility of today's market (and likely increased volatility in the future) presents you with an opportunity: using options as a means for profiting in the market, while also reducing your exposure to market risks. In the past, the use of traditional listed options provided some advantages, but the short lifespan of listed options also curtailed their potential. This problem is solved with the use of the LEAPS (Long-term Equity AnticiPation Securities) option, which exists for up to three years. A single LEAPS contract can be used to control 100 shares of stock; this allows you up to three years to decide whether to buy shares, sell the contract, or simply allow the LEAPS to expire worthless. This illustration may be the most important use of the LEAPS option in modern-day market investing; however, it is only one of the many possibilities.

The three-year term of the LEAPS opens up significant opportunities for both buyers and sellers; it creates many new and potentially profitable strategies; and it helps both speculators and conservative investors to realize their investment goals. While options in general have the reputation of being high-risk vehicles, this is not necessarily true. Some option strategies are high-risk; others are moderate or even conservative.

In this book, we provide you with a series of strategies, broken down by sections and cross-referenced by indexes to specific pages. Part I shows you how leverage works to maximize capital. By using LEAPS as an alternative to buying stock, you are able to control a greater number of shares, make purchase decisions later, and lock in the price of shares that you ultimately buy. Part II expands on this idea by providing many strategies for hedging your portfolio positions with the use of LEAPS options. It includes explanations of timing advantages, alternative forms of controlling stock through LEAPS buy and sell strategies, and more. Part III provides you with four chapters on the all-important covered call strategy. There is more to covered calls than simply selling a call against stock you hold. You also need to consider whether you are willing to accept exercise; which stocks to pick; and how to roll forward and up to avoid exercise when market value begins to rise. Part IV concludes with an examination of secondary strategies: portfolio insurance, application of strategies, and redesigning your personal investment portfolio.

The book also provides you with valuable cross-reference tools. An Index of Illustrations in the back of the book takes you right to a visual representation of the key strategies; and an Index of Strategies helps you to navigate through the book by directing you to the page where each strategy is located.

Throughout this book, the strategies have been designed to emphasize features that every investor needs and wants. Primary among these is the advantage of leverage, the ability to control 100 shares of stock for a relatively small amount of risk. You will discover the many ways that you can use LEAPS options to your advantage. One premise of this book is that *you* ultimately have to determine what risk level is appropriate in your own circumstances.

One of the more intriguing aspects to LEAPS strategies is the *certainty* that they provide to you. Because the LEAPS contract has a limited lifetime, its value is literally predetermined. The time value-that portion of value relating to time rather than to value in the underlying security-decreases in a predictable pattern over the lifetime of the LEAPS contract, ending up at zero upon expiration. Intrinsic value, on the other hand, will track value in the underlying security on a dollar-for-dollar basis. So value is predictable to the extent that we can accurately predict it, given price movement in the stock itself.

With the ever-present limitations of risk, you can apply LEAPS in a variety of ways to improve overall portfolio returns. For those who are already familiar with basic option strategies, LEAPS can be used to expand the potential, because their lifespan is far longer than the better-known listed option. For those new to the market, LEAPS may well change the way that you approach investing in every respect. The challenges of mastering the terminology of the options market, and then becoming familiar with the mechanics of options trading, are necessary steps in mastering this specialized market. However, once those steps have been completed, you will be ready to take a new look at the whole question of how to enhance profits and leverage capital.

The timing could not be better to take a new look at investing. The entire Wall Street culture is undergoing a period of self-examination following the corporate scandals of past years. New regulations and laws are going to change the way that financial statements are prepared and communicated, audits completed, and every investment decision made. Corporate officers are now required to personally certify their statements, so investors have to expect a period of vastly increased volatility, not only in reported revenue and earnings but as a direct result, in stock prices as well. This higher volatility is going to be unsettling for stockholders who have become accustomed to predictability in financial reporting-even though that predictability was achieved through accounting manipulation and, in some cases, outright fraud. In the new, post-reform environment, investors will have to accept a more uncertain year-to-year reporting outcome.

While investors will have trouble in the short-term identifying appropriate stock investments, the volatility causing that uncertainty is an advantage for LEAPS investors. Higher price volatility invariably means greater opportunities for profits in all options, and LEAPS will benefit more than listed options because their contract lifespan is longer.

The interesting new world of LEAPS investing and speculation is one full of opportunities for the thoughtful investor. The traditional process of placing capital at risk-buying shares of stock in increments of 100 shares is no longer the only way to participate in the stock market. In fact, it is not necessarily the smartest way to buy stock, considering the potential uses of LEAPS as a low-risk alternative. Why place capital at risk buying 100 shares, when their market value might decline? Using LEAPS options limits your risk but locks in your contingent purchase price of stock, for up to three years.

Your investing experience is a reflection of your own willingness to expand your knowledge base. No one strategy works for everyone. Clearly, the options market should only be employed by investors who are experienced and who understand the language, trading procedures, and risks of the options market. The LEAPS market is not for the novice, but it does offer great potential to maximize your capital and to provide yourself with clear advantages over investors using only the more traditional strategies.

There are no guarantees for success, of course. This is why an underlying premise for anyone considering using LEAPS options in their portfolio, is that you need to fully understand the risks as well as the potential for profits. As long as you are aware of those risks, you will be able to join the evergrowing ranks of investors who have enthusiastically employed LEAPS in one way or another, not to aim for the goal of 100% success, but to improve your ratio of successful trades. That is where you gain your edge.

Part I

Leveraging Your Capital: Strategically expanding your investment power

Chapter 1

Options as a Specialized Market:
A gateway to higher profits

Are you comfortable placing capital at risk in the stock market? Recent unpredictability, accompanied by well-publicized corporate scandals, has added great uncertainty to the entire market. The traditional strategies and tools—fundamental analysis, diversification, and portfolio management, for example—do not always provide all of the safety that you need. This uncertainty is aggravated by the loss of confidence in Wall Street institutions, analysts, the regulatory structure, and even independent accounting firms.

In this troubling environment, investors can gain an advantage by using their capital to control blocks of stock and leave open the choice of eventually buying or not. An "option" is just that, a choice. You can exercise an option and buy stock at a fixed price, or you can make a choice to not exercise the option; that choice depends on a comparison between the market price of stock and the fixed price of the option. Historically, investors used listed options for up to eight or nine months to control stock in this manner; but that is not a long period of time. In comparison, the LEAPS, or long-term option may continue to exist for up to three years. Every investor knows that in the market, three years is a long time. A lot can happen in 36 months. Consider, for example, the range of trading and index as well as stock prices you have seen over the last 36 months. Then try to predict what potential changes will occur over the next 36 months. This exercise demonstrates the great opportunities that the LEAPS option provides. It is possible to use LEAPS options today for relatively small amounts of capital, defer a decision to buy for many months; and ultimately, to place more capital at risk only if the stock's price does rise. Because the LEAPS option allows you to fix the price of stock, you will be able to buy shares three years from today, but at today's price.

Options in general

The option contract has no tangible value. It is a "right" only, a contract that provides the buyer or seller with the ability to make decisions concerning the underlying stock. So as an option buyer, you have the right to trade in the underlying stock at a fixed price at any time between your purchase date and the date the option expires. If you buy a call option, you are buying the right to purchase 100 shares of stock at the fixed price, or striking price, of the option. If you buy a put option, you are buying the right to sell those 100 shares.

Sellers of options have the opposite rights. If you sell a call, you are promising to deliver 100 shares of stock at the striking price *if* the option is exercised before expiration date. If you sell a put, you are promising to take delivery of 100 shares of the underlying stock *if* the option is exercised.

A few important concepts about options in general are worth review. First of all, options are traded over the American stock exchanges under a system known as orderly settlement. The Options Clearing Corporation (OCC) ensures orderly settlement, which means that investors can be confident that their options will be transacted without problem. Even when the mix of buyers and sellers is not equal, the OCC equalizes the market. They act as seller to each buyer, and as buyer to each seller. For example, if on a given date sell orders outpace buy orders for a specific option by a margin of four to one, the options investor does not need to be concerned about the disparity; the OCC will pay for the excess sell orders as part of orderly settlement.

The idea goes beyond acting as the opposite side of transactions; the OCC also works with the exchanges in setting fair policies for assigning exercised options; and for ensuring that delivery and settlement of option contracts is done smoothly. The uniformity of the American options market ensures liquidity and fair pricing throughout the system.

Each and every option is defined by specific characteristics. These are:

The underlying stock – Every option relates specifically to one stock (or index). They are not transferable; so an option on Xerox Corporation is always associated with that company and cannot be applied to Kodak or IBM.

Striking price – The option is always identified in terms of its striking price, which is the fixed price per share for the underlying stock. If the option is exercised before it expires, it will be exercised at that striking price, even when current market value of the stock is significantly higher or lower at the time. Considering that a LEAPS contract has a lifetime up to three years, the potential for greater distance between market price and striking price is substantial.

Expiration date – Nothing lives forever, including options. The LEAPS expires at a specified year and month. Once it expires, it ceases to exist and instantly loses all of its value. This predictability ensures that the market value of options will be reflected accurately by expiration, by comparing the market value of the underlying stock to the striking price of the option. If a stock's market value is four points above a call's striking price at expiration, that call will be worth four points ($400); if the stock's market value is at or below the striking price, the call will be worthless. For puts, the same arguments apply, but in the opposite direction. If the stock's market price is lower than striking price by three points, the put will be worth three ($300) at expiration. If the stock's market price is at or above the striking price, the put will expire worthless.

Call or put – Each option is also identified in terms of whether it is a call or a put. A call gives its owner the right to buy 100 shares of the underlying stock at the specified striking price and before expiration. A put gives its owner the right to sell 100 shares of the underlying stock at a specified striking price and before expiration.

The basic strategies for calls and puts is the same whether you employ traditional short-term listed options or LEAPS options. The only difference is the duration of the option itself. There are four basic strategies and all advanced or combined strategies grow out of these. To review:

> ***Strategy # 1 – Basic long bull position*** *Take a long position in calls to (a) profit from increased premium value or (b) exercise to purchase stock.*

Buy calls – The purchaser of a call acquires the right to buy 100 shares of the underlying stock at the fixed striking price, at any time between purchase date and expiration. The buyer may either exercise the call and buy 100 shares, or close the call by selling it and taking a profit or loss.

> ***Strategy # 2 – Basic long bear position*** *Take a long position in puts to (a) profit from increased premium value or (b) exercise to sell stock.*

Buy puts – The purchaser of a put acquires the right to sell 100 shares of the underlying stock at a fixed striking price, at any time between purchase date and expiration. The buyer may either exercise the put and sell 100 shares, or close the put by selling it and taking a profit or loss.

> **Strategy # 3 – Basic short bear position**   *Take a short position in calls to (a) profit from decreased premium value or (b) accept exercise.*

Sell calls – The call seller, or writer, promises to deliver 100 shares of stock at the fixed striking price on or before expiration if that call is exercised. The call seller may await exercise or expiration, or close the call by entering an offsetting buy order and taking a profit or loss.

> **Strategy # 4 – Basic short bull position**   *Take a short position in puts to (a) profit from decreased premium value or (b) accept exercise.*

Sell puts – The put seller, or writer, agrees to accept 100 shares of stock at the fixed striking price on or before expiration if that put is exercised. The put seller may await exercise or expiration, or close the put by entering an offsetting buy order and taking a profit or loss.

The option seller may wait out expiration as long as the risk of exercise is relatively low. For example, if a call seller's option has a striking price of 50, but the stock's market price is now only 35, there are 15 points between the two. As long as the call's striking price is higher than current market value, it will not be exercised.

Option sellers go through the sequence of trades in a direction opposite the well known long position sequence. When you are in a long position, you *buy, hold, and then sell*. When you are in a short position, you begin the series with a sell order and you close the position with a later buy—the sequence is reversed to *sell, hold, and then buy*. This applies whether you go short on stock or write options.

The basic characteristics of calls and puts are compared and summarized in Table 1.1.

CALLS	PUTS
Buyers own right to buy 100 shares	Buyers own right to sell 100 shares
Sellers may have 100 shares called away	Buyers may have 100 shares put to them
Calls are in the money when stock trades above striking price	Puts are in the money when stock trades below striking price
Buyer benefits when stock rises	Buyer benefits when stock declines
Seller benefits when stock declines	Seller benefits when stock rises

Table 1.1 – Attributes of options

These features distinguish the two types of options as well as showing the differences between buying and selling:

- Buyers acquire the right to buy (with calls) or sell (with puts) 100 shares of the underlying stock; each option contract applies to 100 shares. Sellers grant the right to buyers, to call away 100 shares (with calls) or put 100 shares to them (with puts). These possible forms of transaction occur at the option's striking price.
- An in-the-money option is one in which the striking price is lower than current market value of the stock (for calls) or higher than current market value of the stock (for puts).
- The majority of options are not exercised; they either expire worthless or are closed out before expiration. A buyer can make a profit when the stock rises (for calls) or when the stock declines (for puts). A seller profits

when the stock declines (for calls) or when the stock rises (for puts).

Striking price and expiration

The attributes that every option buyer or seller accepts as part of the contract include striking price and expiration. The striking price is the fixed price at which 100 shares will be traded in the event of expiration; the variance between striking price and current market value of stock defines option value. The greater the distance between these two values, the higher the premium value of the option. Of course, depending on the direction of the variance, either buyers or sellers will benefit. Because the LEAPS option lasts far longer than the traditional short-term option, there is more time for these values to develop.

Example: You purchased a LEAPS call and paid 3 ($300), with a striking price on the underlying stock of 50. Today the stock is selling for 62 and the LEAPS call is about to expire. The current value of your LEAPS call is 12 ($1,200). Because the stock is 12 points in the money and the call is about to expire, the option has grown in value. As a buyer, you have a choice of exercising the call or selling it. Were you to exercise, you would buy 100 shares of stock for $50 per share, even though today's market value is $62 per share. If you sell, you would realize a profit of $900 (purchase price of 3 versus today's value of 12). (Note: All examples are given without consideration for the cost of transactions. In practice, you will need to take this cost into account on both sides of the transaction.)

Example: You sold a LEAPS call several months ago for 8, and at the time you had $800 credited to your brokerage account. The stock has not moved much since then and today, the call is worth 2 and is about to expire. You may either wait out expiration, or close out the position with a buy order. If you let the option expire, your entire $800 would be profit; but you continue to leave yourself at risk in the event the stock were to rise above the call's striking price, in which case it would be exercised. In that event, you would be required to deliver 100 shares at the striking price, even though that price would be lower than the stock's current market value. Your second choice is to close out the LEAPS call. It is now worth 2 and you originally sold it for 8; if you buy the contract today, you will realize a profit of $600.

As you can see, the fixed striking price determines premium value for every LEAPS contract. The market value of stock moves but the option's striking price remains constant. This, combined with the pending expiration date, determines not only the value of the LEAPS option, but also the timing of subsequent actions on your part. If you are risking growing losses, you can cut those losses by closing a position; or if you have earned a nice paper profit but risk losing it, you can take your profits now.

Example: You bought a LEAPS put a year ago and paid 11. Today it is worth 8 and the stock appears to be strong and on an upward trend. Because you are long on a put, you risk further decline in value if the stock continues to rise. You decide to sell at 8 and accept the $300 loss, rather than risk losing more value.

Example: You sold a LEAPS call a few months ago and received a premium of 7. Today the LEAPS' premium value has fallen to 2. You decide to enter a closing purchase order and take your profit of $500, out of concern that the underlying stock could begin to rise in value. Were that to occur, your profit could be wiped out very quickly.

Expiration also determines the value of the option as well as your timing. As expiration draws closer, the stock's rising or falling price may affect the LEAPS' value directly. If your option is in the money (meaning the stock's price is higher than the call's striking price or lower than the put's striking price) then the option's market value is going to change point for point with changes in the stock's price. This point for point change is most likely to occur closer to expiration, when time value has evaporated from the option's premium.

Time value and intrinsic value

The option premium consists of two parts: intrinsic value and time value. Intrinsic value can also be called in-the-money value because it only exists when the stock's price is higher than striking price of the call, or lower than striking price of the put. Time value is a reflection of the advantage (or disadvantage) of time remaining in the option lifetime.

This feature of the LEAPS option makes premium value predictable, given the variable of the underlying stock's ever-changing market value. The more volatile the stock's trading pattern, the more likely the LEAPS option value will be higher as a consequence. So the volatility factor, which may also be described as an immediate form of market risk, will have a direct effect on the LEAPS as well.

Intrinsic value is calculated using a simple formula. The striking price is subtracted from the stock's current market value—as long as market value is higher than the striking price (for a call), or lower than the striking price (for a put). When a call's striking price is higher than the stock's market value or, when a put's striking price is lower than the stock's market value, there is no intrinsic value.

Time value is the difference between total option premium and intrinsic value. When the LEAPS contract is out of the money, the entire premium is time value. For buyers, time value is a continual problem because, as time passes, it declines. So even when a stock is inching upward, it may only offset what the buyer paid for the option.

Example: You paid 6 for a LEAPS call several months ago. At that time striking price was 40 and the stock was selling at $38 per share. Your 6 points were all time value. Today, the call is nearing expiration. The stock is selling for $41 and your option is worth only 1 point ($100). Even though the stock has risen three points during the time you owned the LEAPS call, your option has declined five points, all representing loss of time value.

For sellers, time value is a great advantage. Because it evaporates over time, sellers can profit even if the stock moves only a few points or not at all. Given the example above, if you had sold the call a few months ago, you would have received $600. Today, you could buy the option to close the position and take a profit of $500.

Time value changes in a predictable pattern. The LEAPS has a lifetime up to three years, so time value will not change significantly in the early months. As expiration date approaches, though, the decline in time value accelerates and reaches zero at the point of expiration. This pattern of rapid decline in time value is illustrated in Figure 1.1.

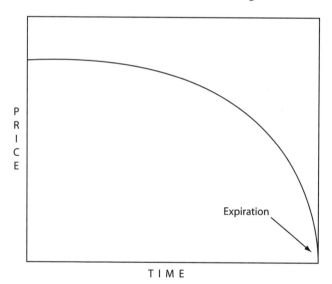

Figure 1.1 ■ Time value course

Sellers can time their trades so that they are exposed in a short position for the least amount of time possible, but to maximize the advantage of declining time value. Buyers, in comparison, need enough rise in intrinsic value to not only gather value, but also to offset declining time value itself. With this in mind, it makes sense to look at the duration of a LEAPS option in a different way. The early months are advantageous to the buyer, because time value declines slowly; but the later months are very disadvantageous, because time value declines more rapidly.

For sellers, the opposite argument applies. Being short on a LEAPS contract for the full three years can be a disadvantage because the stock's price can change a lot during that time. But selling options within four to six months of expiration is a wise strategy, because time value is going to decline rapidly in those later months.

Time is an advantage to the seller, but a disadvantage for the buyer. Regardless of your reasons for trading in LEAPS options, this inescapable fact will dictate your timing and strategies and, ultimately, will also determine whether you earn a profit or suffer a loss. Advanced ideas, such as offsetting buy and sell orders for options on the same stock, or writing covered calls (meaning you own 100 shares of stock for each call you sell) mitigate risks and, in some strategies, ensure profits.

Long strategies and short strategies

Perhaps the most appealing aspect of LEAPS investing is the flexibility this product provides. You are able to identify strategies that fit your personal risk profile precisely; alter your strategies based on changes in the market; and use LEAPS to hedge other positions, insure your portfolio against losses, and combine long and short strategies in any number of ways.

Long strategies—those based on an opening "buy" of options—include the purely speculative and the very conservative. For example, simply buying calls or puts and waiting out price movement in the stock is a very speculative approach. The greater the time until expiration, the better your chances of profiting in this way; you have up to three years for a long speculation to work out. If you are buying options close to the money, you will pay more for time value, and the time value premium will naturally be greater when a corresponding longer time remains before expiration. For the long position, time is the enemy; but with LEAPS options—especially compared to the more traditional short-term option—you have more time for the stock to move in the direction you want.

An example of the time value issue shows the degree of the problem: If you buy a LEAPS option today and there are three years to go until expiration, your premium will be all or mostly time value. This is especially true if you buy an option whose striking price is at or near current market value. So if you buy an option for 12 and it is all time value, you will need the stock to move 12 points up (if a call) or down (if a put) just to break even by expiration. While that is three years out, it is still a considerable move. When you consider the possibility that the stock will not move 12 points or more, and that if it does move it will not always do so in the desired direction, it is obvious that buyers of options face a problem.

> **Strategy # 5 – Long insurance purchase**   *Buy puts to protect a long position in stock from a downward movement.*

An alternative long strategy involves buying puts as a form of insurance for long stock positions in your portfolio. For example, if you own 100 shares of stock, you may purchase a put at or near your original purchase price. In the event that the stock's market value were to fall below that level, your put would increase in value one point for each point of decline in the stock. This is a wise strategy when you want to hold onto the stock but you are concerned about short-term price decline during the next one to three years. Once the insurance put expires, you will need to buy another to continue this protection.

> **Strategy # 6 – Short insurance purchase**   *Buy calls to protect a short position in stock from an upward movement.*

Another type of insurance involves buying one call for every 100 shares you are short on a stock. If the stock's market value were to rise above the striking price of the call, the call would increase in intrinsic value one point for each point lost in the stock short position.

From a practical point of view, buying calls or puts for insurance may not be cost effective. The cash you spend insuring your stock positions adds a requirement for break-even or profit. If investors are concerned about losses, the alternative may be to close out their stock positions until the perceived threat passes.

Short positions involving options are interesting because time value is an advantage. In fact, the greater the time value premium, the higher the profit potential from selling options. Because the seller receives a payment at the opening transaction, especially rich options yield a higher time value premium. In this case, buyers will have difficulty recapturing their investment because time value evaporates over time; this disadvantage for the buyer is an advantage for the seller.

If you sell calls, you face a potential unlimited risk. A stock could rise to any possible market value, especially if given three years to do so. If your short call were to be exercised—and exercise, LEAPS investors should understand, can occur at any time—the short position holder would be required to deliver 100 shares at the fixed striking price.

Example: You sell a call with a 35 striking price when the stock is selling at 32. You receive a premium of 4. But a few months later, the stock begins rising quickly. Within only a few trading days, the market value climbs to 52, or 17 points above the striking price of your short call. If the call were exercised at that point, you would lose $1,300 ($1,700 minus the $400 you received when you sold the call).

> **Strategy # 7 – Basic conservative short** *Sell calls covered by shares of stock to (a) profit from decreased premium value or (b) accept exercise.*

Most investors will not be willing to expose themselves to this much risk. Even though that level of increase in market value is rare in the short term, it does occur so the risk is very real. As an alternative, a highly conservative strategy is selling *covered* calls. In this scenario, you own 100 shares of the underlying stock for each call you sell. Assuming your basis in a stock is 32 and you sell a 35 call for 4, you receive $400, which effectively discounts your basis in the stock down to 28 (32 purchase price less 4 call premium). In this case, exercise would tie in a profit of 7, or $700 (4 points for selling the call plus 3 points in stock profit). That's nearly 22% return, not a bad outcome. Other possibilities are found with covered calls as well. At the time of selling the call in the example above, all four points represent time value. As long as the stock's market value remains at or below the striking price of 35, all premium remains time value. As expiration approaches, the short seller can allow the option to expire worthless, or close the position with a buy order and take a profit on the difference. Once the position is closed, the investor is free to sell another covered call—one further one in expiration date, and with higher time value. As long as the stock's market price remains at or below striking price, this process can be repeated indefinitely. A yield of 4 points on a stock purchase for 32 is 12.5% return—and it could be repeated two or three times per year with proper timing.

You can also sell puts; however, you cannot cover a put the same way that you cover a call by owning stock. When you sell a put, you are exposing yourself to the risk that you will be required to buy 100 shares at the striking price—even if the current market value is lower. For many investors, short puts are not as risky as uncovered short calls. This is true because, while a stock's price may rise indefinitely, it can only fall so far—to zero in theory. In practical terms, a stock will have a safety area, or resistance level based on trading history, book value, and investor perceptions of value. So selling puts is not as risky as selling calls. As long as the stock's market value remains at or above the striking price of the put, it will not be exercised.

Example: You sell a 45 put on a stock currently selling at $46 per share, and receive a premium of 7. As long as the stock remains at or above $45 per share, the put will not be exercised. Without considering trading costs, your risk level in the stock is at $38 per share (striking price of 45 less 7 points you received for selling the call). As long as the stock's market value remains at or above 38, you won't lose money on the short put (not counting the cost of entering and exiting trades).

Combinations

The four basic option strategies—buying calls, selling calls, buying puts, and selling puts—can also be used in many different combinations to form straddles and spreads. These combinations are familiar to traders in short-term options; the same strategies apply to LEAPS contracts as well, with the added flexibility derived from the long-term nature of the LEAPS option.

> **Strategy # 8 – LEAPS spread**   *Buy or sell LEAPS and/or short-term options with different striking prices or expiration dates.*

A *spread* is the purchase and sale of different options on the same stock, but with different striking prices or expiration dates. For example, you create a spread when you buy a call and sell a call at the same time. If the striking prices are different but expiration dates are the same, it is called a vertical spread. If the striking prices are identical but expiration dates are different, it is a horizontal spread. When both striking price and expiration are dissimilar, that is called a diagonal spread. The three configurations of spreads are shown in Figure 1.2

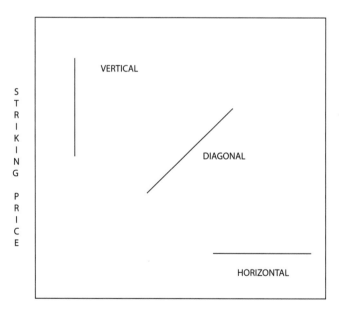

Figure 1.2 ■ Types of spreads

Note that a diagonal spread may have an upward slant (as shown) or a downward slant. An upward slant indicates that the later-expiring side of the spread has a higher striking price.

Spreads can be further distinguished as *bull* or *bear* spreads. A bull spread is designed to creates profits if and when the value of the underlying stock rises; a bear spread is designed to produce profits when the value of the underlying stock declines. The outcome is determined by whether calls or puts are employed in the spread, and by whether the positions are dominated by the "buy" or "sell" side of the spread. Another variation, the *box* spread, is a complex combination involving the simultaneous opening of a bull and bear spread. This combination limits losses but also limits profits.

Spreads of any type have always been difficult strategies when using short-term options, because time itself is so limited. With the LEAPS option, though, the potential uses of spreads is far more flexible and interesting. Employing ratios—having a dissimilar number of options on one side than on the other—is not only possible but practical with LEAPS options, for example. Many strategies for LEAPS options are demonstrated in Chapter 7.

> ***Strategy # 9 – LEAPS straddle*** *Buy or sell LEAPS and/or short-term options—both calls and puts—with the same striking prices and expiration dates.*

A *straddle* is a technique involving the simultaneous purchase and sale of both calls and puts, with the same striking price and expiration date. The basic straddle is meant to have a profitable outcome when the stock moves in either direction. The price movement would have to involve enough points to offset the net cost of opening the option positions in cases where the cost of buying exceeds the cost of selling option contracts. In this case, also called a *long* straddle, the position involves profits above and below a middle range. If the options were to expire within that middle range, losses would be limited to the net cost of the open positions.

A *short* straddle is the opposite: It is designed to produce a profitable outcome if the stock moves only within a medium range. If the stock were to move above or below that range by expiration of the option positions, a loss would result; the more price movement, the greater the loss. Short straddles are normally not desirable because they offer only limited profit potential, but increasing risk of losses on both upside and downside.

Figure 1.3 shows how both types of straddles work, given the possibility that stock prices remain in a limited range; move up; or move down.

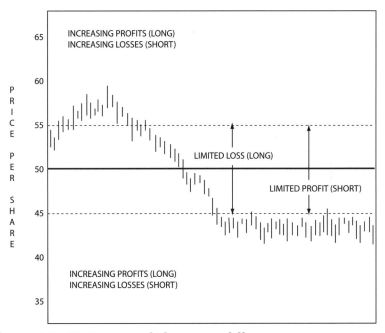

Figure 1.3 ■ Long and short straddles

In the example shown in the figure, we assume that the net receipt or payment for the straddle was five points and that the striking price was 50. For example, when buying options in the straddle, if the put costs 2 and the call costs 3, the total cost is 5; and when selling options in the straddle, if you receive 2 for the call and 3 for the put, you receive a net of 5.

Because the net payment made or received is five points, the straddle creates a five-point limited loss range (in a long straddle) or profit range (in a short straddle). This range will extend in either direction away from the striking price. Once the stock's price moves above 55, the long straddle would produce profits and the short straddle would creates losses. The same is true on the downside; if the stock's price were to fall below 45, the long straddle would produce profits and the short straddle would produce losses. The farther away from striking price the stock's price moves, the larger these profits or losses.

All combination strategies have to be undertaken with the realization that transaction costs have to be considered as well. The example above is given as a demonstration of how the basic strategies work; but when potential profits are marginal, the cost of going in and out of positions can add up quickly and may often make the difference between marginal profits and outright losses. With transaction costs in mind, single-option spread and straddle strategies might simply not be practical. Using multiple LEAPS contracts would produce an economy of sorts, while also increasing both potential profits and risk of losses.

Speculation with options

Once you examine the wide range of possible strategies involving LEAPS contracts, it becomes clear that any number of approaches can be used. More to the point, you can shift from a bull to a bear stance instantly, and visa versa. This flexibility—as well as the potential to employ combinations designed to profit in many different scenarios—lends itself well to speculation.

Most investors will view speculation as too high-risk to fit within their own risk profile. However, even moderate or conservative investors may wish to speculate with a small portion of available capital; and to do so would violate the more permanent investment policy that each individual establishes based on risk analysis. For the outright speculator, interested in better than average yields and willing to accept higher than average risks, the LEAPS contract is both flexible and long-term. In comparison with short-term listed options, which expire in a matter of weeks or months, the opportunities to maximize the speculative approach are limited and rare, and in many cases simply don't materialize. When options are so short-term, opportunities for rapid changes due to deteriorating time value, rapid stock price change, or hedging of other portfolio positions, are impractical. Short-term profit margins often do not justify the risk exposure in these short-term instances. In comparison, the LEAPS option has a lifetime up to three years and many of the speculative strategies work far better.

For speculators, the LEAPS approach makes more sense than short-term options using the same strategies. If a speculator specializes in near-expiration contracts, the predictable changes in time value are going to be identical whether using short-term options or LEAPS options; and if speculators benefit from longer-term time spans, then LEAPS just make more sense, especially when speculators adopt a long position.

Example: You want to speculate by buying options and waiting for stock prices to change enough so that the positions can be closed at a profit. However, with short-term options, time value tends to evaporate far too quickly and, even if stock prices do change in the desired direction (price rise for calls, or decline for puts), the declining time value offsets the gains and it is difficult to profit. With LEAPS, though, you have as long as 36 months to offset time value and have the underlying stock move far enough to produce profits. Using LEAPS contracts for this strategy, you pay more time value premium; but that added time—especially in the earlier months when time value changes more gradually—is a clear advantage.

Conservative strategies

The LEAPS option provides even more benefit to the conservative investor. Of course, buying calls and puts is not usually considered a conservative strategy, and everyone agrees that time works against the buyer. But you can also use LEAPS to insure other positions in your portfolio against loss. Buying calls on securities in which you are short protects you in the event the stock rises; losses in your short stock will be offset dollar for dollar by rises in the in-the-money LEAPS call value. Buying puts on securities in which you are long provides downside protection. If the stock's market value falls, the decline in price will be matched dollar for dollar by increased value in the in-the-money LEAPS put.

One cost feature of insuring portfolio positions is the LEAPS premium itself. While this cost affects your basis and reduces ultimate profits, remember that the LEAPS has a longer life. So as opposed to utilizing short-term options, where the premium has to be repaid every three to six months, you can pay a LEAPS premium once every three years. For many conservative investors, the security of insurance is well worth the relatively small premium cost.

The most profitable conservative strategy is the LEAPS covered call. When you sell a call on a stock and also own 100 shares, the short position is covered. In the event of exercise, you have the 100 shares for delivery, so your risks are limited. You may argue that in the event a stock's price rises significantly, you would prefer to take the profits from increased stock values, over trading that away for a LEAPS call premium. However, you do not necessarily have to accept exercise as an inevitable consequence of rising stock prices. The stock's price may fall back out of the money before expiration; while exercise may occur at any time when in the money, it is more likely to occur closer to expiration. When the stock's price does not rise above striking price, the covered call provides downside protection by reducing your basis in the stock. For example, if you purchased 100 shares at $35 per share and later sold a call for 6, your basis is reduced to $29 per share—because when you sell a call, you receive cash when you open the transaction.

> **Strategy # 10 – Exercise avoidance** *Roll forward and up (for calls) or forward and down (for puts) to avoid exercise of short LEAPS positions.*

You can also avoid exercise by rolling up and forward. For example, if you sell a 35 call and the stock later rises to 38 or 39, you can close out the 35 option and sell a 40 option with a later expiration date. In many instances, the net difference will be a wash or even a credit. You gain more time value by going out farther, so the rolling technique is effective in avoiding exercise, or in deferring it. With short-term options, rolling is limited to a few months; with LEAPS, you can roll forward significantly, producing ever-higher striking price levels *and* increased credits. As long as the stock continues to rise, your covered position can be notched up so that you can avoid exercise or ensure that, in the event of exercise, your profits will be higher. For example, if you originally write a call at 35 and later roll up to a 40 call, you would earn $500 more in the event of exercise.

The flexibility for conservative investors is even further enhanced when working with multiples of options. For example, if you own 800 shares of a particular stock, you may begin a strategy by selling a single covered call. When the stock price rises and goes into the money, you close out the original short position and replace it with three calls with higher striking prices (and, perhaps, a later expiration as well). The net receipt from selling the three calls should be greater than the payment you are required to make to buy and close the original single call. At this point, you would be covered on 300 shares. This scenario can be repeated over and over until all 800 shares are committed to short calls.

This strategy would assume that the stock's price continues to rise indefinitely. If it does, you can avoid exercise while adding substantially to the contingent sales price in the event of exercise. At the same time, there is always the chance that the stock's upward climb will eventually level out, at least temporarily. At that point, your covered calls may be allowed to expire worthless or purchased below their sales price (due to deteriorated time value), producing an overall profit. Once the positions are closed, you would be free to begin a series of covered call transactions all over again.

The covered call strategy produces higher yields than are possible by merely owning stock, in the majority of cases. It is certain that an occasional missed opportunity will arise and some stock will be called away below current market value. That is a trade-off for consistently high returns employing covered calls. By being able to repeat a profitable strategy many times, the potential for conservative investors is worth serious consideration. Overall returns will have three components: capital gains on shares of stock, dividend yield, and of course, profits from option premium.

When you consider the 10 specific strategies we have introduced in this chapter, you can appreciate the flexibility of the LEAPS option as a pool to protect and enhance your portfolio. But this is only the beginning, and there is much more to come. The initial idea of the LEAPS spread and straddle can be expanded upon to help you protect your capital while continuing to expose yourself to opportunities for profit. The fact that you can use options in any type of market—rising, falling, or flat—demonstrates the potential you find in the basic strategies. From there, you are able to explore many more interesting ideas, with varying levels of risk. Chapter 2 begins this exploration, showing how you can use LEAPS to control stock as an alternative to placing your capital at risk by purchasing shares.

Chapter 2

A New Approach:
Strategic buying with LEAPS

C an we depend on our traditional institutions and regulators to protect our interests? Or do we, as individual investors, have to accept the responsibility for risk? Based on what we have learned in observing how the market works, a balanced approach makes sense.

The SEC and the stock exchanges have made great strides to reform their policies and to prevent the types of abuses that have occurred in the past. The Sarbanes-Oxley Act requires personal certification of financial statements on the part of corporate officers; provides strict guidelines for corporate behavior and imposes controls; and goes a long way to prevent conflicts of interest among executives, boards of directors, analysts, and accounting firms. Even so, it is not practical to invest in the market without performing our own due diligence. We need to be aware that even an audited financial statement does not eliminate risk, and that we cannot trust stockbrokers or analysts to protect our capital as carefully as we do ourselves.

Options investors have to gain a level of sophistication, just to master terminology and strategic concepts. That being said, it also makes no sense to depend on outside advisors in the design of portfolios or selection of options for various purposes. By definition, anyone who uses options is going to have to be able to act quickly, to be in charge of their strategies, and to work without dependence on an advisor. To succeed in the market, we need to maintain a positive attitude concerning the culture of the market itself. This does not mean we need to trust blindly or to merely assume that reform is going to fix all of the problems. It does mean that we need to be in charge of our own capital, and to create profitable opportunities for ourselves.

Traditional methods-buy, hold, sell

In the uncertain world of the market, everyone has to make choices. You may invest only in the stock of long-standing, well-known firms; however, even that is not foolproof as an approach to the market. It narrows your potential profitability, because it leaves out up-and-coming new firms with strong competitive motives, new products, and ambitious growth plans-often the best growth investments themselves. You cannot perform fundamental analysis using traditional methods because-we have discovered-skilled accounting professionals are able to falsify the operating results through manipulation, off-balance sheet subsidiaries where liabilities can be hidden, off-shore partnerships that don't show up anywhere on the books, and even outright fraud. The old fundamentals are not adequate to always identify such problems. You also cannot rely solely on technical analysis, which concentrates on price trends, not enough for the more comprehensive approach you need.

The traditional method of "buy-hold-sell" for stocks has to be qualified in the new investing environment. No longer can traditional tests be used without some adjustments. An emerging point of view about corporate reporting is the idea that adjustments need to be made to what corporations report to identify "core earnings"-those earnings related only to the company's primary business. For example, pro forma earnings for pension plan assets would have to be removed from the earnings or re-stated on a more conservative basis; and earnings would have to be reduced to report incentive stock options given to executives and employees. Adjustments to arrive at core earnings can make a substantial difference in reported earnings versus a more realistic picture-but the calculation is important. Standard & Poor's Corporation makes the adjustment using its own core earnings formula to rate corporate debt. This is a major development in the reform trend underway in today's market.

The "buy-hold-sell" approach to investment may continue to be the dominant method for the majority of market transactions. Institutional investors such as mutual funds are often committed to tradition and, because their trades represent the majority of each day's business, the individual has virtually no direct influence on short-term stock price movement. Under the traditional approach, the individual has no choice but to follow the trends that are effectively set by institutional investors.

> **Strategy # 11 – Basic contingent purchase**   *Buy LEAPS calls as a primary form of "contingent purchase" of stock.*

In the new market environment, there may be two distinct and different methods at work. First is the traditional, still dominated by institutional investors. Under this approach, shares of stock are purchased following thorough analysis and held in the diversified portfolio. When signals change or if the estimated growth does not materialize, the institutional investor sells off those shares and places its capital elsewhere. Second is a new approach to investing, primarily suitable for individuals who understand the workings of the market well enough to employ LEAPS options as part of their basic strategy. Rather than outright purchase of shares of stock, the "new investor" buys LEAPS calls in place of stock. With up to three years to go before expiration, this approach locks in the purchase price. If the stock's value declines or remains in the same price range over the three-year period, there would be no reason to exercise the LEAPS call. But if the stock were to rise steadily, the call can be exercised, and the investor then acquires 100 shares per LEAPS contract, but at the fixed price per share that is well below current market value.

Example: You have $10,000 to invest. You can take the traditional approach and split up the $10,000 among one, two or three stocks, buying 100 shares of each. You are especially interested in two issues, one selling for about $40 per share and the other for $60. Under the traditional approach, that would be the obvious move. But you are concerned with the uncertainty and volatility of today's market; so as an alternative, you identify 10 LEAPS calls that you could purchase today, with an average cost of 10 ($1,000) each.

This example is summarized in Figure 2.1

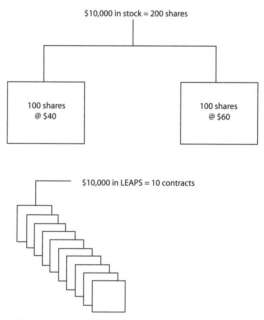

Figure 2.1 ■ **Comparison, stock purchase and LEAPS**

In this scenario, you invest $10,000 in the market whether you buy stock directly or buy LEAPS calls. In the first case, either stock may decline in value and you would lose purchasing power. Your entire $10,000 would be at risk in only two stocks. In the second case, the LEAPS call locks in the striking price on 10 different stocks. Over the next three years, any number of outcomes could occur. Some stocks will rise while others will decline; and some may also just stay within their current price range. You need only a few of the 10 stocks to rise in order to realize a profit on your $10,000 investment. In Chapters 6, 8, and 9, you will also see how the initial long position in several LEAPS can itself be used to create profits between opening the positions and expiration, further enhancing this basic strategy.

The contingent purchase using LEAPS

Using your capital to buy long-term calls instead of shares of stock may be thought of as a type of "contingent purchase" plan. The greatest danger in investing-in any market-is the possibility of loss. This may come about for a number of reasons:

- poor selection of stock based on the fundamentals
- inaccurate or unreliable information provided by analysts or corporations themselves
- poor timing in the market itself
- unforeseen problems, such as expensive lawsuits or labor problems
- cyclical profitability patterns for a specific industry

In modern application, "timing" has a broader problem as well. The markets today are in a state of great uncertainty. This has grown out of a combination of reasons: one was the most expensive scandal in history, the decade-long growing range of problems that has come to be known as "Enronitis." It encompassed a wide range of problems in several industries: the investment market and associated advisors, planners, and other professionals; self-regulatory agencies within the markets; Wall Street firms and their investment banking and research arms; the government, both federal and state and the regulatory industry; the auditing and accounting profession; and the entire business world and its leadership culture. Another was the terrorist attacks of 9/11, which had disastrous effects not only on world events, but on the economy and the markets as well. The attacks and military actions that followed put the markets into a state of uncertainty and, as most observers remind us, investors do not like uncertainty. This has been reflected in the volatility and weakness of the stock market in the years following the 9/11 attacks.

Following periods of scandal or uncertainty, history has shown that a period of unrest is inevitable. The greater the chaos, the longer the period of unrest is likely to be. No one can know how long it will take for the markets to return to "normal" by any measure. We can only look for ways to continue operating as investors without being exposed unnecessarily to market risk. Ironically, the volatility and uncertainty of the markets, while a clear disadvantage for equity investors, can also be a great advantage for those using LEAPS options in place of stock.

Volatility, often used as the most important measurement of market risk, may be a major factor in determining time value levels for LEAPS options. Stockholders view unpredictability in stock prices as one reason to avoid a particular stock. However, as new rules become implemented, stockholders are going to experience greater volatility in stock prices, due to more volatile fundamentals. Among the new rules under the Sarbanes-Oxley Act of 2002 is a requirement that the CEO and CFO of listed companies must personally certify their financial statements. Failing to do so can result in both civil and criminal penalties. This new rule is going to make corporate executives far more conservative in their accounting decisions; so as a result, financial statements are likely to be far more volatile. Revenues and earnings will be less predictable than in the past, because it will be less likely that the numbers will be manipulated to achieve forecasted outcomes.

This volatility in the financial statements will translate to greater volatility in the stock price as well. As stocks become more volatile, Wall Street analysts will need to change their definition of relative volatility. As even the most stable of companies (by traditional measurements) becomes increasingly volatile, stockholders will have growing trouble finding low-risk stock investments (as defined by volatility). Many changes will have to occur in the basic methods that investors use to compare and judge stocks and to assess risk.

The increased volatility (and by traditional definition, risk) of buying shares of stock will require a period of adjustment for stockholders. At the same time, investors who begin using LEAPS call options to lock in prices will not only avoid market risk to some degree; they also will be able to diversify among many different stocks for the same capital investment. So the LEAPS call purchase can be used as a means for reducing market risk while also diversifying their holdings, or at least, their "contingent" holdings represented by locked-in striking price.

The LEAPS life span of up to three years is an extraordinary advantage over the short-term listed option. As most investors already know, a lot can happen in three years. If a stock does decline in value, your loss will be limited to the amount of cash paid out to buy the LEAPS contract. However, if that stock's value rises, the income potential is equal to that of buying stock directly. So using LEAPS options in place of direct purchase of stock eliminates the very market risk that is at the heart of the problem most investors face today. Using traditional short-term listed options, time value decline makes it very difficult to use long calls consistently; there simply is not enough time. With LEAPS calls, the time span up to three years makes the same strategy far more appealing-as well as practical.

The stock buyer's dilemma-capital risk

Let's examine market risk a little further to identify the scope of the problem it poses. Investors understand price volatility quite well, and tend to equate volatility with market risk. This is a purely technical indicator, since it involves price volatility; that can be caused to some degree by fundamental uncertainty, but is far more likely to be the result of non-fundamental causes.

The market's tendency to operate from and react to technical indicators obscures the importance of fundamental analysis. Even those investors who identify themselves as working from fundamentals tend to react and make decisions based on technical indicators: volatility, changes in market indexes like the Dow Jones Industrials, S&P 500, or NASDAQ, and price targets announced by analysts. None of these are fundamentals; it is price itself that *leads* the market, not financial reports. By allowing analysts to establish earnings forecasts and to set price targets, the market as a whole has given far too much power to the establishment of Wall Street, often at the expense of common sense.

Market risk as it is commonly defined has always been price-related and short-term in nature. To be accurate, however, *real* market risk should be value-related and long-term in nature. The disparity between these two contradictory points of view is where LEAPS investors may have their real advantage over stockholders.

Value investing refers to picking investments based on corporate strength and growth potential and is, of course, a long-term effort. Volatility, in comparison is a factor of price trends and is short-term in nature. The short-term is unreliable as a measurement of a trend, a belief that is agreed by the two major schools of thought, the Dow Theory and the Random Walk Hypothesis. Under both of these viewpoints, short-term price change *must* be ignored in the attempt to spot trends, continuation patterns, or reversals within the market. Even so, it is that very thing-short-term price-that defines market risk itself.

Keeping in mind the important distinctions between fundamental and technical approaches to evaluating investments, the LEAPS investor may wish to redefine "market risk." Putting aside the price-oriented and commonly used definition, try this alternative:

> ***Market risk*** *is the exposure that you, as a stockholder, accept in the long-term ownership of stock. The degree of risk is determined by the corporation's ability to create and maintain long-term growth and value to stockholders. This fundamental version of market risk is based on the corporate model of growth and equity strength (revenue projections, maintenance of strong earnings, and careful control over the mix of equity and debt capitalization, for example). The serious long-term investor who bases decisions on these fundamental values chooses stocks based not on short-term price or volatility trends, but on fundamental potential itself.*

This definition serves as the basis for intelligent selection of stock investments. Chapter 11 offers further recommendations for picking stocks; for now, the point to be made is that market risk, the immediate and most obvious measurement of stocks, should be forged as a fundamental test rather than yet another study of price alone.

In selecting stocks based on long-term fundamental understanding of market risk, you will improve your portfolio's overall performance. Even so, you still face the short-term price dilemma that every investor faces: How do you time the selection of stock purchases, given the unreliability of price movement in the immediate future? So much of the difference between profit and loss has to do with timing. For example, investors who entered the stock market *after* the big value declines of 1929 through 1933 made significant profits; but those who put their money into the market in the summer of 1929-when a lot of people did invest-lost most of that value, and the market did not recover its pre-1930 value until the 1950s. This illustrates the potential problems associated with timing.

Even if you are able to identify a handful of companies you consider excellent long-term growth candidates, your timing could be off, even by only a few months. Whenever you buy shares at the market peak, it is going to affect your portfolio's value for a least a few months, and possibly for several years. Using LEAPS calls in place of direct purchase overcomes this problem.

When you lock in a price, your capital can be diversified over many more issues; at the same time, you are not committed to buying shares; that is only a choice you can make in the future. So if it turns out that timing was poor on some stocks, you would not exercise those calls; you would concentrate on those issues whose shares appreciate between the time you open the LEAPS call and expiration.

Overcoming market risk

The strategy of buying LEAPS calls instead of shares of stock, may be thought of as a way to protect yourself against poor timing. This is the key to overcoming, or in some cases eliminating market risk.

No investor can claim to produce 100% profits; that cannot ever be a realistic goal. The wise observation concerning the market is: being right more often than wrong is a reasonable goal. As long as you can reach it, you will profit consistently and be able to make your portfolio grow rather than watching it shrink. Imagine, for example, what a difference it would have made in the year 2000 for investors to buy Enron LEAPS calls instead of stock (and, of course, diversify at the same time by buying calls in other stocks as well). The large number of stockholders who bought up Enron stock had lost most of their capital within two years. This was poor timing and more; the misleading financial statements made the stock look far safer than it was. The point, though, is that buying shares in any company, including Enron, is always going to contain an element of market risk-whether defined in terms of price and timing or in terms of long-term fundamental analysis. No method of stock selection can ensure accurate timing, or even a foolproof method for picking financially strong companies. The case of Enron proves this point; without any doubt, the individual and institutional investors who bought Enron stock believed it was a sound investment, whether based on price trends or fundamental analysis.

Looking backward is always easier than projecting forward, of course. The point to be made here is that using LEAPS calls, with up to three years life span, the short-term problems of technical market risk and timing can be mitigated. You are safer picking 10 stocks and purchasing 10 LEAPS calls at 10 each, than you are buying $10,000 in shares. The outcome is safer as well; you will exercise only those LEAPS calls whose current share price is higher than the locked-in striking price of the calls. That won't necessarily happen in all 10 stocks; but you only need two or three winners to make a profit on the strategy.

Is it wise to put all of your capital into an intangible product such as the LEAPS call? Some traditional advice has to be seriously considered here. Before the days of the long-term option, conservative investors recognized the troubling time value problem associated with going long in options. Even if the underlying stock rises, the declining time value premium offsets at least part of the gain; and it requires a considerable price move in a short period of time, just to break even. For those using short-term options, going long is a high-risk strategy and is not recommended for most investors.

The whole question of risk is different when using LEAPS options, however. This does not mean that it is *always* wise to invest most of your capital in the intangible options market; in some situations, it does not make sense. For example, when the market is over-bought and prices are inflated across a broad market selection of stocks, you could time the purchase of LEAPS calls poorly, even to the point that you would not be able to recover your investment within three years. A slow recovery of price following a market tumble, aggravated by the problem of declining time value, would make even long-term options a poor choice.

When the market is broadly volatile or when prices have been depressed for many months, the opportunities are greater to profit using LEAPS calls. Those who follow market trends know that primary market movements are characterized by pauses and even contrary indicators. If you follow the short-term price trends and recognize these lulls and false indicators within primary trends, you can use LEAPS to better time your entry into stock positions-again, not by going long in stock but by carefully selecting LEAPS calls. This locks in the striking price without risking a larger amount of capital in a volatile market.

It is that very volatility that prevents investors from better timing their purchase decisions. If you were able to always identify buying opportunities, profits would be easy. But in practice, what looks like a low point in today's price trend could quickly become a resistance level for an extended period of soft prices. The opposite is true as well; today's one-year high could easily become the new support level for an entirely new trading range in that stock.

To ensure that you do not miss the opportunities for stocks whose price is going to climb, LEAPS calls are a sound alternative to the risk of buying stock. To avoid the risk of poor timing in stocks whose price ends up depressed over coming months and years, using the LEAPS call prevents you from losing value in large segments of your portfolio. Conservative and moderate investors will shun the common view of options as highly speculative. They will rather come to recognize the strategy of contingent purchase as a method of capital management, and reduction of short-term market risk.

Everyone wants the best of both worlds: excellent short-term timing to avoid technical market risk, with accurate selection of stocks that take advantage of long-term fundamental growth. This is where the use of LEAPS calls to leverage your portfolio expands opportunities while helping to manage those risks.

Leverage advantages

The immediate advantage of buying LEAPS calls is the leverage it creates. In our previous example, we demonstrated the differences between buying 100 shares in two companies through purchase of stock, versus picking up 10 LEAPS calls averaging $1,000 each. Clearly, the LEAPS investor is able to lock in prices on far more equities using this strategy.

Is the trade-off worthwhile? Considering that the LEAPS contract is going to expire, but stockholders can wait out timing problems, the risks associated with long LEAPS positions cannot be ignored. The trade-off is worthwhile assuming several key elements are present:

1. *Stocks are selected properly and carefully.* There is no substitute for picking the right stocks, even if you will be buying LEAPS rather than shares. The fundamental analysis that you perform should be directed toward finding well-managed, competitive, growing corporations whose long-term prospects are better than average. This "value investing" approach is a more practical way to proceed than the more popular price-trend orientation based on technical market risk. Attempting to time the market through a study of price alone tells you nothing about the fundamental strength or weakness of the company; and because short-term price trends are unreliable for picking strong growth stocks, the selection process has to be based on fundamental strength rather than on price trends.

2. *The market is not broadly over-bought.* At times when prices have run up quickly, perhaps to the point that the market is described as over-bought, it is far more dangerous than when prices are depressed. Optimism is dangerous because, (a) it is contagious, (b) it clouds your judgment, and (c) decisions made at such times are invariably wrong. Most people buy at the top and sell at the bottom, so a generally contrarian approach is wise. When prices are high, putting a lot of capital into LEAPS calls makes no sense. (At such times, an alterative strategy is to buy LEAPS puts-see Chapter 4.)

3. *You do not over-commit to the intangible approach.* No single strategy works well in every market, and no single strategy should be used exclusively. Just as it is a mistake to invest all of your capital in tech stocks or retail, it is also a mistake to use LEAPS calls as your only strategy. A diversified portfolio works, but only when you also employ a diversified strategy. Some core stocks should remain in your portfolio, others may be

purchased at certain times, and a portion of your capital can then be used for contingent purchase using the LEAPS method. The temptation to use any one approach because it was profitable last month or last year, should be resisted. The ever-changing environment of the market means that no one strategy is ever safe all by itself.

<blockquote>

Strategy # 12 – Close to the money position
Balance considerations of cost with likely appreciation.

</blockquote>

4. *You select calls realistically in every respect.* No strategy is foolproof. It is all too easy to buy LEAPS calls unwisely, just as it is easy to buy the right stock at the wrong time. Two elements have to be balanced carefully. First, even when you have three years until expiration, you do not want to pay too much for time value. When interest is very high in a stock, and when price volatility is high, there is a tendency for time value to be inflated as well. (This is a great opportunity for *selling* covered calls as described in Chapters 6, 8, and 9, but a poor situation for buying LEAPS calls). Second, you need to select LEAPS calls whose striking price and market value are not too far apart.

<blockquote>

Strategy # 13 – Far out of the money position
Reduce premium cost by picking low-priced LEAPS options.

</blockquote>

You can pick up LEAPS calls far out of the money for very little investment, because the chances that those will be profitable are remote; the farther out of the money, the more remote the chances for profits. So there must be a balance between proximity between striking price and current market value on the one hand, and price on the other.

> **Strategy # 14 – In the money position**   *Seek point-for-point movement with leveraged investment in in-the-money LEAPS options.*

Yet another strategy is to buy only in-the-money LEAPS calls, so that the calls will change in value dollar for dollar with movement of the stock (with gradual loss of value due to declining time value premium). The use of out-of-the-money LEAPS options involves less cost because no intrinsic value exists at the time of purchase; however, you need to consider how much time you want to remain in the LEAPS call. If you buy a call with the full three years remaining, you will have to expect to pay more for the benefit of that time; if you buy shorter-term calls, you will pay less but also risk not having enough time for the underlying stock to move significantly.

Remember, the reason for using LEAPS calls is to lock in a price and use capital in a leveraged manner to reduce short-term technical market risk. Doing this properly will require careful balancing between the attributes of the call: premium price, proximity of striking price to current market value of the underlying stock, and time until expiration. By carefully balancing the premium cost with all of these considerations, you will be able to narrow the zone of purchase and maximize the leverage, resulting in solid diversification of the contingent purchase strategy.

Diversification advantages

The concept of diversification applies to LEAPS strategies as with any other method of placing capital at risk. Diversification itself is often misunderstood or underestimated. It has to be more than simply buying many different stocks, if it is to be effective. The purpose to diversification is to mitigate risks and to avoid catastrophic losses that would result from singular causes.

With this distinction in mind, it is not effective to buy several stocks that share the same economic and competitive traits. Whether you buy stocks directly or use LEAPS calls to leverage capital, you will still need to diversify the range of stocks. For example, it would make no sense to buy tech or retail stocks exclusively, as those sectors' stocks would tend to experience similar economic and calendar cycles. So even when leveraging capital to purchase LEAPS calls and lock in striking prices, be sure to diversify among stocks and sectors.

Diversification needs to be put into effect on many levels. On an overall portfolio, you will need to diversify among different markets-stocks, real estate, and money markets, for example. Within a specific market, diversification can and should be accomplished not only by buying in different sectors, but also by buying varying levels of risk. For example, when considering technical market risk, you might wish to diversify among stocks with different volatility levels. If you are primarily interested in long-term growth based on fundamental analysis, diversification can be done by selected stocks in different competitive positions; in sectors with dissimilar markets and potential new product development growth); in stocks with diversified product and service lines of business; or in terms of the management philosophy between different companies.

Diversification can and should take many forms in order to work effectively. While all of these observations apply to stocks, they also apply with equal importance to the selection of LEAPS calls. Remember, the purpose of buying calls is to make contingent purchases, so stocks should be selected not only for the cost levels of the LEAPS contract, but also with the idea in mind that shares of stock may ultimately be purchased and held in your portfolio.

Another, less obvious type of diversification should be made between tangible and intangible products-a distinction that could also be called permanent and finite. Shares of stock are tangible, or permanent investments because (a) they represent real ownership, (b) they require full payment or margin financing, and (c) there is no expiration or deadline. LEAPS options are intangible and finite; they represent a contractual right rather than ownership; (b) they do not require payment of the full price of 100 shares of stock; and (c) there is a specific expiration date, after which the option expires worthless.

It would not be prudent to use all of your capital to buy or sell intangible LEAPS options. However, by the same argument, it also makes no sense to commit all of your capital to long equity positions. If the market moves in the wrong direction, both strategies will fail. The prudent form of diversification allows you to cut losses through LEAPS contract limited commitment; or to wait out a temporary softness in the market by simply holding shares of stock and waiting out the market. Both of these strategies make sense, but neither works effectively if all of your capital is tied up in a single strategy.

Contingent purchase does not always work as effectively as the outright purchase of stock, given the two features unique to stock ownership: your ability to hold shares indefinitely without pending expiration, and dividend income. In volatile times, contingency planning involving the use of LEAPS calls can help you to leverage *and* diversify the use of your capital, which is smart defensive investing as well as good strategy.

It always makes sense to evaluate strategies based on a comparison between risk and potential. This involves worst-case planning (see the next chapter) as a means for ensuring that risk is recognized equally with opportunity. There is a tendency to always see the potential for gain, without recognizing the accompanying potential for loss. This is the most common downfall for investors, who tend to always believe in a stronger future. Worst-case planning can not only protect our positions in the market; it can also open up a series of strategies that you can employ when markets are weak.

Chapter 3

Worst Case Planning:
Strategies for tough times

No strategy is foolproof. The goal of any investing system should be to reduce losses by being right more often than wrong. Experience has shown that following the crowd mentality, taking expert advice, and developing schemes to get rich quick, all fail the ultimate test: performance when you have money at risk.

Theories of investing, whether long-standing and well established, or based on a new twist of an old idea, are just that: they are theories. Intelligent and objective analysis takes us to the unavoidable conclusion that it is impossible to forecast the future, and that any effort to do so can serve to deceive rather than enlighten us. Technicians look for mathematical or price movement patterns to predict short-term price direction. Fundamental analysts study moving averages of revenue and earnings—all trying to arrive at that one, simple, basic piece of knowledge: What is going to happen next?

Under any system or plan, we are going to have losses. If your money is at risk, you have no assurance of being right all of the time, and even if you diversify your capital in the best possible manner, you are exposed to losses. Clearly, some investing decisions expose you to more losses than others. Being short while the market price is rising, for example, is an expensive situation. It can be hedged in many ways, but it remains true that when the market moves in a direction you did not expect (or when it does not move when you need it to) some portion of your portfolio is going to lose value.

We cannot expect any return on investment without exposing ourselves to risk. We struggle continually with the dilemma: We want maximum profits, but we cannot afford to violate our risk tolerance level. This never-ending balancing act between profit and risk characterizes all investing. Successful plans do not aim at eliminating losses altogether; they do include contingency plans to (a) avoid risk, (b) reduce exposure, and (c) take secondary actions when losses do occur.

Studying outcome scenarios

Investors who limit their market exposure to stocks are aware of possible outcomes. The one that all investors seek involves buying at a low point, followed by rapid rise in price and a sale at the top of the market. A second scenario involves selling with a loss to free up capital for reinvestment elsewhere while also avoiding further decline in value. A third scenario involves holding stock for the long term, either because the investor believes in potential growth, or because shorter-term goals have not been met.

LEAPS investors not only face scenarios for their option positions, but also for combinations involving both stock and options. For options alone, outcomes will include a range of possibilities:

1. *Rapid paper profit in the open long position.* As a purely speculative move, the simple purchase and sale of a LEAPS option—like the more familiar listed option—is a desirable outcome because (a) profits can develop very quickly and (b) they tend to be significant in comparison with the amount invested. It is entirely realistic

to expect some portion of speculative long option positions to produce double-digit returns within a matter of days or weeks. The real challenge is in producing such profits consistently. The speculative move is likely to produce more losses than profits. Some speculators fail to take profits when they are available, or to cut losses when it becomes clear that the chances of profit are remote. Remembering that time value is going to offset profits to a degree, you will need more than price movement to make the speculative play worthwhile. For most investors, speculating in rapid price appreciation by going long in LEAPS options is a poor strategy.

2. *Stagnant or losing position in the open long position.* A more common scenario for the speculative long position is the inability to build profits in the open position. With LEAPS, you have a significant advantage over shorter-term listed options, because so much more time is involved; however, the challenge of time value remains. The closer you get to expiration, the more rapidly time value is going to fall. Even when the underlying stock holds its value or appreciates, time value may offset that appreciation. If you paid 5 for a long position call, for example, you break even only if and when the underlying stock moves five points above striking price by expiration. To yield a profit, the stock will have to move more than those five points.

3. *Acceptable profit in the uncovered short position.* If you write short LEAPS calls or puts, you accept considerable risk, but time works for you instead of against you. Writing a short call without also owning the underlying stock exposes you to the risk of exercise. The short call writer hopes that time value will fall out of the premium so that the call can be closed with an offsetting purchase transaction, with the net difference represent-

ing profit. For the uncovered call writer, profit is limited to this difference (unless the call is held until expiration, in which case profit is limited to the amount received when the LEAPS call was sold). An important evaluation to be made is this: Given the limited profit potential in writing uncovered calls, is the risk worthwhile? In many situations, it is not. You may be exposing yourself to significant potential losses in exchange for rather limited profits.

For put sellers, the same guidelines apply with two notable observations. First, the seller of a LEAPS puts should be willing to have 100 shares of the underlying stock put to them at the striking price. In other words, the strategy is sensible when you think of the striking price as a reasonable price, even though market value would be lower if and when the put were exercised. Second, the risk to selling uncovered puts is limited to the difference between the striking price and the realistic book value support level. In theory, the stock could decline to zero, but it is more realistic to consider the underlying company's tangible book value as the real support level. So in all likelihood, the maximum risk in uncovered put selling is the spread between striking price and intrinsic book value, minus premium income received for selling the uncovered put.

> **Strategy # 15 – Short put tangible risk analysis**
> Study the difference between discounted striking price and tangible book value per share, to judge the risk of selling LEAPS puts.

This realistic assessment of risk may be called the "short put tangible risk." As shown in Figure 3.1, the striking price represents the price at which shares will be put to the seller in the event of exercise. The basis in stock would be the striking price, minus premium received for selling the put. The "tangible risk" is the difference between adjusted basis in the stock, and the tangible book value per share. It is conceivable that this tangible risk could be minimal or even non-existent. For example, in cases where the striking price is relatively close to tangible book value, it is also possible that the time value in a LEAPS put will match or exceed the tangible risk price range.

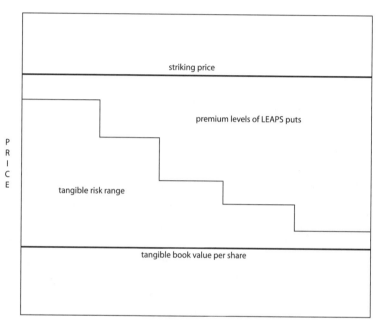

Figure 3.1 ■ **Short Put Tangible Risk**

4. *In-the-money status in the short position—avoiding exercise.* The short seller, always at risk of exercise, may wish to avoid it altogether. This is especially true when (a) exercise will create a loss, or (b) in the covered position, avoiding exercise presents an opportunity for higher profits. A loss can be avoided when a LEAPS option is in the money by rolling forward. Because the roll creates greater time in the replacement option, it is accompanied by more premium as well. It is possible to roll with a net credit or very small debit; when the roll

also goes up in striking price (for calls) or down (for puts), in addition to a later striking price, exercise would require an additional five points in movement.

> **Strategy # 16 – Rolling for striking price levels**
> *Roll forward and up (for calls) or down (for puts) to create higher profits in the event of exercise against short positions.*

An in-the-money short LEAPS call can be rolled forward and up to avoid exercise. This creates a double benefit. In avoiding exercise, the new position may produce a small credit; and by rolling up, the covered call writer creates an additional five points of striking price. This means that even if the new position is eventually exercised, that outcome would produce an additional $500 profit.

> **Strategy # 17 – Acceptance of exercise** *Enter into short positions to encourage exercise, programming profits in both LEAPS call and the underlying stock.*

5. *In-the-money status in the short position—accepting exercise.* Short sellers, as part of their risk evaluation, should be willing to accept exercise as one possible outcome in their position. This may be not only acceptable but desirable at times. For example, a covered call writer who sells a LEAPS call rich with time value receives premium that discounts the basis in the underlying stock. In the event of exercise, the writer will also have a capital gain. So profits would be derived from three sources: capital gain, option premium and dividend. It is not unusual for covered call writers using appreciated stock to receive double-digit returns upon exercise.

Put sellers cannot cover their short positions; however, they may be willing to accept exercise of their LEAPS puts. If the premium received includes substantial time value, that discounts the true price of stock that is put to them. The risk is limited, unlike the same risk associated with selling LEAPS calls; and as described in Chapter 4, the strategy of selling puts and accepting exercise can work as a profitable two-phase strategy.

6. *Offsetting profit and loss in a combination of LEAPS options.* With the many possible combinations—straddles, spreads and hedges—available using LEAPS options, it is entirely possible that a profit in one position is going to be offset by a loss in another. This is the purpose of the combination to a degree: reducing risk exposure while also accepting reduced profit potential. The problem for those using complex LEAPS strategies is the possibility that the degree of risk exposure is not justified by the relatively limited profit potential itself. Some worst-case analysis often reveals this disparity, and the serious LEAPS investor will soon be able to avoid the lost opportunity and unnecessary risk exposure that can arise all too easily.

How the LEAPS trader minimizes losses

In any LEAPS transaction, proper planning and analysis includes developing a contingency plan. You need to evaluate all possible outcomes. The purpose is to avoid any surprises, because surprises most often lead to losses.

As a LEAPS trader, you have the benefit of predictability. You can estimate the decline in time value over the life span of the LEAPS contract; and you know that intrinsic value is going to track changes in the underlying stock on a point-for-point basis. While aberrations occur in time value premium, they tend to be temporary and may represent profit opportunities. The only permanent introduction of uncertainty arises from not properly anticipating likely outcomes in the transaction.

LEAPS traders minimize losses in several ways, including:

1. *Evaluating all possible outcome scenarios.* Any LEAPS strategy can result in a number of different outcomes— it all depends on the direction and degree of movement in the price of the underlying stock and, of course, the time factor. In studying how a position may end up, LEAPS traders have to be continually aware of how time affects their positions. In addition to possible outcomes given price movement occurring in the right time frame, the ever-present outcome that is most significant will be expiration of the contract. This consideration has to rule most heavily in the analysis, and yet many novice LEAPS traders overlook this. For buyers, time is the enemy because price movement has to not only go in the right direction, but also move strongly enough to offset diminishing time value premium. For sellers, time is the big advantage. As long as price movement does not occur by expiration, sellers will profit.

2. *Hedging within LEAPS positions.* Using straddles and spreads as well as complex variations of those strategies, helps you to mitigate risk. To the extent that loss exposure is reduced, income potential is usually reduced as well. The smart strategy is to identify methods for fixing a minimal loss in one outcome, in exchange for potentially rising profit in another outcome. Another way to hedge is by using LEAPS options in conjunction with equity positions. The most conservative strategy is the covered call. The 100 shares held in your portfolio can be given up in the event of exercise, so that the only real risk is lost opportunity, in the event the stock's price rises. This is a minimal risk because (a) by rolling forward and up, you can avoid or defer exercise, and (b) the strategy should always be programmed so that having shares called away is an acceptable outcome.

> **Strategy # 18 – Contingency strategies** *In studying outcome scenarios, identify subsequent actions to increase profits or reduce losses.*

3. *Developing follow-up strategies.* The LEAPS trade should not necessarily be viewed in isolation. Given the long-term life span of the contract, you have an opportunity to play a position in either direction. A follow-up or contingent strategy is always possible. For example, you can buy a long-term LEAPS call and then write shorter-term, higher striking price calls against it. This is technically a spread; however, it is also referred to as writing a covered LEAPS strategy; the long position is covered by the higher short position. Another variety of a follow-up strategy is writing a LEAPS put and (a) waiting for it to expire or (b) accepting exercise and buying 100 shares. As a follow-up, you can then write LEAPS covered calls against those shares. In this example, you are first short with puts and then with calls. That creates two forms of premium income with minimum market risk.

4. *Seeking conservative and low-risk strategies.* For the pure speculator, LEAPS options are the perfect vehicle. They require very little initial investment, but can yield short-term double-digit returns. At the same time, though, the exposure to various forms of risk cannot be ignored. For most investors, LEAPS options in speculative applications are not going to be acceptable. For the more conservative investor, safer strategies can and should be used. The covered call—applied against 100 shares of stock or a long-term LEAPS call—is a conservative strategy. You may also buy a LEAPS call as a form of contingent purchase and reduce the cost by selling calls against it while waiting out the course of price movement in the underlying stock. Fortunately, many low-risk strategies are available for the conservative investor.

5. *Sticking with a smart plan.* Discipline is always at the core of the intelligent LEAPS program. Evaluating outcomes in advance and knowing what to do in each scenario, is the key to the successful program. There is always the temptation to violate your own standards, to go for higher profit or delay making the indicated choice. Because time is always running, LEAPS traders have to follow their plan when certain events occur, or they will end up with losses where they should have had profits. For example, if you have gone long on a LEAPS contract, you might decide that you will close the position if you are able to double your money. However, when premium value rises, you might hesitate, thinking it might produce even more profits; as a consequence, the profits erode as time value falls, and those paper profits are lost forever. This outcome occurs frequently—because the LEAPS trader either does not establish clear policies or does not enforce them.

Alternatives in profit situations

LEAPS traders can reduce or even eliminate losses through hedging strategies or, when writing calls against stock, downside protection (the premium received reduces the basis in stock, creating a price cushion). The other side of the problem—deciding what to do when in a profitable phase—is equally interesting. Just as LEAPS traders need to evaluate possible loss scenarios and follow-up reactions, they also need to decide what actions should be taken when profits exist.

There are three likely methods for dealing with profits:

> ***Strategy # 19 – Profit-taking approach*** *Close positions when they become profitable, and then look for new opportunities.*

1. *Take the profits and close the position.* Perhaps the most obvious action is to simply close the LEAPS option and take profits. If you are long in a call or put, you simply sell and the difference is profit. If you have gone short, a closing purchase transaction also creates profits. In either case, the decision to close frees up the risk exposure and capital to then seek out a new position. It makes sense to close positions if and when alternative strategies would make more sense. For example, if you have sold a LEAPS option and are now in a profitable stance, closing that short position not only eliminates risk and ensures the profits; it also makes it possible to transfer risk to another position that seems more promising in terms of potential profits. If you enter a LEAPS position purely for speculation, it makes sense to also identify a profit target and to take action when that target is reached. It's important to remember that profits can appear and disappear quickly.

> **Strategy # 20 – Long option exercise** *Exercise and then develop additional strategies employing the stock position with LEAPS strategies.*

2. *If long, exercise the option.* Purchasers of options have three possible outcomes: if the value of the underlying stock never exceeds striking price, it will expire worthless. If it is profitable, it can be sold and profits taken. (In some outcomes, the holder will sell because some intrinsic value exists near expiration, but not enough to justify exercise; in this instance, taking a partial loss is preferable to taking a complete loss.) Finally, an in-the-money option can be exercised. As part of a program of contingent purchase, the buyer holds LEAPS calls with the idea that those calls fix the price in the event of exercise, but do not require commitment of capital in the event of a loss. Another version of contingent

purchase involves selling puts (see Chapter 4). Those who buy LEAPS options for the purpose of exercise will either buy 100 shares of stock at the fixed striking price of a call; or they will sell 100 shares of stock at the fixed striking price of a put.

> **Strategy # 21 – Profit cushion position**   *Use existing profits to augment your position, such as the creation of expanded spreads.*

3. *Use the profit cushion to create new strategic LEAPS positions.* The third choice—expanding upon the profit by moving into new positions—is the most complex but also the most sophisticated outcome scenario. Having a paper profit in an open LEAPS option expands the possibilities greatly. The contingent purchase strategy is most profitable when the underlying stock value rises well before expiration; and when you then enter into a spread by selling higher striking price calls (see Chapter 6). This strategy achieves several advantages. First, the cash received for selling the call reduces the original cost of buying the first LEAPS call. Second, it is covered in the sense that, if exercised, you can employ the long call to satisfy the assignment, creating an automatic profit (the short call is sold at a higher striking price than that of the long call, so the difference is a net gain.) Third, by timing the short positions well, you get maximum deterioration in time value between opening the position and expiration. Generally, this time range is the last four months of the LEAPS call's life. In theory, you could sell a number of covered calls against the long call during its life span, and still exercise the LEAPS call and purchase stock.

> **Strategy # 22 – Short put to short call conversion**
> *Double up on short position premium income while discounting your basis in stock.*

Many other variations can be used. For example, if you begin with a short put, that can be offset with a lower-striking price long put or, upon exercise, by writing covered calls against shares of stock. When you convert from the short put to the short call position, you double up on premium income while also discounting your basis in the stock. As a result, even though a an exercised short put creates a disparity (your purchase price will always be higher than current market value), that can be eliminated through LEAPS premium.

Why even enter the short LEAPS position if, in fact, you only end up at a break-even outcome? The reason is that, while break-even basis is the goal in the event of exercise, that is a worst-case outcome; in many situations, the LEAPS put can be closed at a profit, avoiding exercise altogether, or it will expire worthless. So the put writer will be able to write many puts and risk exercise, without having exercise occur in every case.

Rolling forward of long positions

Even though you might be fully aware of the range of possible outcomes in LEAPS trades, it does not follow that any of those outcomes would be desirable. As with all investment strategies, not every trade will be profitable; in those cases, the appropriate goal should be to reduce losses by any practical means available.

For those who open long positions, there comes a point where it is clear that the move is going to lose. In that case, it makes sense to close before expiration and reduce the loss, even if it is only a small reduction. Just as those in profitable positions have the enviable task of having to decide which outcome to pursue, those with losing long positions also need to analyze the situation and to determine how to minimize the damage.

For short positions, there are two possible negative outcomes. First is exercise. The LEAPS writer should be fully prepared for exercise, because it can occur at any time that an option is in the money. For put writers, this means having to be prepared to purchase 100 shares at a price above current market value. For call sellers, it means having to sell 100 shares at a price below current market value. In either case, you should be aware of this potential outcome and be prepared to accept it. If you sell puts, be aware of the tangible book value and its proximity to your discounted basis in the event of exercise (striking price less put premium). As long as this is a minimal range, the paper loss can be reduced or eliminated by writing calls against the long stock. If you have sold a covered LEAPS call, you should ensure that exercise produces a profit in the stock; in that way, exercise is a positive outcome. In that regard, while exercise may be viewed as a negative income, it is accompanied by a profit.

The second potentially negative outcome for LEAPS sellers is when the option is in the money. In this scenario, you may wish to avoid exercise by rolling forward. You can roll *and* create a net credit at the same time. For a LEAPS call, you would close the current in the money position and replace it with a later-expiring, higher striking price call. For a LEAPS put, you would close the current in the money position and replace it with a later-expiring, lower striking price put. In both cases, you avoid exercise by replacing in-the-money options with out-of-the money options.

Example: You sold a July call with a striking price of 50, and received 5. Now the stock has risen to 53 per share and you are concerned about expiration. You close the call for 9 for a loss of $400; and at the same time, you sell an October 55 call, receiving a premium of 6. In this case, you earn $200 (a buy which creates a loss of $400, and a sell for $600). This transaction requires paying $300, but it also creates an additional $500 of striking price in the new call position.

Example: You sold a July 45 put and were paid 4. Now the stock has fallen to 43 and you wish to avoid exercise. You close the July put for 7 and take the loss of 3; and you replace it with an October 40 put, for which you are paid 5. You are required to pay out $200 for the net of these transactions; however, you also build in an additional five points worth of striking price with the lower-expiring put.

Both of these examples are summarized in Figure 3.2

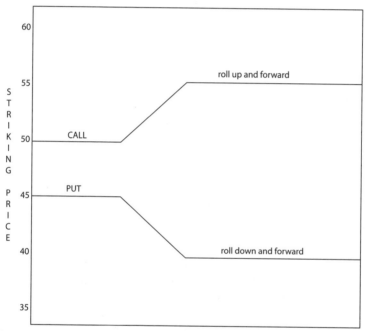

Figure 3.2 ■ Rolling Forward

The roll can be done with the same striking price, in which case you remain in the money but receive a higher premium and a net credit as well; or as demonstrated above, you can roll out of the money as well. Even though rolling out of the money usually requires a net payment, it also enables you to replace the current striking price with a more profitable one.

If this move only serves to defer expiration, it translates to higher profits in the covered call situation; or reduced disparity between striking price and market value in the uncovered put situation.

It makes no sense to roll forward if the move creates a net loss. This has to be defined as a negative effect when differences in premium are considered along with differences in striking price. In the previous examples, it was necessary to pay out additional funds, but those payments were offset by a higher change in future striking price value. An even more favorable outcome is one in which a net credit is created, by rolling forward at the same striking price or by going forward farther than one additional expiration cycle. By rolling forward, you may avoid exercise if the original option is close to expiration, but as always there is no guarantee. By going out two or more expiration cycles, you build in more time value premium, but you extend the period of exposure. Both of these are acceptable as long as you are willing to remain in the modified short position.

In comparison, if you have to pay out a net additional premium that is higher than the future savings in the difference of striking prices, it is not a worthwhile move. For example, if closing a current position requires loss of 9 and you open a new position for 4 or less, then rolling has not accomplished anything—the cost of replacing one option with another is equal to or greater than the potential savings in striking price changes. In such a case, consider going out farther to a later expiration cycle, or just leave things where they are and risk exercise.

> **Strategy # 23 – Roll forward for tax loss** *Use rolling techniques to create a net credit by replacement of options, while creating a tax loss this year.*

When you roll in such a way that the new option does not expire until the following tax year, you also create a tax benefit for yourself. By closing the existing option and taking a loss this year, you can offset other gains and reduce your tax liability; at the same time, profit on the new option position is deferred until the following year. Option profits are taxed or losses deducted in the year the position is closed, even in a short sale transaction. So timing of the roll forward can produce a tax deferral of profit, while also creating a loss in the current tax year.

Letting the LEAPS expire

Is expiration a desirable outcome? It all depends on whether you find yourself in a long or short position, or in a combination. Considering that some profit margins are indeed slim, an outcome can be so close that the difference between small profit and loss comes down to transaction costs. Before entering into a position so close, you should evaluate the risk: Is the exposure justified by relatively small profit potential?

It may be argued that it is only justified to enter *any* LEAPS position when the potential for gain makes it worthwhile, especially when the strategy also minimizes possible losses. The covered call is a fine example of this. As long as the underlying stock has appreciated before the call is sold, virtually all likely outcomes justify the decision. But if the potential margin of profit is slim, it is not a wise move to open a covered call; it involves losing any chance for profit in the event that the underlying stock's value rises significantly, and why risk losing that for marginal profits at best?

In the short position, you may wait out expiration and take a 100% profit on the LEAPS call or put. However, even when the distance between market value and striking price is substantial and chances of exercise slim, it remains possible right up until expiration. So it could occur that the stock's price moves suddenly on the last day and the option is exercised. If you find yourself near expiration with an option holding very little value, it could make sense to close it out, for two reasons. First, you can do so for a minimal cost and it does away with the remote risk of exercise. Second, it frees you to immediately sell another, later-expiring option on the same stock. The sooner you close the previous position, the sooner you replace one with another. It is an individual choice. If you are willing to wait a few days to take 100% profit and avoid the transaction cost required to enter a closing purchase, that is usually a reasonable procedure. It enables you to take a 100% profit with only one transaction cost, rather than the two required to close the position before expiration.

If you own a long LEAPS call or put, the decision to allow it to expire worthless rests with the value, versus transaction cost. If the transaction cost absorbs all of the remaining value, or exceeds it, then you are well advised to just let it expire worthless and take the full loss. This also leaves open the remote possibility that the underlying stock's price will move at the last minute and create a profit, or a small loss rather than a total loss.

Investors have some attributes in common. As a group, they tend to desire a foolproof strategy and that is under-standable. As elusive as that may be, the real purpose in going through the exercise is to mitigate risk. It makes sense to get away from traditional thinking, and to broaden the possible sources for making the most of the market, or for that matter, *any* market. The traditional view is that we make money when the market moves upward, and we lose money when the market falls. LEAPS investors can make money in both markets. The next chapter shows how to profit in a falling market by using LEAPS puts.

Chapter 4

LEAPS Puts:
Betting on the downside

The majority of options traders think in the same terms as stockholders-assuming that prices are going to rise. One of the great flaws among investors in general is the belief that a purchase price-whether stocks or options-is the bottom and that is the point from which prices are going to begin moving upward.

In practice, of course, we know that prices rise *and* fall, and nothing moves continually in an upward line. Even the strongest stocks will experience periods of falling price levels. When price support erodes, a declining price trend can establish itself at least temporarily; this does not indicate that the investment value of the stock has evaporated, only that for the moment, at least, that particular stock's value has declined.

For LEAPS traders, recognizing this reality about the market presents an opportunity to profit, not only when prices are rising strongly, but also when they are falling. In addition to playing price softness using LEAPS puts, even the serious long-term investor interested in acquiring equity can make solid use of puts.

Bear market strategies with LEAPS contracts

The most basic LEAPS put strategy is to buy and wait for prices to fall. As a buyer, the LEAPS trader has the advantage over the listed options trader that up to three years of life span will be involved; however, you will pay for that with increased time value premium.

Just as call buyers have to fight against time value, LEAPS put traders have the same concerns and problems. Your LEAPS put will lose value just due to the passage of time and regardless of what is occurring in the price of the underlying stock. In order to make a speculative profit from buying the LEAPS put, you will need the price of the underlying stock to fall enough to offset time value premium *and* to create enough points of intrinsic value to create a profit.

Example: You bought a LEAPS 50 put when the stock's market value was 53 per share, and you paid 5. Now you have $500 at risk, and the entire premium is time value because the put is out of the money. By expiration, you will need the underlying stock to decline 8 points just to break even. If the stock were to fall to 45 per share, that would yield 5 points of intrinsic value and, at expiration, there would be no time value remaining.

The above example demonstrates that in order for any LEAPS option buyer to earn a profit, a considerable price movement is going to be required. This is a never-ending problem for option buyers in general. The time value is going to reflect the time remaining so that, the longer the life span, the higher the time value premium. That also means you have to experience a higher point spread in the underlying stock before you can expect a profit. Even volatile stocks will not always move in the direction you desire to earn a profit; and limited movement in either direction will do nothing to make the long put profitable.

Any investment in long LEAPS will require a significant degree of movement or a short-term change adequate to create a relatively small profit. The LEAPS speculator can then go in and out of positions and take profits where and when they become available. The problem with this strategy is that earning profits consistently is difficult in long LEAPS. Whether you use calls or puts, you will need to time your purchases perfectly to experience adequate price movement in the right direction.

> **Strategy # 24 – In-the-money put purchase**
> *Select LEAPS puts so that each dollar of decline in the underlying stock will be matched up a dollar of increase in the put's value.*

An alternate strategy is to always purchase LEAPS puts in the money. In this strategy, any price movement will be matched point for point by changes in intrinsic value of the LEAPS put. This is acceptable as long as the underlying stock's price declines in the short term, so the strategy may work when you are convinced that the stock has been overbought. The strategy depends on the market as a whole also recognizing this, and creating enough softness in demand so that prices do fall. Even though the point-for-point change occurs, it is still possible that time value premium will offset part of the momentary profit in the LEAPS put. So even when the strategy is well-timed, it will not always produce the same degree of profits as would be experienced if time value were not a factor.

While in-the-money puts will naturally be more expensive than out-of-the-money puts (because you will be paying for intrinsic value), this remains one form of leverage worth considering. It requires far less risk than the alternative of selling stock short. In the event you time short sales of stock poorly, you could experience significant losses. For a relatively small amount of capital at risk, the purchase of a LEAPS put makes far more sense. It exposes you to the same market opportunities without the same risk. The offsetting consideration is time value and eventual expiration of the LEAPS put; but with a three-year window, that argument is not as serious as the same argument made in reference to short-term listed options.

> **Strategy # 25 – LEAPS puts buy alternative**   *Buy LEAPS puts to achieve the same market position as that of selling uncovered calls, but without the risk.*

Buying puts also opens up the same profit opportunities as selling calls. However, selling uncovered calls is recognized as one of the highest-risk options strategies. In comparison, buying puts limits your risk to the premium you pay. Call sellers are paid a premium while put buyers have to make a payment, so comparing risks has to be adjusted by the spread between these two premium cost/receipt factors.

Example: You are comparing the sale of an uncovered call for 5 and the purchase of a LEAPS put at 4. As a first point of comparison, you acknowledge the potential risk of uncovered calls associated with the risk that the underlying stock's price will rise and the call will be exercised. As a put buyer, you would not be exposed to the same risk. A second point worth considering is the importance of time value premium. As a call seller, you are far more likely to profit due to the decline in time value, so that the position could be closed at a profit even if little or no movement occurred in the underlying stock. As a put buyer, time would work against you. Finally, the premium situation also affects your decision. As a seller of a call, you would receive a payment of $500; as purchaser of a LEAPS put, you would be required to pay $400. This spread of 9 points provides a form of cushion favoring the call sale over the put buy. Now the question you need to address is: Will one strategy be safer or more profitable than the other, with all of the risk and profit factors in mind?

This is the type of analysis that every LEAPS trader needs to undergo in order to determine which strategy makes the most sense. Depending on your personal risk tolerance, you may choose to accept the higher risk of call selling with the greater likelihood of profit due to declining time value (plus the 9-point cushion in the example above); or you might consider uncovered call writing as far too risky, and decide in the alternative to buy the put.

This entire question becomes quite different when you also own 100 shares of the underlying stock. In that case, selling the call would be covered rather than uncovered, which is recognized as one of the safest LEAPS strategies. In that case, selling the call is clearly preferable to buying the put-assuming that the purpose is limited to the creation of profits and not to otherwise hedge the long position in stock. The ownership of stock eliminates the most common risk of selling calls, that the stock will rise significantly and you will have to make up the difference between an exercised market price and the far lower striking price. When you own shares to satisfy the exercise, the covered call is far more preferable to the long put.

The expectation of falling prices

Using puts in anticipation that the underlying stock's price is going to fall, requires a keen sense of market timing. If you are able to estimate the point at which prices have peaked and you know when the stock is overbought, then buying puts is a smart strategy.

> **Strategy # 26 – LEAPS puts buy in place of stock short**   *Buy LEAPS puts to achieve the same market position as that of shorting stock, but without the risk.*

Going long on puts is preferable to shorting the stock. Even though time is going to be a factor, short selling is a high-risk strategy and exposes you to the same risks as those of selling uncovered calls. Considering that the LEAPS put goes out as far as three years, the traditional comparisons between short selling and put buying are not entirely applicable. When comparing short selling to the traditional short-term listed put, a valid argument could be made that the short life span of the put made it an unrealistic alternative to short selling. This argument cannot be used with the long-term LEAPS put. Even with a higher premium for time value, a lot can occur in three years. As long as you are confident that the stock's outlook within the next three years is bearish, then buying puts provides less risk, a high degree of leverage, and greater flexibility.

The LEAPS put is less risky because your loss is going to be limited to the cost of the premium. No matter what kind of movement takes place in the underlying stock, you can never lose more than your premium cost. The shortcomings of long positions in LEAPS are unavoidable and you have to fight ever-declining time value. The only way to overcome this problem is to wait until time value has declined, meaning there is less time remaining until expiration. You may also limit your speculation in long LEAPS puts to those that are far out of the money, meaning the striking price has to be many points below current market value. The farther out of the money, the cheaper the premium cost. Of course, this also requires more point movement in order to create a profit. Again, if you are confident that the trend in the underlying stock is to move to the downside, this strategy gives you three years for a profit to appear in the long LEAPS put.

Leverage is always a significant feature to long positions in LEAPS options. When you buy a put, you have control over the right to sell 100 shares. So if you own those shares, the put gives you the right to sell them at the fixed striking price even if market value has declined far below that level. As a pure speculative move, buying long LEAPS puts opens up the possibility of significant profits for relatively small investment and risk. For example, if a put that cost you 3 points makes an in-the-money downward move of three points immediately after you buy, that is a 100% short-term profit.

As is always the case when you have the potential for big profits, you also face the risk of big losses as well. Even though the capital at risk is relatively small when compared to short selling 100 shares of stock, the risk of loss is always present.

As a purchaser of long LEAPS puts, you also enjoy great flexibility. Of course you can sell at any time and take profits or cut losses. You also can exercise the put and sell 100 shares at the fixed striking price. Or, as yet another alternative, you can create a spread or a straddle, converting the solitary LEAPS put into party of a more complex strategy. You also can buy 100 shares of the underlying stock, recognizing that the LEAPS put protects you against the downside. If the stock's price rises, you make a profit; but if it declines, you can use the put to fix the sales price.

So the long put can work as much more than a purely speculative move. It can also be used to time a series of offsetting strategies when you time your decisions in a volatile market. If you have a good sense of the short-term up-and-down trends of a particular stock, you can alternate between long calls and long puts to maximize profits. A few points of movement in the right direction enables you to take advantage of short-term volatility without placing large sums of capital at risk. By using LEAPS options in this manner, you convert short-term volatility from a negative market factor, into a positive one.

Alternative form of contingent purchase

In Chapter 2, the idea of using LEAPS calls as a form of contingent purchase was introduced. LEAPS puts can be used in a very similar manner, and with better cash flow as well.

When you employ a LEAPS call, you take a long position for up to three years. This requires investing a sum of capital in the hopes that the underlying stock's price will rise. If you are right, you can either sell the LEAPS call at a profit or exercise it and purchase 100 shares at the striking price. This is a well understood use of long LEAPS calls. However, it requires placing capital at risk and, unavoidably, some portion of that capital is going to evaporate due to deterioration in time value premium. It is possible, in fact, that even a well selected stock could produce only small gains, placing you in the worst possible position: ending up with an in-the-money LEAPS call that has less value than you paid for it. Do you sell and accept a loss, or exercise? If you exercise, the cost of the LEAPS call will be greater than the spread between market value and striking price, so you end up in a loss position. This is the problem with using LEAPS calls as a form of contingent purchase. While the strategy makes sense in a volatile market, and is a sensible alternative to placing large amounts of capital at risk in buying stock, there is an even better alternative: selling LEAPS puts.

> **Strategy # 27 – Secondary contingent purchase plan**   *Sell LEAPS puts as a form of contingent purchase of stock.*

By selling LEAPS puts, you place yourself at risk. If the underlying stock's value declines below the striking price of the put, it could be exercised and you will have 100 shares put to you at the higher striking price. Unlike the uncovered call, where the risk is potentially unlimited, the very worst case outcome would be the range between striking price and zero. As a practical matter, the real risk has to be defined as the difference between striking price and tangible book value, minus the premium you receive at the time of sale.

Example: You sell a LEAPS 35 put and receive a premium of 7; the stock's current market value is 36. Tangible book value is $22 per share. Your maximum risk is:

Striking price	$3,500
Less: Tangible book value	2,200
Less: Option premium received	– 700
Net risk	$ 600

In this example, the market value of stock was $36 per share, so the entire put premium is time value. So were the stock to remain above striking price, this entire premium would disappear by expiration. This means that for the exposure, in practical terms, of 6 points, you are very likely to be able to close out the short put and realize a profit.

If, as an alternative, you simply purchase 100 shares, you would pay $3,600 given today's market price. If that price rises, then you would make a profit based on your stock purchase. However, in a volatile market, you might be unwilling to risk $3,600. You may decide instead to sell the put and receive the 7-point premium. In the event of exercise, this gives you 7 points of downside protection, to $28 per share. So if the put were exercised in the range between 28 and 35, you would not have any loss; in fact, your adjusted basis would depend on the exact market price. So if the stock were at 30 at the time of exercise, you would purchase the stock 5 points above current market value; however, your 7-point premium absorbs the difference and provides 2 additional points. In this situation, and not allowing for transaction costs, your true basis in the stock would be two points higher than your discounted purchase price.

As a method for making cash flow in a volatile market, selling puts close to the money brings in healthy time value premium and opens up the chances for short-term profit (from closing positions when time value has declined); and also for buying stock at or near market value when exercise does occur. You may lose some opportunities to buy stock today that will appreciate in value in the near future; but which stocks are going to rise? How can you pick winners every time? Of course, in a volatile market, it is that very problem that keeps so many people out of long stock positions. The concern that short-term price weakness could take months or even years to recapture, is a potentially serious problem that many would-be stockholders cannot afford to risk.

Selling puts cannot be undertaken without limit. You will not be allowed to write uncovered puts without placing capital with your brokerage company to satisfy exercise. So some percentage of your total risk will have to be left on deposit, either in cash or other securities. The strategy works best when you have a base of portfolio stocks you want to hold for the long term and not touch; these can be used as security for your short put strategy.

Exercise is acceptable in this strategy as long as you select puts carefully, and with an awareness of time value premium and the distance between striking price and tangible book value. You can also avoid exercise if desired by rolling forward, a strategy in which you replace the current LEAPS put with a later one with more time value and a lower striking price. This is a wise move when the underlying stock's market value has declined and you see avoiding exercise as a smart move. By moving downward in striking price, you further reduce your real risk, because five points come off the calculation of the difference between striking price and tangible book value.

Example: You sold a 35 LEAPS put and received 7. Tangible book value was $22. However, the underlying stock's market value has declined from 36 down to 31. To avoid exercise, you close the 35 put with a buy of 5 (4 points intrinsic value and 1 point time value); and you sell a later 30 put, receiving a premium of 6. In this example, you receive a net of 1 point but trade out of the 35 striking price and replace it with a 30 striking price. To calculate your net basis in this roll forward and down, calculate the differences using the original premium and adjust for the new premium, but base the real risk on the new striking price:

Striking price	$3,000
Less: tangible book value per share	−2,200
Less: profit on original LEAPS put:	
Sale	$700
Purchase	− 500
	− 200
Less: Sale of new LEAPS put	− 600
Net risk	$ 0

In this example (not allowing for trading costs) the roll forward and down eliminates the risk altogether. If you use tangible book value as a form of fundamental price support, then the market risk is limited to the remote chance that market value will fall below tangible book value. It can and does happen, but the risk is remote.

One problem with the use of short LEAPS puts as a contingent purchase strategy is that the choice is not yours. Exercise is left to the buyer, and that occurs only when the underlying stock's value has declined. In comparison, when you buy calls, you would exercise only in the more desirable situation where the stock's value has risen. With this in mind, an alternative is to combine short puts with long calls.

> **Strategy # 28 – Combination, short LEAPS puts with long LEAPS calls** *Maintain control over the right of exercise, with reduced premium cost by creating a call-put straddle.*

This call-put straddle overcomes the problems associated with using only calls or only puts. With calls, your concern is with diminishing time value *and* the cost involved. With puts, the problem is that even though you receive the premium, exercise is someone else's choice and it occurs only when the underlying stock's value has fallen. With the call-put straddle strategy, the cost of the call is offset by the premium you receive from selling the put. As a result, the true net cost will be relatively small but you will have both open positions, a long call and a short put. If the stock's value rises, the put will lose value and can be closed or allowed to expire; at the same time, you have the choice of selling the call at a profit or putting the contingent purchase into effect and buying 100 shares. If the stock's value falls, the put will be exercised and the contingent purchase goes into effect when the buyer decides; you end up owning 100 shares. If the stock does move enough in either direction, you can close out the put and take a profit; as a result, you still own the call and have up to three years for value to build in the call.

This combination is a smart strategy because it reduces or eliminates your cost while presenting profit opportunities; and still keeps the choice of purchase in your hands if and when the underlying stock's market value rises.

Converting naked puts to covered calls

Selling uncovered LEAPS puts is an excellent form of contingent purchase, even though it leaves the choice of exercise up to someone else. It produces income rather than expense, and exposes you to the same market potential and risk as buying long LEAPS calls. When inadequate movement in the stock is experienced, the LEAPS call buyer loses value. In the same situation, the LEAPS put seller has the chance to close the position at a profit and then sell another put with higher time value.

> **Strategy # 29 – Conversion, put exercise to covered call** When an uncovered LEAPS put is exercised, reduce basis using covered LEAPS calls.

In the event of exercise, the strategy does not have to end. It can be expanded into a three-part program to further discount your basis in the stock and create current income. The three stages are (a) sell the LEAPS uncovered put, (b) take exercise and buy 100 shares, and (c) use the long position in stock to write covered calls, reducing your net basis in the stock.

If you enter into the short position with this three-part plan in mind *and* if you select LEAPS puts with an awareness of the proximity of striking price to tangible book value, then your selection will be made with complete awareness of the likely outcome. You may even wish to sell in-the-money LEAPS puts to maximize premium income, a choice that makes sense when you consider that premium discounts your basis upon exercise. When you sell in-the-money LEAPS puts, you receive a larger premium so, in the event the stock rises, the lost intrinsic value can become immediate profit if you decide to buy out of the position. If the stock's market value remains below striking price, you *invite* exercise by employing only in-the-money puts.

For example, you may compare two different LEAPS puts on the same stock. One is at the money and sells for 4, and the other is five points in the money and sells for 9. The difference of 5 points is all intrinsic value. Upon exercise, the extra 5 points discounts your basis, so it makes no difference which put you sell if exercise is acceptable in your expanded strategy. Remember, too, that if the stock does rise, that intrinsic value will fall point for point with movement in the stock. That could be a quick exit profit for you if that would be a secondary acceptable outcome under this strategy.

Exercise is the second of three steps. You are required to buy 100 shares at the striking price which, at the time of exercise, will be higher than current market value. Here again, if you sold an in-the-money put, you have a greater chance of exercise; but the higher premium income also discounts your basis in the stock. So if you sell an in-the-money put for 9, your basis in the stock will be 9 points *below* striking price.

The third phase in this strategy is selling a covered call against your newly purchased 100 shares. If properly selected, the covered call can offset the paper loss created upon exercise. The combination of the original uncovered put, and the new covered call, both create income and may create a net basis higher than current market value *and* higher than your net cost.

Figure 4.1 presents an example of this strategy. Note the seven points highlighted on this illustration.

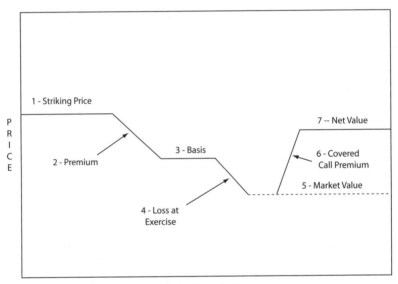

Figure 4.1 ■ Recapturing Short Put Loss

1. This is the original striking price of the LEAPS put.
2. The discount is created by the premium you receive for selling the put.
3. Upon exercise, your adjusted basis would be the striking price minus premium.
4. When the put is exercised, it may occur when market value is lower than your adjusted basis in 3, above.

5. Market value is the current value per share after exercise.
6. The covered call provides additional income, bringing your basis higher than current market value.
7. The net value level represents the difference between current market value and the covered call premium; in the example, this level is slightly higher than the basis.

If you use a call-put straddle to enter this position, the strategy would be identical; the only difference would be that step 2, the discounted price to arrive at basis, would be different. If the put yields more income than the call costs, then the discount would be minimal; if the call costs you more than the put yields, then basis would be higher than the striking price. This trade-off is justified, however, by the fact that in the straddle, you have the opportunity to pick up 100 shares at a discounted basis or, if the stock rises, for little or no net premium cost.

Puts used for portfolio insurance

Yet another practical use for the LEAPS put is to provide insurance for long positions in your portfolio. Anyone who owns stock in a volatile market faces a continual dilemma. Selling stock is undesirable, either because it is below basis or you believe it has long-term growth potential. Still, given the volatility of the market, selling seems like the only sensible course.

> **Strategy # 30 – Long LEAPS put insurance**
> *Manage stock volatility by using long LEAPS puts as form of insurance on long stock positions.*

One solution is to use LEAPS puts to insure your position. One put per 100 shares protects you in the event of a downside movement in market value. The premium cost may be relatively small compared to the potential losses you could suffer. Because the LEAPS put lasts up to three years, the annual cost of insurance is relatively small, especially when compared to the use of short-term listed puts for the same purpose.

The LEAPS put can be structured so that it provides insurance, enabling you to recapture losses in the stock's market value. One strategic solution is to create a buffer between striking price and original cost, so that some or all of the put premium will be recaptured if and when you exercise the put. If market value falls below striking price, you can exercise your long LEAPS put and get rid of the stock, also recapturing premium cost at the same time.

> **Strategy # 31 – LEAPS puts for premium cost insurance**   *Recapture all or part of the put premium if you decide to exercise.*

Example: You bought 100 shares of stock at $29 per share. The value has risen to $37 and you would like to continue holding these shares, protecting your basis. You purchase a LEAPS 35 put and pay 6. If the value of stock were to fall to your original basis or below, you could exercise the put and receive $35 per share. That would replenish your original basis *and* the cost of the put:

Original basis in stock	$2,900
Plus: cost of LEAPS put	+ 600
Exercise price of LEAPS put	$3,500

In this example, the LEAPS put is used to protect the original basis, even though current value of the stock is $37 per share. Were you to buy a 40 LEAPS put instead of the 35, you would receive $500 more upon exercise; but to determine whether that would be worthwhile, you would need to evaluate the additional cost as well. If it were $500 higher in cost, it would not be worthwhile, considering that exercise would only be a contingency at this point. Remember, too, that paying $1,100 for the put would raise your basis to 40. However, if the 40 put could be bought for only 3 points more than the 35, then your basis would be adjusted to 37, which is current market value. In this case, a decline would keep the put in the money, enabling you to exercise at a profit; but if the stock were to rise in value, you could sell it at a profit as well. The "worst" possible outcome in this scenario would be for the stock to remain at exactly $37 per share until the expiration of the LEAPS put, which would leave you at a break-even point.

While you could ignore the use of the LEAPS put altogether and simply sell the stock for an 8-point capital gain, that does not address the larger concern for long-term investors: wanting to retain ownership of stock with long-term growth potential as long as its value is rising-and at the same time being able to offset short-term losses in the event the price does fall. In the more volatile market environments, even long-term investors will be concerned with short-term price decline. By definition, a volatile market is one in which you cannot safely identify support or resistance levels in the underlying stock. This is a serious problem for stock investors, but a situation that opens up many profit opportunities for those using LEAPS options.

You can expand the viewpoint that market prices have to have a bottom and a top, and that transactions are best timed in the traditional manner-buy low and sell high. As the study of puts demonstrates, it is equally possible to buy high and sell low and still earn a profit. When you look at the market through the put looking-glass, you realize that at times, a market high serves as the point where a profitable move begins. This observation opens up a realm of further possibilities, many of which are examined in the next section.

Part II

Hedging with LEAPS — Adding new dimensions

Chapter 5

Time Is On Your Side:
How time value works for you

Time value is unavoidably the *disadvantage* for buyers and the *advantage* for sellers of LEAPS options. In every LEAPS option, time value evaporates as expiration approaches. The rate of decline in time value helps identify the best possible time to trade in a LEAPS option. The rate of decline depends to a degree on the volatility in the market value of the underlying stock, and whether the option is in the money, out of the money or at the money.

In each case, a study of the trading characteristics of a particular series of LEAPS options is going to depend on the stock itself, recent trading history and volatility, and emerging changes in how that stock and its related options are viewed by options traders.

There is no one formula for the best timing for either buying or selling LEAPS options, so you cannot apply a single formula to every possible situation. For example, time value may be richer on one option compared to another, even though time until expiration is identical. One fact is a constant, however: Sellers have a significant advantage over buyers because time value works to their benefit. As a LEAPS seller, you profit the most when time value starts out as high as possible, and declines as rapidly as possible. The recognition of time value as a strategic feature for open short positions in LEAPS also points the way to many profitable strategies.

Using time value strategically-the ratio write strategy

The short-term listed option is going to expire within a few months. From a seller's point of view, this reality leaves very little flexibility. The opportunity to get maximum out-of-the-money time value is limited and, in fact, exceptional opportunities are rare. However, the life span of the LEAPS option-up to three years-provides many deep discount opportunities in time value premium. For example, writing covered calls over most of the 36-month span could produce triple-digit returns based on the original purchase price of stock. Actual outcomes and yields depend largely on (a) original purchase price versus striking price, (b) which options are selected and whether you seek expiration or wish to avoid it, (c) whether you close profitable positions or wait out expiration, and (d) whether you write one-to-one covered calls or employ a ratio write formula.

> **Strategy # 32 – Ratio write position**   *Sell a ratio of higher LEAPS calls against stock to increase profits with minimal added risk.*

An example of the ratio write is to sell three calls against 200 shares of stock. This could be viewed as two covered and one uncovered call. However, it is more realistic to analyze this strategy as a 3 to 2 ratio write. If a significant amount of time value is involved and the options are well out of the money, the ratio write can be a profitable strategy with minimum risk exposure. If the price of stock begins to rise approaching a higher striking price, the change in option value is not going to be affected on a point-for-point basis until striking price has been exceeded. Given the fact that rich time value premium is going to evaporate or, in a rising stock price situation, remain the same, the excess ratio call can be disposed of if you fear exercise. The ratio write positions can also be rolled forward and up to avoid exercise and to extend the opportunity to profit from declining time value.

> **Strategy # 33 – Ratio write roll** *Convert one-to-one covered calls into ratio writes when rolling forward, or rolling forward and up.*

Another profitable use of the ratio write is in expanded one-to-one position. For example, if you write two covered calls against 200 shares of stock, one technique for rolling forward and up is to expand from two to three calls. This creates the ratio write without requiring that you pay out additional cash to avoid exercise. While it increases your risk, it is a viable strategy if the stock tends to experience price volatility-meaning that a current upward movement is likely to be offset by a stabilized trading range or a price decline. In such situations, higher volatility stocks also tend to have richer time value premium, so those investors willing to employ the ratio write can also significantly enhance their covered call writing yield.

The ratio write is a strategy that works well when structured with time value premium in mind. If time value is minimal, it will be difficult to justify the use of the ratio write, since risk is present but potential profit will be limited. As long as you are willing to remain in the "ratio risk" status for several months (meaning you also need to monitor the position regularly), you can not only avoid exercise, but allow that time to work for you. To mitigate risk exposure while maintaining the advantages of being in a covered call position, you can also transfer back and forth from straight covered call status to ratio write status.

Example: You wrote two calls against 200 shares of stock two months ago. As of today, the underlying stock's market value has moved through the striking price and is now 2 points in the money. Simply rolling forward and up will require either additional payment on your part, or going out much farther than the original expiration. A solution is to replace the 2 calls with 3 that are an increment higher in striking price and three months farther out in expiration date. This requires no additional payment and yields a small credit after trading costs.

As long as the stock is in a swing trading pattern, the ratio position can be eliminated as soon as time value declines enough to sell off the extra option. Even if the stock were to rise an additional three points between now and expiration, no change should be expected in time value premium. Given the fact that the roll forward also bought an additional five points in striking price, this provides you with a potential extra $1,000 profit in the 200 shares that are covered. So even if you were to lose on the ratio portion, you have some protection in extra profit built in to the ratio write.

A later roll up and roll forward can also be used to further avoid exercise; however, expanding the ratio in an ever-increasing market value situation could be a dangerous move. It could wipe out your profits and create a net loss eventually. At some point, it would make sense to either accept exercise or sell the excess call and revert to a one-to-one covered situation. However, the ratio write often helps avoid exercise without additional premium costs, create additional profits, and take advantage of the underlying stock's trading pattern. The ideal stock for the ratio write is one with a moderately broad trading range and a tendency toward a wave pattern between the extremes of support and resistance. The ratio write can be used repeatedly while avoiding exercise, turning a sound long-term stock investment into a short-term cash cow. For accepting the possibility of exercise, covered call writing invariably produces double-digit returns when properly structured (see Chapter 9). The ratio write can convert double-digit returns into triple-digit returns-admittedly for a higher level of risk, but with proper management and control, that level of risk can be controlled and managed.

LEAPS traded against listed options

Another strategic approach designed to maximize time value is to create straddles or spreads between LEAPS and short-term listed options. To avoid exposure to uncovered positions, the long side should expire later than the short side. For example, you could sell a short-term listed call and buy a long-term LEAPS call. If the short-term call is exercised, you can use the LEAPS call to satisfy that exercise.

> **Strategy # 34 – LEAPS short-term straddles or spreads**   *Combine LEAPS with traditional options in spread or straddle position, when advantageous.*

The problem with creating such positions is that you will normally have to pay more to buy the longer-term LEAPS than you will receive for selling the shorter-term call. Solutions to this problem include:

1. *Using the ratio write.* You can reduce the cost (or even create a net credit) by using the ratio write. Instead of staying with a one-to-one strategy, write more options short-term than you buy long-term. For example, you could sell three calls expiring in three months, and buy two calls expiring in six months. As long as the net difference in premium is minimal, this reduces your cost. However, it does leave you partially exposed to the danger of exercise against your one uncovered short position. As with any ratio write or uncovered call position, you can avoid exercise by (a) rolling forward and up and (b) selling the excess call or calls in the ratio when time value declines enough to take a small profit or break even.

2. *Shorting on puts when you are willing to accept exercise.*
   Reversing the expiration sequence solves the cash flow
   question and also finances potential future put
   strategies. For example, if you buy a short-term put and
   sell a long-term LEAPS put at the same time, the
   straddle can work to your benefit. The long-term short
   position more than pays for the short-term long
   position, which might end up being profitable (or
   providing insurance for shares of the underlying stock
   that you already own). Once the long-term put expires,
   you can also close the LEAPS put or hold it and revert to
   the contingent purchase plan described in Chapter 4. If
   time value has declined adequately by the time the
   short-term put expires, then the LEAPS put can be
   closed at a profit. If you would prefer to hold the short
   put to wait out time value or to accept exercise, then
   you have that choice as well. You can also avoid exercise
   of the short LEAPS put by rolling forward and down.

3. *Setting up combinations when you own stock to cover the
   short side.* You have a variety of choices when your
   combination serves more than one purpose. For
   example, you could sell a call and buy a put at the same
   time when you own 100 shares of the underlying stock.
   The put provides temporary insurance against the
   downside, while the covered call provides income to (a)
   pay for the put, (b) increase cash flow, and (c) provide
   downside protection. In this case, you can use long-
   term LEAPS calls to maximize time value along with
   LEAPS puts of varying expirations to provide insurance
   or the potential for short-term profits. You can also
   select puts with a different striking price than the calls,
   to minimize the cost while still providing insurance
   protection for your long position in stock.

4. *Pick options to maximize short-side premium and minimize long-side premium.* In analyzing varying premium values of LEAPS and short-term options, your incentive will be to find viable short positions with maximum time value; and viable long positions for minimal premium cost. By combining both expiration date and striking price variations, you can create diagonal spreads and calendar spreads that take advantage of the time premium variation. For example, if you buy a LEAPS call expiring in 15 months and it rises five points, you can take advantage of the paper profit by selling a higher-expiring call that expires in five months. This gives you immediate profit; if the shorter-term call is exercised, you can use the longer-term call to satisfy expiration. For example, you previously bought a 50 LEAPS call that expires in 15 months, when the underlying stock was at 48. Today, the stock's market price has risen to 53 and you sell a short-term 55 call expiring in five months. If the call is exercised, you will be required to sell 100 shares at 55; but you also own the 50 LEAPS call, which you can exercise. The outcome: you purchase 100 shares at 50 and sell them at 55, in addition to keeping the premium on the short call. As long as your net cost for the original option, less the premium you received for selling the short-term call, nets out below 5 points, this will be a profitable transaction. Even as a "worst-case" scenario, breaking even in this strategy is not a negative outcome. When you own the long-term LEAPS call, you have the potential for profit from rising premium or for contingent purchase; as long as short-term calls are not exercised, you can sell them over and over (see Chapter 6). So if there is an exercise of the short position, you have programmed in a break-even outcome to protect

against those risks. In this way, risk is eliminated while profit potential is retained.

Rising market strategies

Any analysis of the strategic use of time value has to be made with market conditions in mind. The strategies in various markets will have to be altered because rising or falling stock prices have everything to do with option values.

Sellers benefit from declining time value; in rising markets, however, it is not time value but intrinsic value that becomes a problem. The seller depends on time value evaporating enough to either offset rising intrinsic value, or to create profits before the stock's price moves beyond striking price. Sellers do not want to be exercised unless that is a part of the strategy itself.

The rolling technique is essential in a rising market. The goal is to avoid exercise without having to give up potential profits. So if you have to pay more to roll forward, that erodes the potential profit that is to be derived from the option premium. For example, if you sell an option for 4 and later roll out of it and pay 6, then you have lost $200. However, if you expand the striking price range and sell a new option for more than 6, that creates a net credit (more profit later upon purchase to close, or upon expiration) *and* avoids or defers exercise.

In a rising market, buyers of options hope that the intrinsic value gains outpace the inevitable time value declines. The buyer benefits from a rising market only when the price rise takes place substantially enough and quickly enough to create the needed profit or to justify exercise if that is the eventual goal. Put sellers also benefit from a rising market for the same reason; however, they are hoping that the stock's market value remains at or above striking price because as sellers, they are hoping for the rapid deterioration of time value. The goal for put sellers is to close the position by purchasing the put for less than they paid; or having the put expire to create a profit.

The most serious problems to be overcome in a rising market are those faced by the sale of a LEAPS call. The call seller may have one of several possible outcomes, including:

1. *Accept and even welcome exercise.* Every LEAPS trader acknowledges the realities of the market. If you go short, there is always a chance the position will be exercised, automatically or at random. This can take place at any time the underlying stock is in the money, although it is increasingly likely as expiration approaches. Option sellers may have a sense of relative immunity from exercise when a lot of time remains until expiration, and this is only a delusion. While the chances are better closer to expiration, you need to be able to accept exercise if and when it happens. In some strategies, exercise is a welcome resolution to the short position. For example, if you own shares of stock that have appreciated significantly, a properly selected striking price would, upon exercise, produce a nice profit. In this situation, exercise is the most profitable exit strategy, because your profits would consist of capital gains on the stock *and* from selling the option.

2. *Wait out the rise in price, assuming that prices may again fall.* You may also hold onto the short LEAPS call position, in the belief that the rise in price of the underlying stock is only temporary and that it is likely to retreat. You only need one retreat for intrinsic value to disappear entirely; and as long as time value has fallen as well, the short position can be bought to close it out at a profit. If your calculation is wrong, you risk exercise. However, if your position is covered, then you will profit from the combination of 100% of the option

premium you received upon sale, and the capital gain on stock.

3. *Balance time value decline against intrinsic value rise, and speculate on intrinsic price movement alone.* As expiration approaches, time value becomes increasingly insignificant. As long as the amount of intrinsic value is less than what you received when you entered the short position, it can be closed at a profit. For example, you sold a LEAPS call a year ago and received 12. Today, the stock's price is 8 points above market value and expiration is coming up soon. You are certain that the call is going to be exercised. If that did occur, you would be required to deliver 100 shares of stock at the striking price, which is eight points lower than current market value. Considering that you were paid 12 for the call, this could be worthwhile as long as the stock's price either falls or does not rise more than three points beyond its current level. You can speculate on falling intrinsic value or wait out exercise; or you could close the position now and take the 4-point profit. Once time value is no longer a factor, you have the opportunity to speculate in this manner, knowing that the option's value is going to mirror movement in the stock's price on a point-for-point basis.

4. *Roll up and forward to avoid exercise.* The standard method for avoiding exercise is to sell more time value while also rolling out of the original striking price and into a higher one. By doing this, you expand your risk exposure period to the later expiration; at the same time you maintain your cash position or even improve it. If your call is covered, eventual exercise brings additional gains in the stock when you roll up diagonally. If your position is uncovered, rolling forward

and up helps you escape the in-the-money status and avoid exercise.

Some option writers like to remain in the risk position indefinitely as long as the market is rising, knowing that they can usually avoid exercise while increasing their profit by perpetually selling time value. For covered call writers, this is an intelligent and conservative method for increasing current income with no market risk to speak of. The major risk is that of a significant decline in the stock's value (a risk you face whenever you own stock). This risk is mitigated by receiving premium for selling the covered LEAPS call. A secondary risk is that of lost opportunity; if the stock were to rise and your 100 shares were called away, you would not receive the total possible profits you would have had if you had not written the LEAPS call. However, experienced call writers know that the potential revenue from selling covered calls is worth the occasional lost opportunity in a rising market.

Falling market strategies

When prices are falling, LEAPS traders need to employ different strategies and timing. For those investors who own shares of stock, selling covered calls provides a degree of downside protection because the premium income discounts their basis in the stock. In fact, a long-term stockholder is able to sell LEAPS calls repeatedly without experiencing exercise and, over time, the net basis in stock can be reduced substantially.

Given that argument, the LEAPS trader still needs to employ different strategies in falling markets than those that work best in rising markets. If you have not owned stock for many years, selling covered calls provides only a limited discount; so if the stock's price falls farther than the option premium, you end up with a loss position in that stock, and will then need to either wait out a reversal in the price trend, or another option strategy.

> **Strategy # 35 – Reverse contingency plan**   *Use a reverse sequence of the short put loss to recover basis when a covered call is exercised.*

When your stock's value has fallen farther than the discounted basis, you can make up the difference by selling a put and entering into the put-based contingent plan explained in Chapter 4. In the falling market, you employ this strategy in reverse. The original idea was to begin without owning the stock; sell the put; accept exercise; and then recover the basis by selling a covered call. In the falling market, the same strategy follows a reverse course: buy 100 shares of stock; sell a covered call; sell a put to recover the net basis. This reversed version of the strategy is shown in Figure 5.1

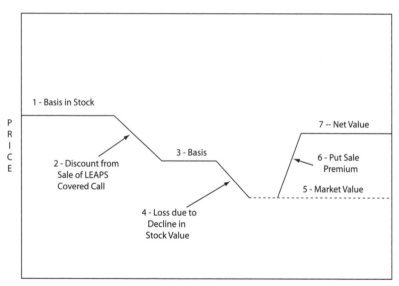

Figure 5.1 ■ Recapturing Covered Call Stock Loss

Note that the structure of the strategy is identical to the explanation in Chapter 4, but the outcome is derived from different causes:

1. We begin with the basis in stock.
2. The basis is discounted by the sale of a LEAPS call.
3. The basis is established below the original purchase price of stock.
4. A net loss occurs when the underlying stock's value falls below the discounted basis.
5. The market value of the underlying stock now resides below the discounted basis.
6. The paper loss is recovered by the sale of a LEAPS put.
7. The net value of the position now is greater than the discounted basis.

This position leaves you with 100 shares of stock as well as two short positions: a covered call and an uncovered put. The call is not going to be exercised as long as the stock's value remains in this range, since market value is lower than striking price. If the price does rise, then the put would not be exercised. Because the call is covered, eventual exercise would be a profitable outcome.

It may be more troubling if the stock's market value continues to fall and the put is exercised. In that scenario, you end up with more shares of stock, and overall market value is lower than your basis. As with any short strategy involving uncovered LEAPS puts, you should ensure that the distance between net basis in stock assuming exercise of the put, and tangible book value per share is not too great. In the example shown in the illustration, basis in the stock would be the average of two purchase prices:

a. the original basis in stock, discounted by the covered call *and* further discounted by premium from selling the put.
b. the striking price of the exercised put.

When this average is calculated and compared to the tangible book value per share, you can calculate whether the strategy is sensible or not. Remember, too, that while tangible book value per share is an estimated "real" bottom for a short put strategy, that does not mean market value will never fall below that level. It is unlikely because as a general rule, stock prices are found at a premium above tangible book value, and this is why this represents a practical support level for the market price. It is an assumed safety point, and not a guarantee. You may also view tangible book value as an identification of bargain price. If market value of stock falls below that level, it is selling at a bargain and picking up additional shares is a smart move.

This argument assumes that tangible book value per share is accurate. As every investor discovered in the year 2002, corporate financial statements can be unreliable. The misleading results reported by Enron, WorldCom, and others demonstrate the on-going need for due diligence. Any case to be made for a LEAPS strategy has to be based on the premise that-before anything else takes place-you have faith in the fundamentals of the company.

That being said, we also need to remember the important distinction between buyers and sellers, with time value premium in mind. The traditional stockholder hopes that at the time of purchase, the stock price is relatively low, and that as soon as possible after purchase, that price will begin to rise. This is a logical premise, but from the point of view of the LEAPS trader, rather unimaginative. With options, you can profit whether markets rise, fall, or remain in a narrow trading range. The buyer's worst enemy-time value premium-works as the most valuable ally of the LEAPS seller. Nowhere is this more true than with the covered LEAPS contract. This is the topic of the next chapter.

Chapter 6

The "Covered" LEAPS Contract:
Lowering the cost of going long

A rather creative approach to the long LEAPS is to enter a "covered" strategy. Because the LEAPS call is long-term, it can be covered, in a manner of speaking, just as 100 shares of stock. So you purchase a LEAPS call, pay a premium, and wait to see whether the stock's price rises or falls. In this initial strategy, you face two problems. First, time value is going to evaporate over time; and the longer the time, the more you paid for time value. Second, you had to pay to buy the long-term LEAPS and you probably would like to get your money back-even if the LEAPS call doesn't hold its value.

Neither of these problems are deal killers. In fact, by using the covered LEAPS strategy, you can eliminate a good part of the cost, and perhaps *all* of the cost. You may even be able to repay your premium cost and still profit from the long LEAPS position. The strategy involves thinking of the long LEAPS call as though it were shares of stock. The traditional "covered call" is created when you own 100 shares of stock and sell a call against it. In the event of exercise, you are required to deliver the 100 shares at the striking price. Because the LEAPS call has a life span up to three years, it can also be "covered" in a sense. Once you own the LEAPS call, you can write shorter-expiration, higher striking-price calls on the same underlying stock. This strategy is the creation of a combination, but it is easier to understand if it is treated just like a covered call-the only difference is that you cover the long LEAPS call instead of 100 shares of stock.

The Covered LEAPS Strategy

The method involved in covering a long LEAPS call is identical to that in covering 100 shares of stock. The major difference is that you are going to be required to have cash or securities on deposit whenever you go short on any option. Policies vary by brokerage firm. As a general rule, a short position also requires deposits; however, some firms may allow an offset between later-expiring long positions and shorter-expiring short positions in calls with equal or higher striking prices. If you are required to also leave securities on deposit, you can satisfy that with stocks held in your portfolio.

> **Strategy # 36 – Covered LEAPS calls** *Sell shorter-term, higher striking price LEAPS calls against existing long LEAPS calls.*

In the basic covered LEAPS strategy, you will purchase a LEAPS call with a life span up to three years. This may be either a speculative move or a contingent purchase (see Chapter 2). As long as the stock holds its value or rises, the value of the LEAPS call will change only to the degree that time value changes and, in the very early stages, this change will be minimal.

The second step involves selling a LEAPS call on the same underlying security, with the same striking price or with a higher striking price. The short LEAPS call will have an expiration that precedes the long LEAPS call position. Thus, if held until expiration, the exposure in the short position expires before the long position. Only in this situation can it truly be called a covered LEAPS call. If the short position has a lower striking price, then you are at risk to the degree of the point spread. For example, if your long LEAPS call has a striking price of 50, and your short LEAPS call is a 45, then you have a five-point exposure. You could justify this risk if, for example, you receive more than 5 points at the time you sell the call. If the option ended up in the money by expiration and was exercised, the position is still covered by your long LEAPS call. However, the covered call strategy is based on the assumption that the short position striking price will be higher and expiration will be shorter.

Example: You purchase a LEAPS call expiring in 32 months with a 40 striking price; the stock's market value is 38 and you pay a premium of 13. The stock moves up to 43 within one year. You sell a LEAPS 45 call on the same underlying stock that expires in six months, and you receive a premium of 6. This premium consists entirely of time value. You expect to close out the position before expiration when time value has declined.

In this example, you could also wait out expiration and the entire $600 would be profit. Or, if the premium value declined to 2, for example, you could close and take a profit of $400. In either event, once you close the short position, you could repeat the strategy, selling another LEAPS call expiring in under six months. As long as the long LEAPS call expires later than the short position, you can enter and exit the short position as many times as you wish. So in this strategy, if you can realize a profit in a matter of days or weeks, it is reasonable to take that profit and then repeat the move again.

> **Strategy # 37 – Rolling short LEAPS calls**   *Close short LEAPS call positions and replace them to increase premium income.*

Example: Given the same facts as in the previous example, the short call is sold for 6. A month later, its value has fallen to 2. You purchase to close and take a profit of $400 (before transaction costs). You immediately sell another LEAPS call, perhaps with a later expiration date (but not later than the expiration of the long LEAPS call). Because expiration is farther away, you receive more in premium.

It is entirely likely that, as long as the underlying stock holds its value, you would be able to sell a series of LEAPS calls covered by the long LEAPS position, and recapture the entire investment cost of the original purchase.

Example: Your long position required an original premium cost of $1,300. If you sell a call against this position for 6, you have already recaptured nearly half your cost. If the short position expires within six months (versus your long position expiring in 32 months), you could repeat this strategy at least five times without trouble. If you began five months after opening the long LEAPS call, you could execute a short position at months 5, 10, 15, 20, and 25 (with the idea of closing the short position and replacing it at each five-month interval. In each case, the short position would expire six months later in this example, providing you time value premium that is perpetually extended with each subsequent sale. If the stock held its position, and you were able to make a net of 4 points on each transaction, that would be a pre-transaction cost profit of 20 points-against the original investment of 13.

The ideal situation, of course, is one in which the value of the underlying stock increases just enough so that time value falls out of each short position, but does not go in the money; and when you are able to receive a premium on ever-increasing striking price levels above the striking price of the long call. In this ideal situation, you have many advantages:

1. You can still carry out your contingent purchase plan using the long position, with the fixed striking price; in the situation where the stock's price rises over the life span of the LEAPS call, you will have a basis below market value when you exercise that call.
2. You recapture your original investment in the long LEAPS call by selling a series of short LEAPS calls with equal or higher striking prices and shorter expiration dates.

3. Exercise is avoided by ensuring that you select out-of-the-money short calls; if the LEAPS calls go in the money, they can be closed or rolled forward. While this may reduce your profit on the short positions, the faster than expected rise in the value of the underlying stock means (a) greater profits in the long position and (b) more flexibility and future profits in selling short LEAPS calls before expiration of the long position.

This scenario is summarized and illustrated in Figure 6.1. Note that the 32-month life span of the long LEAPS call provides an opportunity for five short positions to be opened at five-month intervals between months 5 and 25. In each case, the premise is that the short position will be closed at the fifth month and replaced with a new short LEAPS call with expiration six months later. At each five-month interval, the previous short position is replaced with the new one. Each point at which a new short position is initiated, is marked with a black rectangle.

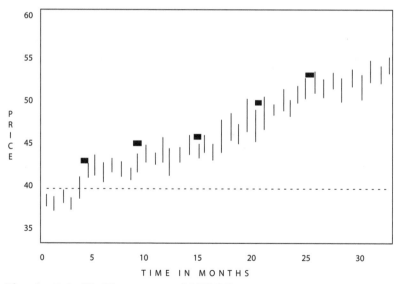

Figure 6.1 ■ The covered LEAPS strategy

In practice, the timing of your decision to close an existing short position and replace it would be based on movement in the underlying stock, and on the status of the short call's value. If you can make a profit relatively quickly, it also makes sense to move in and out of short positions as frequently as you can.

This example is the ideal, involving the case of a stock gradually moving higher with each short LEAPS call position. Of course, if the underlying stock's value were to decline temporarily, the strategy will not work as smoothly. The perfect situation enables you to recover the full cost of the long LEAPS call and even to exceed it; in the life span of the long LEAPS call, it is equally likely that the underlying stock's value will not always rise consistently.

Strategies when the stock's price falls

The illustration involving stock that holds its value or rises over the life span of the LEAPS long position is ideal. When the stock's market value falls, a different strategy has to be employed. We can illustrate how to profit in rising markets, but the reality is that markets may move in any direction. It is most likely that the market for a specific stock will move in both directions during the life span of a LEAPS option-and this is where LEAPS traders have the greatest advantage.

> *Strategy # 38 – Deferred replacement roll*   *Close short LEAPS call positions and wait out subsequent price rises, and then re-enter the covered position.*

In a situation in which you have covered a long LEAPS call with a higher-striking price, shorter-expiration LEAPS call, the temporary downward price movement in the underlying stock is an opportunity. By closing the short position once a downward movement has occurred, you are able to take profits; once the position has been closed, you are free to sell yet another short LEAPS call and re-cover the same long LEAPS position. In theory, you could "ride the wave" of stock price movement, selling short LEAPS calls as prices rise and taking profits as they fall, and continue the pattern for the entire life span of the long LEAPS call.

As long as prices move gradually upward-meaning the trading range is on the rise over time-it is possible to sell a series of covered LEAPS calls and then close them on short-term price corrections. Figure 6.2 shows an example of the underlying stock's ideal trading range and price pattern.

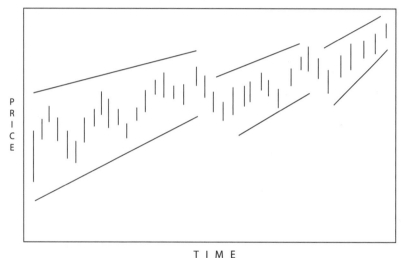

Figure 6.2 ■ Ideal trading range and price pattern of the underlying stock

In this case, three major upward movements each contain several price movements within their trends. Both support and resistance are dynamic over the indicated time, so that two desirable events are underway. First, the long LEAPS call will be increasing in value since its striking price is fixed. Second, a series of LEAPS calls can be sold and covered over time, with each position closed and profits taken as prices test support during the upward trends.

In a less perfect scenario, the stock's price remains within a static trading range or gradually falls over time. If the stock's price remains static, the original contingent purchase plan for the long LEAPS call is in jeopardy, especially as expiration approaches. Even with as long a period as 36 months until expiration, the LEAPS trader needs to evolve a strategy to mitigate or recover the cost of the long LEAPS call.

This is accomplished by selling a series of short LEAPS calls with shorter expiration and higher striking prices-just as in the rising price scenario. However, by selling calls in this manner, two points have to be remembered. First, because they have higher striking prices than the long position, they probably are in the money, which increases the possibility of early expiration. Second, the basic strategy remains intact-buy to close when time and/or intrinsic value have declined. In the event of expiration, the higher striking price of the short call ensures some profit. You would use the long LEAPS call to satisfy assignment of the short LEAPS call; so you buy at a lower striking price than you sell. This strategy depends on calculating your break-even point in the two positions.

Example: You bought a long LEAPS call and paid 11, and later sold a LEAPS call with a striking price 5 points higher. You received 7. At this point, your net cost for the two LEAPS positions is 4 ($400) before trading costs. In the event of exercise, you would also earn a $500 capital gain (exercising your long LEAPS call to satisfy exercise of the short LEAPS call five points higher). Your pre-transaction cost profit would be $100.

If you are able to sell a series of LEAPS calls and close them without exercise, your profits make it increasingly easier to build in the future profits, even when the stock's price is not rising. So this strategy enables you to reduce the net cost of the long position, and perhaps even completely wipe out the net debit; at the same time, exercise would create a profitable exit strategy in those situations where contingent purchase does not work out.

The whole idea of contingent purchase is to actually exercise the LEAPS call and buy stock, but only in those cases where the underlying stock's price rises well above the call's exercise price. In the case of stock not appreciating, the series of sales of LEAPS calls provides the solution: offsetting the contingent purchase investment while creating exercise at a profit. Even though the profit may be small, it wipes out the risk of contingent purchase.

> **Strategy # 39 – Long LEAPS cost reduction**   *Sell a series of short LEAPS calls to offset the original long LEAPS call investment.*

When the price of the underlying stock falls, you cannot afford to sell a series of higher striking price LEAPS calls indefinitely. There comes a point where exercise would create a loss. In this scenario, you certainly can continue to sell LEAPS calls and reduce the cost of the original contingent purchase-as long as exercise would recover the net cost of the entire strategy. If you continue to have faith in the long-term value of the underlying stock, you can also revert to the contingent purchase plan involving puts described in Chapter 4. That would reduce your net investment in the long call while opening up the possibility of having stock put to you at a price above market value. So it is possible to combine the purchase of a LEAPS call (original contingent purchase strategy), the sale of a LEAPS call (covered LEAPS) and the subsequent sale of a LEAPS put (secondary contingent purchase strategy), all at the same time. The creation of the short straddle (LEAPS call and put both open at the same time) reduces the cost of the long position. If the price of the stock is less volatile in either direction, it is likely that both the short call and the short put can be closed profitably.

As long as one or both of the short options have been closed, you can then sell another with a later expiration date (but not later than the expiration of the long position) and gain profit by selling more time value, further reducing your net cost. If you are using the secondary contingent purchase plan, you could even extend beyond the long LEAPS call's expiration-assuming that you continue to view the underlying stock as a desirable long-term investment.

> **Strategy # 40 – Bear market ratio write**   *Sell short LEAPS covered calls against long position LEAPS calls, using the ratio write in a falling market.*

You can manage the falling stock scenario by selling calls in a ratio write. For example, if you have purchased two LEAPS calls, you can sell three LEAPS calls with higher striking prices and shorter expiration dates. This exposes you to greater risks because part of the whole position is uncovered; but in situations where the stock's price has been falling or remaining static, that risk is often manageable. As long as you monitor the ever-changing status of the ratio write, you can sell off the excess call if and when the underlying stock begins to rise and approaches striking price. You also can roll up and forward out of some or all of the ratio write short positions. This avoids the in-the-money status, picks up additional striking price points, and may even create additional net credit. The ratio write is a practical solution to the low-volatility stock whose price is level or falling. However, the astute LEAPS trader is aware of the unpredictability in the market. Today's low-volatility, lackluster stock can change suddenly into a very successful, high-volatility issue.

In the ratio write, actual risk is not the same as it would be with a simple uncovered LEAPS call. Because striking price of the long positions are lower than striking price of the short positions, the potential loss in a rising market situation is limited to the net difference. For example, if you own 2 calls and sell three calls in a ratio write, each point of in-the-money rise is a 3-to-2 loss (rather than a 1-to-1). Even this is not entirely accurate; the 3-to-2 loss is reduced somewhat by falling time value. So as long as the rate of price growth does not outpace the decline in time value, it is likely that the time value will be replaced by intrinsic value, at least to some extent. (The richer the time value premium, the more padding you have in this price differential). With LEAPS options, the time value premium tends to be higher than for comparable short-term listed options, because time until expiration is much farther away; this provides the ratio writer more flexibility, and greater ability to avoid exercise. This occurs through replacement of time value with intrinsic value, possibly with little or no change in net option premium value; and by rolling up and forward to escape the in-the-money status.

The Conversion Strategy: Covered LEAPS to Covered Calls

For those LEAPS traders using the contingent purchase plan, the strategy is not limited to simply buying the LEAPS call and hoping the underlying stock's market value rises. As shown already, you can also sell LEAPS puts as a secondary strategy; combine short positions in calls and puts; and employ the covered LEAPS strategy to reduce the long position's cost.

> **Strategy # 41 – Conversion, long LEAPS to short**
> *Upon exercise of a long LEAPS call, use acquired shares to create stock-based covered calls.*

The contingent purchase strategy employing LEAPS calls can be successfully converted in one of two ways. First is to exercise the LEAPS call and purchase 100 shares of stock. Second is to buy the stock and then sell covered calls. The great advantage to the conversion strategy is that in either case, the purchase price of stock is lower than current market value. This may be viewed simply as downside protection, or as an opportunity to sell covered calls with more flexibility.

The degree of downside protection depends on the net cost of the original long LEAPS call. For example, if you bought the call for 11 and exercised it when stock was 15 points higher than striking price, you have only 4 points of net downside protection. Given the same circumstances, downside protection is increased for the net premium you received for selling calls covered by the LEAPS long position. For example, if you bought the long call for 11 and earned an overall net of 8 by selling calls, your net cost for the long LEAPS was only 3. If the stock's market value is 15 points higher than the striking price at the point of exercise, then your downside protection is 12 points.

It is even possible to increase downside protection *beyond* the price spread between current market value and striking price of the LEAPS call. If you are able to earn more premium from selling covered calls than you paid for the LEAPS call to begin with, then the downside protection is increased by that point spread.

The conversion strategy involving becoming a stock-holder and then selling calls is summarized in Figure 6.3

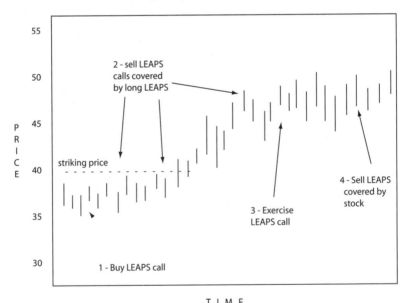

Figure 6.3 ■ The conversion strategy

There are four distinct segments in this strategy:

1. Buy the LEAPS call. In the illustration, the striking price is slightly higher than current trading range of the stock. This holds down the original premium cost, so that no intrinsic value is being purchased. As the trading range begins to grow, time value may fall out but it will be replaced by intrinsic value.
2. During the period following the purchase of the LEAPS call and eventual exercise, one or more LEAPS calls are sold, covered by the long LEAPS. The net receipts from these LEAPS sale premiums reduce the net cost of the long position. Each short position is either bought at a lower premium level than the sale, or held to expiration.
3. You decide to exercise the LEAPS call, picking up 100 shares of stock at the striking price.
4. You sell LEAPS calls against shares of stock, the traditional covered call strategy.

This four-part strategy can have significant profit potential, with likely profits derived from numerous sources:

1. Capital gains on stock and/or long LEAPS
2. Premium from sale of LEAPS calls covered by long LEAPS calls
3. Dividend income, if applicable, earned after exercise of the long LEAPS call
4. Premium from sale of LEAPS calls covered by shares of stock
5. Premium from sale of LEAPS puts if alternative contingent purchase is used

The value of the conversion strategy goes beyond downside protection, and the importance of this feature should not be overlooked. The entire strategy is an outgrowth of the contingent purchase strategy itself. By using short position sales to reduce or entirely eliminate the premium costs associated with contingent purchase, the risk of loss in the long position is also reduced. This frees you to pursue many more contingent positions involving long LEAPS and short LEAPS calls together; the outright sale of short LEAPS puts; or a combination of both. By employing any and all available strategies, the potential for a diversified approach to contingent purchase is going to be limited only by brokerage policies and deposit requirements. As long as the brokerage firm demands that securities or cash be left on deposit in the event of exercise against a short position, the potential is limited to the capital you have available.

This becomes an issue if you use short puts as a primary means of contingent purchase; or if you modify a call-based strategy by creating a straddle to offset paper losses. If you have substantial value in your portfolio, it can be used to protect the brokerage firm against possible losses in the event of exercise. If your primary strategy involves covered LEAPS calls, the requirements on the part of your brokerage firm may be more liberal. As long as the long position has a lower striking price and a later expiration, the firm may allow you to sell calls without any deposit requirements beyond keeping the long position open until (or in case of) exercise of the short LEAPS calls.

Once you complete the four-phase conversion strategy, you can take several different approaches in covered call strategies:

> **Strategy # 42 – Forced exercise** *Program maximum profits when you want to sell shares of stock, by selling LEAPS calls deep in the money.*

1. *The forced exercise approach.* Once the long LEAPS call has been exercised, you pick up 100 shares of stock at a price below market value. This paper profit can be used in many ways, including the "forced exercise" approach. This means that you sell calls that are deep in the

money. This increases premium income through the combination of time and intrinsic value. In the event of exercise, your return is substantial. However, if the market price of stock falls before exercise occurs, you can trade out of the short call position. Because you will gain a one-to-one profit for lost intrinsic value, this strategy provides downside protection in the alternative. Once you trade out, you can await further price changes and sell a call, repeating the strategy.

> **Strategy # 43 – Maximize premium and avoid exercise** *Select covered calls following conversion to take advantage of time value premium while avoiding exercise.*

2. *The out-of-the-money approach.* A more conservative and traditional approach is to sell calls to get maximum time value, but avoid in-the-money contracts. The idea here is that you trade strictly on time value. As time value begins to fall, the contract is bought and closed, freeing you to repeat the procedure with a later-expiring call whose time value is also higher. If the stock's price moves higher than striking price, you can close the call, wait out exercise, or roll forward to avoid exercise.

> **Strategy # 44 – Roll to avoid exercise** *Select covered calls following conversion that have maximum time value, and avoid exercise using rolling techniques.*

3. *Avoiding exercise by rolling indefinitely.* A third technique is to sell calls with maximum time value premium. These usually will be longer-term and closer to the money, if not a few points in the money. While the risk of exercise will be greater, longer-term life span also means less likelihood of early exercise-especially if only

a few points in the money. Under this strategy, you wait out time value and then roll forward. If the stock's market value remains in the same range or falls, you roll forward with the same striking price. If the stock's market value is rising, you avoid exercise by rolling up and forward, striving to select striking prices at or above current market value. Rolling up and forward can be done as often as practical, as long as the net change is a credit or breakeven, and as long as it helps avoid exercise.

> **Strategy # 45 – Timing changes in value**   Select covered calls following conversion to time changes in the stock's price on a short-term basis.

4. *Using covered calls to time the market.* Many people have observed the tendency of some stocks to experience price waves over time. Price tests support and resistance levels without actually breaking out of the trading range; this tendency may involve only a few points over a number of weeks, or double-digit point changes within a few days. The higher the volatility, the more profit opportunities for LEAPS traders, but the more uncertainty as well. Timing a stock's price swings requires a degree of dependability as well as a sense of the time involved in these cycles. If you own the 100 shares, the opportunity for selling covered calls arises whenever prices swing upward; and those short positions can be bought and closed when the stock's price swings downward. If you use long-term LEAPS in this strategy, you will probably have the greatest success when timing the market using intrinsic value. In long-term LEAPS calls, time value tends to be far less responsive to minor point swings in the stock, whereas intrinsic value follows the stock's market price on a point-for-point basis.

Decisions: Exercise or Trade Out

In each open long position involving a LEAPS call, you will come to the point when you need to decide whether to exercise and buy shares, or take the profit in the LEAPS call. For the short position covered call, you have the reverse decision: to accept exercise or to trade out with a roll forward strategy. For some traders, the day may arrive in which exercise becomes desirable.

We may classify option writers in one of two ways. Whether you are covering a long LEAPS or 100 shares of stock, you may wish to avoid exercise. However, in some cases, you will fit into the second category, that of traders who have programmed their position so that maximum gain is achieved when their short position is exercised.

Avoiding exercise is a popular and potentially profitable approach to call writing. The maximum profit is probably possible when you are long on a LEAPS call or 100 shares of stock, and you use the long position as a "safety net" for a series of short sales. In the ideal situation, you are able to write a series of calls and take the profits, without experiencing exercise. The combination of good timing, proper selection, and constant monitoring ensures that in most instances, you will be able to roll forward and up to avoid exercise, thus trading profitably on time value over and over again.

If you employ ratio writes, your interest in avoiding exercise will be even more avid. While the one-to-one call writer views exercise as a profitable potential outcome, the ratio writer is exposed to a risk. It is a mitigated risk; however, the trader will want to avoid exercise by rolling away from in-the-money status, selling the excess call when exercise appears unavoidable, or accepting exercise with a trading loss.

Accepting exercise is the second possible approach to the covered call strategy. Every trader who employs a covered call strategy needs to evaluate the possible outcomes in profitable situations, and then determine which outcome is most desirable. You may use covered call writing as a means for the profitable sale of stock or offsetting covered LEAPS with little or no net investment (due to offsetting cost and benefit from buying and selling calls on the same stock but taking advantage of striking price spreads).

The calculation of "return if exercised" for covered calls involving stock includes profit on the premium from selling the call, dividends received from owning the stock, and capital gain on the stock. If you cover a long LEAPS call, the calculation includes the *net* cost or benefit of premium on both calls, and the striking price spread.

The calculation for "return if expired" involves only the profit on the short LEAPS call in cases involving stock. If you cover a LEAPS call, the calculation should be modified so that income from the short sale reduces the cost of the long LEAPS call position. The ultimate outcome depends on what happens to the long position. However, in order to compare possible outcomes, the expiration of the short call would cause a 100% return, since the entire amount of premium would be profit.

Finally, "return if sold" is relatively easy to calculate. If you sell a LEAPS call and later purchase to close, the net difference will be your profit or loss.

In all of the three possible outcomes, you will need to also calculate the net effect of transaction costs. If your LEAPS trading involves the use of multiples of contracts, then the per-contract cost will be lower, although the capital requirements and risks will be higher.

All returns should be compared on an annualized basis in order to reflect them realistically on a comparative basis. For example, if you hold a short position LEAPS call for 36 months until it expires, your overall return will be 100%, but the annualized return would be one-third of that, or 33 $\frac{1}{3}$%. If you go short and close the position within two weeks and earn 15%, the annualized return would be 26 times higher, or 390%. Of course, because it is unlikely that such a fast turnaround is going to be possible every two weeks, a triple-digit return should not become a hard and fast expectation. LEAPS traders can and do earn triple-digit returns, but not on every trade. The purpose in annualizing return is to be able to analyze potential outcomes and to select the one considered most desirable. You may determine that taking a short-term return on a LEAPS sale makes less sense than holding off until more time value has gone from the position; or the immediate profit may be viewed as the best outcome, because you can immediately enter into another covered position.

The easiest method for annualizing return is to divide the return by the period the position was open (or will be open) and then multiply by either 12 (months) or 365 (days). This procedure can be applied to closed positions or in the analysis of possible outcomes before entering the positions. If you have an open position for only 6 days, and you earn a 5 percent return, annualize using the "days" method:

$$(5\% \div 6) \times 365 = 304\%$$

If you have an open position for a period longer than one month, you should use the "months" method. For example, if a position were open for $2\frac{1}{2}$ months and you earned a 5% return, the annualization would be calculated as:

$$(5\% \div 2.5) \times 12 = 24\%$$

Although both examples yielded a 5 percent return, the annualized outcome is vastly different.

Predictability of Time Value Premium

As a writer of LEAPS covered calls, you hold a tremendous advantage over buyers. The time value premium will decline over the life span of the short LEAPS call and this is a predictable outcome. Intrinsic value is also predictable in the sense that we know its movement will mirror price change in the underlying stock; however, that change is unknown to you in advance.

The very predictability of time value is the key to profits in LEAPS trading. A few smart rules to follow ensure that you will succeed with this strategy. These include:

1. *Pick the stock carefully.* No matter what strategies you employ, the underlying stock should meet your fundamental and technical tests. If the stock is highly volatile, then the options will be volatile as well. You may view this as high-risk or high-opportunity. By the same argument, you will observe that stocks with a narrow trading range will offer very little time value premium. So while a short position will be relatively safe, you will not experience much profit from selling calls against LEAPS long positions. Depending on your personal risk tolerance level, you should select stocks that not only meet your long-term investment requirements (assuming your underlying strategy is contingent purchase), but also offer an appropriate volatility level to justify option strategies.

2. *Buy the LEAPS call with covered writing in mind.* When you pick a particular call for a long purchase, you need to be aware of three aspects. Cost and time to expiration is the first; proximity to striking price is the second; and potential for covered LEAPS calls is the third. The most desirable long position is a LEAPS call that is less than five points out of the money, with maximum time until expiration, and with the lowest possible cost. You may not be able to attain all three of these elements. You also need to review relative premium levels for LEAPS calls at higher striking prices and with shorter expirations. Because striking price is higher and expiration comes up sooner, premium value for potential short LEAPS positions will be less than what you pay for the long

LEAPS. However, this can change quickly if and when the stock's market value rises. Ideally, you look for the stock to rise soon after you buy the LEAPS call, so that you can sell a richer covered LEAPS call against it. Even though expiration will come up sooner and striking price is higher, the increased market value of the underlying stock vitalizes interest in the call you wish to sell. The strategy you use to time both the long-term purchase and the shorter-term sale of LEAPS calls determines how profitable the strategy will be.

3. *Be willing to accept exercise as one of the possible outcomes.* Any time you sell a covered LEAPS call, you should be prepared to accept exercise. As long as the striking price of your short position is higher than the striking price of the long position, you have no market risk if the short LEAPS call is exercised. However, you need to ensure that the difference in striking prices is greater than the net cost of the long and short LEAPS positions; otherwise, you could experience a loss. It is not always possible to build in this profit, so in writing a short LEAPS, you need to accept the possibility of a net loss in the event of exercise. If you are able to sell a series of short positions covered by the longer-term LEAPS call, you can eventually create the net profit in the event of exercise.

4. *Decide whether you want exercise or want to avoid it.* Every trader in short LEAPS calls needs to decide whether they seek exercise or wish to avoid it. The strategies are entirely different, so it is not enough to define possible outcomes and settle for either. The specific strategy you select will determine whether you will employ ratio writes, whether or not you roll forward to avoid exercise, and how you pick the short LEAPS positions. If you want exercise, you may sell deep in-the-money calls rich in both time and intrinsic value; if you

wish to avoid exercise, you will be more likely to attempt to pick out-of-the-money LEAPS calls with the highest possible time value, and then monitor positions to decide when and if to close them out or to roll them forward.

5. *Compare the profits in various outcomes.* LEAPS traders have to approach the market analytically. The selection of a particular strategy has to depend on a study of various outcome scenarios. This is partially a risk analysis exercise because you have to consider how to deal with a decline in stock price; and what actions to take in a situation where the stock price remains the same or rises. It is more than risk analysis, too. The comparative study of outcomes also defines whether you are interested in contingent purchase, or simply want to speculate in LEAPS options with purchase one of several possible outcomes. The concept of covered LEAPS trading going on indefinitely is appealing because cost can be quite minimal and risk can be managed effectively at the same time. The potential for profits from contingent purchase extend far beyond the mere question of whether or not to buy the stock. Using LEAPS calls helps you avoid tying up a large sum of money in stock that does decline in value. Those cases in which you exercise the LEAPS call and buy stock enable you to then write covered calls against appreciated stock, which is the most desirable situation and potentially the most profitable as well.

6. *Devise a strategy in case the underlying stock's market value falls.* Perhaps the most common mistake made by options traders is to forget that stock values often fall or remain unchanged within a narrow trading range. For those seeking profits from long LEAPS calls, the poor performance of a stock can defeat the strategy-not only because the long LEAPS call does not appreciate, but

also because the available premium on higher striking price LEAPS calls is too little to open positions. In this situation, several possible alternate strategies can be used to reduce the cost of having entered the long position. These include selling puts as a secondary method of contingent purchase, or using the ratio write to increase higher striking price LEAPS call profits.

7. *Determine whether it will be possible to pay for long positions with short ones.* In the best of all worlds, the underlying stock's value begins rising steadily right after you buy a LEAPS call. This provides you ever-richer call premium for higher striking price contracts, so that your covered LEAPS strategy works brilliantly. Even if your stock holds its value without increasing substantially, you may still be able to sell a series of higher striking price calls, and use the profits from declining time value to pay for the long position. This is desirable as an alternative to completing the contingent purchase plan. You would exercise the long LEAPS call only if the stock appreciated during that call's life span. Simply waiting out the life span without any additional action, you would stand to lose the premium paid for that long position. This is a better alternative than tying up capital in the purchase of 100 shares, without any doubt. However, it is possible to pay for the long position by writing that series of covered LEAPS calls. If the market for the stock does not materialize, contingent purchase saves your capital from a poorly timed decision; and using the time value of covered short positions also reimburses your premium cost. This strategic approach provides you with a double benefit: control over 100 shares of stock for up to three years, with little or no net cost in the event the stock's value does not move upward.

As advantageous as the covered LEAPS strategy is, there is even more to think about. For purposes of illustration, most of our examples have involved single contracts. When you begin adding multiples, you can also expand your strategic control over the LEAPS position, offsetting long positions with staggered writes, ratio hedges, and other attractive devices. The next chapter goes through an expansion of the initial covered LEAPS and shows how this creative idea can be taken even farther.

Chapter 7

Hedging Strategies with LEAPS:
Stretching your investment dollar

In most instances, the use of a LEAPS option will involve leverage of capital, coverage of one position with another, or straight speculation. All of these strategies should be considered seriously, as they may have a place in your portfolio. The variables include risk tolerance and experience in the options market, current market conditions, available capital, and specific investing goals-both short-term and long-term.

Going beyond the ideas presented in previous chapters, the LEAPS strategy may be designed for more complex applications. The lifespan of the LEAPS is considerably longer than the traditional listed option, so that many more advanced strategies that were previously good in theory alone, now have a practical side as well.

Using multiple option contracts

The advanced straddles, spreads and combinations that have been known for many years often could not work using short-term options as time value was limited in points, expiration was invariably looming within a few months at best, and premium values often were not high enough to justify those strategies with marginal potential. When trading costs were added to the equation, many potentially profitable strategies simply could not work out with the traditional listed option. The only alternative was to use multiple contracts to offset trading costs. The problem with that idea is that the use of multiple options also increases overall risk.

While risk and profit opportunity are invariably associated, the question of how many multiples to use is ever present. Whether you use short-term options or longer-term LEAPS contracts, you also need to decide how to expand your strategies. The examples in this book are primarily limited to single-contract examples. This simplifies the argument and also demonstrates the pre-transaction cost outcome in various scenarios. In practice, you may decide to use several options; this also expands the possibilities.

For example, when undertaking a typical covered LEAPS strategy, you will sell one call for each long contract purchased. Expiration comes more quickly and striking price is higher; this is the ideal strategy in a condition where market price is rising over time. Consider the potential when you sell 10 contracts. Of course, exposure to possible loss is multiplied by 10, but at the same time your profit potential is increased as well. Furthermore, you have far more flexibility. Instead of selling only a single call, you can sell a range of calls with varying striking prices and expirations. As long as the 10 long contracts have lower striking price and later expiration, you are not limited to a single short position.

> **Strategy # 46 – Multiple LEAPS shorts**   *Employ a range of short call positions against a number of long positions; enter the covered LEAPS position using a spectrum of short positions to maximize profit potential.*

There are numerous advantages to this variation. While risk exposure is greater, the profit potential is not the only offsetting factor to remember. On the basis of comparative risk and reward, the dollar amounts are higher, but you will also experience far lower trading costs. This alone provides the edge that could make a significant difference in outcome of the strategy.

Beyond the trading cost advantage, you also have far greater trading flexibility. For example, in the single-contract strategy, you are limited to writing a single short call against the long position. When you use many long positions originally, you do not have to limit the short positions to a single expiration and striking price; you can create an array. With this method, some of your short positions may produce maximum profit from time value deterioration; others may deteriorate more slowly over time; some could be exercised, so that the assignment would be satisfied with a portion of your long position holdings; and some may need to be rolled forward and up to avoid exercise. In all of these scenarios, you will earn a profit from selling calls against the long LEAPS call position.

In the multiple-LEAPS strategy, you can offset the long position with a variety of shorts, as illustrated in Figure 7.1

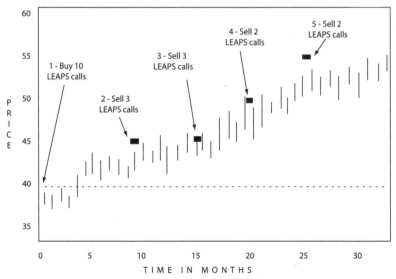

Figure 7.1 ■ The covered LEAPS variation strategy

In this example, you opened the position by buying 10 LEAPS calls with a striking price of 40, expiring in 30 months (step 1). Then at the same time or shortly thereafter, a series of calls were sold against the long LEAPS position, as follows:

- 3 of the 45 calls expiring in 10 months
- 3 of the 45 calls expiring in 15 months
- 2 of the 50 calls expiring in 20 months
- 2 of the 55 calls expiring in 25 months

Consider the potential in this array. The longer-out LEAPS calls will tend to have greater time value, but offset by the higher striking prices, that overall value may be lower. This brings us to yet another variation of this strategy: the timed sale of calls against a long position.

> **Strategy # 47 – Staggered short writes** *Rather than selling calls at the beginning of the strategy, sell some right away and hold off on selling others, pending changing developments.*

In this variation of the strategy, you wait out price movement in the underlying stock before deciding which calls to sell. Referring again to Figure 7.1, we present the ideal situation: the stock's price is moving upward over a 30-month period, meaning at the end, you will be able to either sell the long position call at a profit or exercise it and purchase stock at the fixed striking price. In the example, the stock's price at the end of the term is about 55, but you would be able to exercise the LEAPS call at 40.

This price pattern is by no means guaranteed. So with that in mind, the timing of the short call positions is going to depend on subsequent price movement of the underlying stock. You might have to wait out a period of accumulation; price might fall before rising again; or in the best of all worlds, the price of the underlying stock could rise much faster than assumed in the scenario shown in Figure 7.1

The decision to sell calls against the long position can also assume a form of market timing in which you sell against assumed overbought status of the stock; and close out those positions when the stock's price falls. Under this strategy, you ride the waves of interim price movement, with the longer-term trend continuing to the upside.

> **Strategy # 48 – Timed short writes for overbought and oversold conditions**   *Time the sale of covered short calls to price peaks, and close out those positions when stock prices fall to the low range.*

This strategy works best for those who follow both fundamental and technical indicators. Both can provide insight and timing advantages if used well. The basic technical theory concerning trading range can be used in this strategy. In the example shown in Figure 7.1, the trading range is climbing but is confined generally to a five-point distance between support and resistance. You can time the decision to sell LEAPS calls at assumed price tops, and close out the positions as stock prices swing back down to support levels.

In the example of 10 long positions, it makes sense to still limit the number of options in short positions, for several reasons. First, you want to be able to take advantage of strong price trends by selling still more calls against a strong time value; second, if the price continues rising rather than falling back, you will want to roll out of the short position; in that scenario, you may replace 3 short calls at one striking price with 5 new ones at a later expiration, for example. In this procedure, you create a net credit but still avoid exercise.

> **Strategy # 49 – Limited call coverage in rolls**   *Sell covered calls against multiple long positions, with the ability to roll forward or forward-and-up to avoid exercise while creating continuing net credits.*

Example: You are long 10 LEAPS 40 calls that expire in 30 months (Step 1). You sell 3 LEAPS calls expiring in 10 months at 45 (step 2). The stock's price continues rising, so that the short positions are in the money. To avoid exercise, you close the three short positions (step 3) and replace them with 5 short positions expiring at a later date (step 4). The stock's market value continues to rise so you avoid exercise by closing the 5 short positions (step 5) and replacing them with the sale of 10 short positions with later expirations and higher striking prices (step 6).

In *all* of these replacement moves, you create a net credit on the trades between steps 3 to 4 and steps 5 to 6. What does this accomplish? You receive net premium from the sale of calls against the long position, creating an overall profit. However, all of the short positions have higher striking prices than the long position, and all expire before the long position. Thus, coverage is true in the sense that, upon exercise of any short calls, you are ensured of having long calls available to offset the assignment. The example is illustrated in Figure 7.2

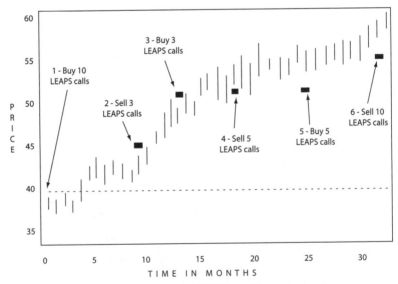

Figure 7.2 ■ The covered LEAPS roll-out strategy

Incidentally, since this strategy extends over 30 months, the losses created at steps 3 and 5 are deductible as capital losses in the year they occur; however, the gains or potential gains that occur at step 6 are not taxed until those positions are closed at a profit or allowed to expire.

In the scenario where the stock's price rises so far that you can no longer roll out without losing coverage, you still make a profit; the premium you receive upon sale of the calls is yours to keep. In one sense, this is the "worst case" outcome as the long calls are needed to satisfy assignment rather than to buy stock. The timing of the sales of calls, however, should produce more than enough premium to offset the initial cost of the long position. While you would lose the ultimate right to exercise the long positions in this example, you are still able to manage the outcome adequately.

Yet another strategy is useful in the event that the stock's price continues to rise beyond your initial expectations: allowing exercise of a few short positions while waiting out price movement before deciding what else to do.

> **Strategy # 50 – Limited exercise exposure**   *Alter the previous strategy when the stock's price rises and accept exercise of a limited number of calls.*

Example: Referring back to Figure 7.2, when step 2 is completed-the sale of three short calls-and the stock continues to rise, you can simply wait out the situation to see what occurs. If the stock price remains high and continues rising, the three calls will be exercised and offset with long positions, leaving you 7 long LEAPS calls. When the stock's price seems to reach a top, more calls can be sold, a decision you would make later based on that outcome. The price of the stock may also retreat, so that your short calls will go out of the money and will not be exercised. In that case, you may decide to sell a few more short calls against the long position, selecting a later expiration and higher striking price-a return to the previous strategy. This strategy enables you to reserve the majority of your long positions for the ultimate goal, purchase of shares of stock. Thus, the "worst case" of a rising stock price becomes a true purchase advantage, in which you will be able to buy 700 shares well below current market value.

The contingent sale strategy

Most of the strategic discussion using LEAPS to this point has involved contingent purchase. Another strategic area worth mentioning is that of the two methods of contingent sale of stock.

You can use puts or calls to accomplish the contingent sale strategy. The use of short calls is one of the topics in Chapter 8. For now we limit the discussion to the use of LEAPS puts to enter a contingent sale strategy, and to expand on the use of the long put by "covering" with lower-striking price, shorter-expiring short puts.

> ***Strategy # 51 – Contingent sale***   *Protect yourself against downside stock price movement using LEAPS puts.*

Anyone who owns stock faces a double dilemma. Do you hold while prices are rising or stable, hoping to gain more profit when prices move upward? Or do you take profits today, fearing the loss of paper profits if and when prices move downward? Stockholders worry about this constantly. It is a matter of knowing when to time decisions, and to reconcile the long-term hold strategy with the natural desire to realize a profit and to time the market effectively.

No timing strategy is perfect, so we can again turn to LEAPS contracts for the solution. The strategy of buying LEAPS puts provides a twofold advantage. First, it protects you against the possibility of a price slide in the stock; as long as you own the long put, you can exercise at the striking price even when the market price has fallen well below that level. Second, it opens up an opportunity to create covered puts, a strategy that is the reverse of the covered LEAPS call, but one that works in the same way.

> **Strategy # 52 – Short put cover** *Sell short puts against long puts positions, with lower striking prices and shorter expirations.*

The strategy of covering the put is easily understood when it is viewed as a mirror of the covered LEAPS call. Rather than looking for higher short positions, you seek lower short positions with the LEAPS put cover.

Example: You own 100 shares of stock and you are concerned about possible price decline; at the same time you are not prepared to sell stock just yet, since you realize that there is a possibility that prices will rise. You buy a LEAPS put to hedge against that threat. To reduce the cost of the long position, you sell a series of puts against it, effectively covered by the long put. Each of the short positions has a lower striking price and shorter expiration than the long position.

A second way to recapture the cost of the long LEAPS put is by selling covered calls against shares you own, achieving complete coverage by limiting this exposure to one call per 100 shares of stock owned. The possible outcomes are worth analyzing.

> **Strategy # 53 – LEAPS put combination with covered calls** *Combine the LEAPS long put and a LEAPS short call to create a spread that reduces or eliminates the long put premium cost.*

1. *Stock price rises.* If the stock price rises, the long put will not gain value; but that is not an immediate concern; the price of that put was offset by the premium you

received upon sale of the call. You have a choice. First, you may accept exercise, recognizing that this programs in a profit and accomplishes the contingent sale through the spread. Second, you may continue holding the put as on-going downside protection, while rolling the short call forward to create a net credit, trading time value and probably avoiding exercise as well. If you are able to roll forward and up, you "buy" more profit in the event of exercise.

2. *Stock price remains in a narrow trading range.* In this outcome, the call will lose time value and can be allowed to expire worthless or bought to close at a profit; and then replaced with a later-expiring call with rich time value. This is a covered call, so that you are not concerned with timing; you can continue rolling the cover forward indefinitely.

3. *Stock price falls.* The premium you receive upon sale of calls against stock are yours to keep, so if the call expires worthless, that premium discounts your basis in stock. Once it expires, you can sell subsequent calls (as long as the striking price is higher than your basis, you program in a profit in the event of exercise). A significant decline in price would not only create a profit in the short call; it would also revert to the original strategy in which the long LEAPS put provides downside protection from the put's striking price threshold.

The contingent sale strategy works when you own shares of stock; when you are willing to have them called away as a consequence of writing a short call; or when you want to continue holding shares, but fear downside price movement. The combination of long puts (alone or offset by short puts), and short calls makes this strategy a viable and potentially profitable one, especially useful when your stock is undergoing exceptional price volatility. That volatility, whether caused by broader market unrest or by fundamental change within the company itself, presents the potential for price growth as well as the risk of short-term price decline. The contingent sale strategy makes sense in these circumstances.

Is contingent sale a wise strategy if you intend to hold shares over the long term? Of course, any option strategy has to be coordinated with broader portfolio intentions. Thus, putting shares at risk of exercise that you have no intention of actually trading, works against that more important goal. However, just as long-term strategies work in a covered call strategy, the covered put aspect of the contingent sale mitigates the cost of gaining downside protection, and makes sense to manage value in the short term. When structured within a spread strategy employing covered calls, the usual caution about call writing has to be applied as well (see Chapter 8). So contingent sale can serve as a useful strategy in these circumstances.

When you hold shares that you are willing to sell given the right conditions, contingent sale makes even more sense. By combining long puts and short calls, you can produce a cost-free situation in which a programmed profit would be created upon sale, which also accomplishes downside protection. So prolonging the time until sale enables you to maximize profit potential with little or no cost, while remaining exposed to potential higher short-term profits. This addresses the often-heard lament of the stock investor who took profits a few weeks or months too soon; who could have made substantially more by waiting; or who is continually worried about the possibility that a decision to take profits will be ill-timed. The contingent sale avoids loss of paper profits while keeping you exposed to market potential.

LEAPS and the long-term hedge

Option traders have always been attracted to the broad range of possible hedge strategies. The contingent sale is one among these; the potential use of puts to protect against the downside in a volatile market is a great advantage. However, with the traditional option, lasting only a few months, premium costs often have made hedging strategies unrealistic.

With LEAPS contracts lasting up to three years, the practical use of options to hedge other positions becomes far more practical. The two methods of insurance were discussed in Chapter 4. These are the use of long puts to protect long stock positions, and the use of long calls to protect short stock positions. You can also use options to hedge other option positions, and there are many varieties and methods available. For example, the "covered" LEAPS call (expressed in quotations because it is not a truly covered position, it just works like one) is a good example. When you buy a long position call or put and then sell other calls or puts against that position, you recover a portion of the premium cost and protect against exercise as well.

In some respects, the mere purchase of a LEAPS contract can also be viewed as a hedge against market risk. Your potential losses are always limited to the premium cost, but potential gains have no such limitation; and you have as much as three years to either sell the option at a profit or exercise it and make a transaction in stock that creates an immediate price advantage.

The concept of hedging, while well understood by investors in theory at least, is not always as easy to put into practice. Many investors make the mistake of failing to continually keep risk in mind; so they are taken by surprise when paper profits disappear suddenly. As a form of consolidation, paper profits are protected through the creation of a "floor" in which the option position ensures that those paper profits can be taken at some point. At the same time, you do not have to close the position and take profits, perhaps sooner than you would like.

> **Strategy # 54 – Paper profit floor**   *Protect unrealized profits by purchasing LEAPS options, to avoid unexpected reversals and resulting losses.*

This strategy solves the age-old dilemma for every investor: the uncertainty of timing. The balance between the desire for profits and the desire to not miss out on *more* profits often leads to the worst outcome: losses.

Example: You have had the repetitive experience of buying stock and seeing steadily increasing market value. Uncertain about when to take profits, you held too long and prices retreated, often falling below your original basis. You have lost many paper profits in this manner.

You decide to use LEAPS puts to protect paper profits. On your next trade, you purchase 100 shares of stock and it immediately rises more than five points in market value. You decide to enter into a program of protecting paper profits using puts. An example of how this works is shown in Figure 7.3.

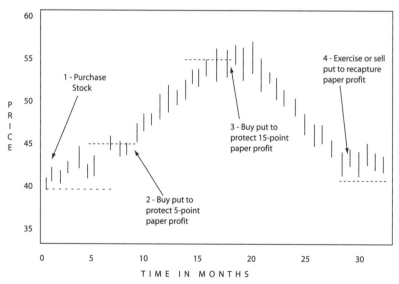

Figure 7.3 ■ LEAPS puts used to protect paper profits

In this example, there are four distinct steps involved. The stock is purchased (step 1) and market value then rises. To protect a five-point paper profit, you buy a put at that striking price level (step 2). The stock continues to rise to the point that your paper profits are 15 points higher than original basis, so you buy another put at the 15-point striking price level (step 3). Finally, the stock reverses and tumbles in a short period of time. At this point, you can exercise the put, selling stock at 15 points above original basis; or you can revert to a secondary strategy, in which you sell the put and recapture lost value from premium gain. This enables you to hold onto the stock with the idea that price may rebound.

> **Strategy # 55 – Lost profit recapture**   *Rather than exercising the put to recapture lost paper profits, sell the put to pick up the value while continuing to hold stock, hoping for a price rebound.*

Under either of these approaches-exercise of sale of the put-you will need to determine how long the put's lifetime should last. Of course, shorter-term puts will be less expensive with less time value involved; but longer-term puts may be less expensive in the long run since you can afford to wait out price volatility without being concerned with pending expiration.

In the second alternative, selling the put to recapture lost paper profits, you probably will not be able to gain *all* of the profits since some time value will have fallen out during the holding period. In some instances, this reduced premium value could be substantial, making this alternative strategy impractical. Unless you truly believe in the continuing long-term value of owning that stock, it makes more sense to exercise the put close to expiration and sell the stock. The question comes down to how you will gain the most. By exercise in the example given, you pick up 15 points of paper profit. It only makes sense to sell the put as an alternative if the point difference is close or better than the 15 points; or if you are willing to take a small loss to continue owning the stock.

Another strategy presents itself in cases where you buy two or more puts, as in the example above. When you own *two* puts, for example, you can not only recapture paper profits, but accelerate those profits as well.

> **Strategy # 56 – Put speculation with price floor**
> *Increase profit potential in the event of a price reversal, by keeping multiple puts held to provide the price floor.*

Example: You own 100 shares of stock as in the example illustrated in Figure 7.3. You first sold a put with a striking price five points above the stock's basis; and then bought a second put at the 15-point striking price level. Since both puts extend for many months into the future, you continue holding onto them. In the event the stock's market value falls below both striking price levels, you would double up on the recaptured profit. Once the price falls below the striking price of the first put, your profit will be two points per point drop of the stock.

> **Strategy # 57 – Conversion, short put to covered put**
> *When initial puts are replaced by higher striking price puts, convert the first puts to a covered put strategy.*

Example: You bought a put at a striking price five points above your original basis in stock, with the idea of providing a paper profit floor. The stock continued to rise so you bought a second put with a striking price 15 points above original basis. At that point, you converted the first put to a covered put strategy.

In the covered put strategy, you hold a long put and sell puts against it. The short puts have lower striking prices and shorter expirations, so in the event of exercise, the original long put is available to satisfy the assignment of the short put. Is there enough premium value to justify this strategy? Since the stock's price is rising in the example provided, the value of lower-level puts is going to be minimal; however, the advantage of time value cannot be overlooked. For this reason-and anticipating the possibility that you may need to replace an original put with a higher striking price put-you may wish to select longer-expiration term puts and pay a somewhat higher price. This provides greater flexibility in the covered put strategy. The longer the term remaining in the short put, the higher the time value premium. Thus, your chances of recapturing premium cost in the original long run are improved when you are able to offset that cost by selling lower-striking price and shorter-expiration puts in the covered put strategy.

Straddle strategies

The straddle involves the simultaneous purchase (long straddle) or sale (short straddle) of calls or puts with the same striking price and expiration date. While the traditional view of the straddle is that the positions are opened at the same time, it is equally likely that an existing open position will be modified so that the straddle is created.

Example: You own a long call and have been waiting to see what price movement will occur in the underlying stock, before deciding whether to cover the call; and if so, at what price levels. Your initial assumption was that the stock's price was going to rise over time. However, recent news indicates that the stock's price might fall instead.

In this situation, you may wish to take advantage of possible downside price movement by buying a put. If you select a put at the same striking price as the LEAPS call and with the same expiration date, this decision creates a straddle.

In the event the stock's price does move downward, the put will increase in value as the call loses value over time. Thus, the straddle would create an advantage if the stock were to move substantially in either direction. The combined cost of the call and put create a price range in which you would not profit. It would be necessary for the stock's price to move above or below that range before you would realize any profit.

Figure 7.4 provides an example of the long straddle. In this case, you purchased a LEAPS call for 4 and later bought a LEAPS put for 7. Your combined cost is $1,100, 11 points. You would need the stock's price to move above or below this 11-point range. Either direction will create the profit; as long as the stock's price remains within the indicated loss zone, you will not realize a profit on either LEAPS option.

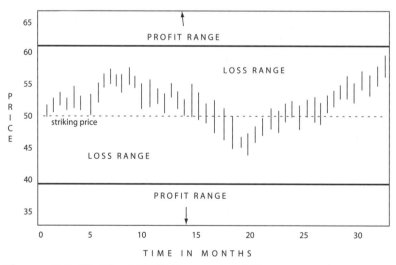

Figure 7.4 ■ The LEAPS long straddle

The advantage of the long straddle is that the loss zone is limited, but potential profit zones are unlimited. Recalling that LEAPS exist for up to three years, you have the advantage of time even in the long position; you can wait for price movement to exceed either upper or lower borders to realize a profit.

A further expansion of the long straddle accomplishes a shrinking of the loss zone. By selling short calls and puts against both sides of the straddle, you increase the potential for profits while maintaining the profit potential of the straddle itself. Of course, at any time that the value decreases in either short position, that side can be closed at a profit and replaced with a richer option having greater time value premium.

> **Strategy # 59 – Long straddle price reduction** *Sell a higher striking price call and a lower striking price put (both with earlier expirations than the long positions) to shrink the loss range of the long straddle.*

Example: You create a covered call *and* a covered put on both sides of the straddle. The long positions both have a striking price of 50 and 30 months until expiration. You sell calls with higher striking prices timed to coincide with price increases of the underlying stock (maximizing premium levels) and you sell puts with lower striking prices timed to coincide with price decreases of the underlying stock. In both cases, the short positions expire sooner than the straddle's long positions.

Your initial premium cost for the two long positions was 11; when you receive 3 points for the short call and another 4 points for the short put, you reduce the loss zone by 7 points. After this, your straddle has profit potential above or below a four-point range, a significant improvement over the original 11 points.

This modified strategy is illustrated in Figure 7.5

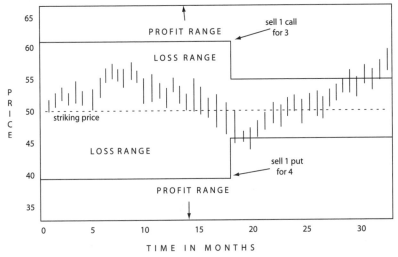

Figure 7.5 ■ Reducing the long straddle loss range using covered LEAPS

LEAPS combined with short-term options

The advantageous spread and combination strategies already introduced provide real potential for profits. The combination of the contingent purchase in its various forms, with the spread (also called the "covered" call or put) solves the chronic problem faced by short-term option investors: How can these strategies be played out for maximum benefit, when time is so short until expiration?

This brings up yet another potentially profitable method for using LEAPS. By devising strategies that combine LEAPS contracts with short-term options, you may be able to take advantage of time value adjustments. In the short LEAPS contract, time value is likely to decrease relatively slowly as long as there remain 20 to 30 months until expiration; and that decline is expected to accelerate in later months.

One sensible strategy for spreads or covered calls is to off-set the long position with short-term LEAPS contracts. By timing the decision carefully, you may be able to select the precise timing for the short position, in which minimum deterioration of time value has occurred; but it will begin to pick up the pace within its remaining lifetime. From a buyer's point of view, this is the most disadvantageous moment to buy an option; but since your strategy will be to offset a long position (in option or stock) with a short LEAPS option, that rapidly declining time value is to your advantage.

When picking options to short in a relatively brief period of time, always compare the available LEAPS contracts with the same traditional listed option contracts. You may discover that, for a variety of reasons, the premium on the short-term option might be richer at the moment. So it is possible to increase your spread advantage by offsetting the long LEAPS with the short listed option.

In the final analysis, it does not make any difference whether you short on listed options or LEAPS, as long as the outcome produces a profit. However, don't overlook the possible value of creating spreads and combinations that include short-term listed options as well as LEAPS contracts.

The possibilities for the creation of long and short combinations is greater when LEAPS are used in long positions, due to the longer lifespan. The same is true when you wish to go short, in which case you desire greater time value. With the lifespan of the LEAPS option greater than the few months of the listed option, you stand to receive far higher levels of premium income. That difference is exclusively represented by time value, so even the basic covered call strategy is more effective-and profitable-when you offset shares of stock with LEAPS calls in place of the standard listed call option. Covered call strategies-the ultimate conservative approach for LEAPS traders-are examined in detail in the next section.

Part III

The Covered Call Advantage: Conservative strategies with low risk

Chapter 8

Covered Calls:
The ultimate profitable approach

Options have the reputation of being high-risk. It is true that speculative strategies like selling uncovered options involve considerable risk. It's also true that going long is risky, because time value declines; so even if the underlying stock's value is rising, it is difficult to get enough price change to overcome time value loss *and* create a profit as well.

Even with the many risky strategies available, there is also a highly conservative way to utilize options. LEAPS, because they are longer-term than traditional listed options, provide the greatest possible return in the conservative strategy. You can design and time the conservative approach to ensure maximum gain with minimal risk, which ultimately is what everyone wants in their portfolio. The covered call-selling a LEAPS call when you also own 100 shares of the underlying stock-is the most conservative of all strategies. You are able to lock in a rate of return higher than the *average* return you would expect to earn by simply buying and selling stock; and without the inherent risks associated with LEAPS long positions.

Among the key elements to keep in mind about covered LEAPS are:

1. Time value works for you as a seller.
2. As long as you own 100 shares, the only risk to selling a LEAPS call is the lost opportunity risk. (While the stock's value may fall, that is a risk that every stockholder faces with or without the LEAPS covered call involved.)
3. Because LEAPS are long-term, the potential for very rich time value premium makes the LEAPS covered call more profitable than the traditional covered call employing listed options.

Two general guidelines to remember in all covered call strategies:

1. *You must be willing to accept exercise.* No matter how carefully you structure your covered call strategy, the call can be exercised at any time. If the position is in the money, you have to be happy with exercise if and when it occurs. You can take steps to avoid exercise, of course; but unexpected price jumps can be accompanied by exercise without warning; this is a reality to covered call writing.
2. *You need to program the strategy to have a profitable outcome upon exercise.* You need to select striking prices that will produce a profit in the stock if and when the LEAPS call is exercised. You can get higher premium by selling LEAPS calls deep in the money, but that is not the purpose to the strategy. Ideally, you would like to use stock repeatedly to produce call income by selling covered LEAPS time and again, but without losing the stock. With this in mind, the "ideal" position for most covered call strategies is to be close to, but out of the money.

The most conservative option strategy

The covered call strategy involves a match between a long position in stock and a short position in the LEAPS call. Since each call is associated with 100 shares of stock, a one-to-one cover involves 100 shares per option. So if you own 500 shares and sell five LEAPS calls, you retain the 100% coverage.

> **Strategy # 60 – Covered call**   *Sell one LEAPS call per 100 shares of stock owned.*

Why is the covered call considered the most conservative of all LEAPS strategies? The risk is limited; the rate of return is assured. When you sell a LEAPS call, the premium that you receive discounts your basis in the stock, providing a limited downside protection as well as cash flow. At the same time, any profits you earn from selling covered LEAPS calls are not taxed until one of three events takes place: exercise, expiration, or a close of the position (to close the position, you execute a closing purchase transaction). So the potential tax benefit includes receiving premium this year, but deferring the tax on profit until a later period. With the LEAPS, which may have as long as a three-year life, the deferral aspect to the covered call could be substantial.

When a specific approach is described as "conservative," we have to define the term carefully. It has different meanings to different investors. Covered LEAPS are conservative in relation to all other strategies, assuming that you already own shares of stock and wish to augment income and discount the basis in that stock. During the time you cover using a LEAPS call, you continue to receive dividend income, and you have the right to close out the position at any time before expiration or exercise. As a seller, you grant the right to the buyer to exercise the call at any time. So whenever you are in the money-meaning, of course, that the current market value of stock is higher than the striking price of the short call-exercise is a possibility. So in the sense that your 100 shares of stock could be called away, one potential form of risk would be having to sell the stock. With this in mind, some preliminary rules should be established as a starting point:

1. *Select striking prices intelligently.* You should only sell calls when exercise would produce a profit in the stock. It would not make sense to sell calls with striking price below your net basis (the net basis is original cost less premium received from selling the call).

2. *Be willing to sell the stock.* The covered LEAPS strategy makes sense only if you are willing to sell the stock. Whenever you go short, that is always one of the possibilities, so any covered call strategy has to be treated like a contingent sale.

3. *Be prepared to hold the stock for the entire period the covered LEAPS call exists.* In entering the covered position, you commit your 100 shares of stock in the event of exercise, so you need to be willing and able to hold that stock as long as necessary in order to go through the covered call strategy.

4. *Be able to accept lost opportunity risk.* The lost opportunity arises when the stock's market price rises far above striking price of the call. This will happen occasionally. Just as the simple ownership of stock involves the potential for high profits due to a price run-up, the covered call-if exercised-involves losing your 100 shares of stock at the fixed striking price. In that outcome, the lost opportunity is the price difference between striking price and market value at the point of exercise. The realist understands that a trade-off is involved, in which you accept the potential for lost opportunity, for the premium

income gained from selling the LEAPS call. Considering the range of possibilities, the realist is likely to profit more from a program of covered LEAPS calls, even considering the occasional lost opportunity.

There are three possible outcomes in the covered call strategy. First, when time value declines, you can close out the position and realize a gain in the LEAPS call; in this scenario, you can immediately sell yet another LEAPS call and repeat the strategy. Second, if stock value rises, the call will be exercised and your 100 shares of stock called away; as long as you have built in a profit under this outcome, you experience the lost opportunity but gain from appreciated stock, option premium, and dividends (if applicable). Third, the LEAPS call expires worthless; in this case, you can immediately sell another call and repeat the strategy.

In all three outcomes, you will experience a profit. The market risk of selling covered LEAPS exists if you own stock, with or without a covered call. That risk is that the market value of the stock may decline. With the covered call, you discount your basis, providing some downside protection; additionally, as long as the price of stock remains below striking price of the covered LEAPS call, you have no risk of exercise. You could close out the position and then sell another call; using an extended expiration date, you would make up at least a portion of the loss with higher time value premium. So you can perpetually trade out of positions and maximize time value profit even when market value of the stock remains below striking price. Later in this chapter, we will also show how you can combine contingent sale through covered calls, with contingent purchase using covered puts. This produces higher premium income, discounts your basis, and provides a useful method for increasing your holdings in a stock you want to hold over the long term.

Time value and the short position

The essence of the covered call strategy is found in time value. Remember, buyers are always at a disadvantage because time value works against them. Even when in the money, a rise in intrinsic value can be easily offset by ever-deteriorating time value premium; so the stock moving in the right direction may not be enough. For the buyer, the stock has to move enough points in the right direction, and do so prior to expiration, just to break even.

For the seller, time value is the great advantage. The higher the time value, the greater the potential for profit. As time value begins to erode, you have a safety net; even if the stock moves above expiration, it will still be possible to close the short LEAPS call at profit or roll out of the position to avoid exercise-as long as overall premium value remains below the original sale price. And that occurs frequently, due primarily to the nature of time value itself.

With the LEAPS, time value tends to be substantially greater than in the shorter-term listed option. With a lifespan up to 36 months, time value can be quite significant, meaning that the total return on covered calls can be far higher as well. Table 8.1 provides some examples of 29-month LEAPS calls (based on August 4, 2003 prices and values for January, 2006 expirations).

Stock	Trading Symbol	Current Price	LEAPS Call	Current Premium	Return
IBM	IBM	80.40	Jan 06 70	19.00	23.6%
			Jan 06 80	13.50	16.8
			Jan 06 90	9.30	11.6
			Jan 06 100	6.10	7.6
Altria	MO	40.80	Jan 06 30	11.10	27.2%
			Jan 06 40	5.80	14.2
			Jan 06 50	2.60	6.4
Wal-Mart	WMT	55.32	Jan 06 45	15.30	27.7%
			Jan 06 50	12.10	21.9
			Jan 06 55	9.70	17.5
			Jan 06 60	7.30	13.2
			Jan 06 65	5.60	10.1
Microsoft	MSFT	25.94	Jan 06 20	8.20	31.6%
			Jan 06 22	6.80	26.2
			Jan 06 25	5.60	21.6
			Jan 06 27	4.50	17.3
			Jan 06 30	3.50	13.5

Table 8.1 – LEAPS values

The rate of return on this table is based on today's market price for each stock. If your actual basis were lower, then the rate of return would be higher. For example, if you had purchased 100 shares of IBM at $60 per share, the January 2006 70 call currently priced at 19.00 would yield 31.7% on your basis. This has to be kept in mind when evaluating options. The current premium yield has to be computed on your basis, and not on current price. The return column is included here only for the purpose of comparative outcomes.

To confine this analysis to only those calls at or close to the money: the 29-month IBM LEAPS call yields 16.8% (again, based on current market price). Since this is entirely made up of time value, it means that even if IBM stock were to rise by 13.5 points or more by expiration, the call would still be worth the same as it is today. That provides many opportunities for you, as a covered call seller, to (a) close out the call at a profit or (b) roll out of the Jan 06 80 call and into a higher-strike price, later-expiring alternative. However, if IBM maintains current value over the coming months, then the time value will begin to erode.

> **Strategy # 61 – At-the-money short**   *Create downside protection by selling long-term at-the-money calls, leaving yourself the alternative of rolling out or accepting exercise.*

The same analysis may be applied to the other stocks on the list. Altria's at-the-money option has nearly six points of time value with a 14.2% yield. Wal-Mart's has almost 10 points and produces current yield of 17.5%. And Microsoft's has $5\frac{1}{2}$ points with a 21.6% yield. All of these are respectable rates of return for at-the-money calls.

When the same type of analysis is applied to out-of-the-money calls-providing you with a cushion for future price growth during the life of the LEAPS call-potential return is just as attractive. For example, IBM's current price is $80.40; the current return on the 90 LEAPS call would be 11.6% based on today's market price. However, upon exercise, you would receive the $9.30 for the call premium plus $1,000 for the 10-point difference between current value and striking price. This profit picture is again based on today's value rather than your actual basis; had you acquired this stock at a different price, then actual return would be different. So under the example given, the total of $1,930 would represent a 24% return on the investment.

> **Strategy # 62 – Out-of-the-money short**   *Combine option premium with potential capital gains to maximize covered call returns.*

The same logic applied to the other three stocks demonstrates what takes place when you cover with out-of-the-money LEAPS calls, if exercised (all based on current stock value):

Altria 50 call =
  $580 premium plus $1,000 stock gain = 38.7%
Wal-Mart 65 call =
  $560 premium plus $1,000 capital gain = 28.2%
Microsoft 30 call =
  $350 premium plus $500 capital gain = 32.8%

In all of these cases, triple-digit returns present the "worst case" outcomes. Exercise of the LEAPS call means stock is called away, creating a capital gain on top of the premium you earn for selling the call. However, given the fact that there are a number of points between current market value of stock and striking price of the option, there is an equal chance that time value will evaporate well before exercise of the calls. You always have the alternative of rolling forward and up to increase income (both from call premium and potential exercise level) and to avoid exercise altogether. The price cushion achieved by selling out-of-the-money LEAPS calls is shown in Figure 8.1

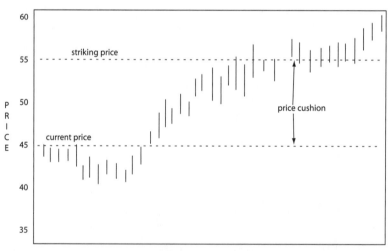

Figure 8.1 ■ Price cushion with out-of-the-money short calls

You maximize the return by selling in-the-money LEAPS calls if you look only to the return on the call itself; this is a smart strategy if the stock's market value falls in the short term. Note that with a 10-point cushion, for example, the stock's market price could range anywhere between current price and striking price without any threat of exercise; this means you could close the position at any time the status remained out of the money. Even when the stock's price crossed striking price, a secondary cushion equal to the premium you received applies, so that exercise itself could still create a profit in your short position. Because the out-of-the-money cushion provides you immunity from exercise, you can either wait out the decline in time value or, if the stock's market price begins to approach striking price levels, you can simply roll forward and up, avoid exercise, and still create a net credit by exchanging short calls.

You need to calculate the overall return in the event of exercise. For example, if you were to purchase 100 shares of IBM at the current price of $80.40 and sell a January, 2005 call with a striking price of 70, you would receive a premium of $1,900. That discounts your basis down to $61.40 per share, a 23.6% return on the $80.40 investment. However upon exercise, what would your net yield be?

Purchase price of stock	$8,040
Less: Call premium	– 1,900
Net Basis	$6,140
Exercise price of stock	$7,000
Net yield	14.0%

You would create a higher profit selling the at-the-money call (16.8%) or the out-of-the-month call (24.0%), given the same assumption that your basis in the stock is today's value. The whole picture is changed if and when your true basis is different; if your net acquisition price is well below current market price, you can willingly sell in-the-money LEAPS calls. That strategy gives you greater downside protection and, upon exercise, creates an acceptable level of profit as well.

> **Strategy # 63 – In-the-money short**   *Program in profits from capital gains and option premium by selling in-the-money calls.*

For example, what if you had purchased 100 shares of IBM at $55 per share? Then the outcome would be much different. This approach assumes that you would be willing to sell your IBM stock if you could create the profit desired today; or in the alternative, you would treat the in-the-money short call as downside protection in case the stock's price were to decline. In the case of a $55 basis, the sale of a January 2006 70 call would produce the following yield:

Purchase price of stock	$5,500
Less: Call premium	– 1,900
Net Basis	$3,600
Exercise price of stock	$7,000
Net yield	94.4%

This outcome is illustrated in Figure 8.2

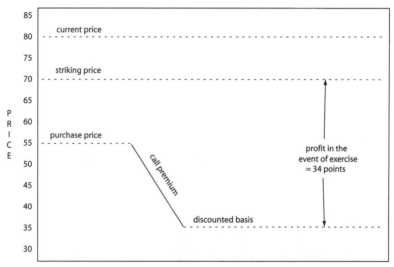

Figure 8.2 ■ Selling in-the-money calls to maximize lower-basis stock profits

If exercise occurs-an outcome you would expect as long as the current market price of stock remained above the $70 striking price-the profit is considerable. A 94.4% return is an outstanding result in this example. However, if exercise did not occur-meaning the market value of stock would have fallen below $70 per share by expiration-then you would be free to sell yet another LEAPS call. The 19-point profit creates a discount in basis to $36 per share, so even a 19-point decline in the stock's value would represent no real loss. That is a very nice downside protection cushion.

Another potential outcome given these same circumstances would be little change in the stock's price but a decline in time value. Looking at the current price of $80.40 per share in comparison to the striking price of 70 for the LEAPS call, a lot can happen in 29 months. One thing is certain; the time value, representing about one-half of the 19-point premium, will decline. So this position could be closed at a profit as long as intrinsic value remained at or below current levels, just from a decline in time value.

That decline in premium value may also occur due to a decline in intrinsic value, bringing up another short-term profit opportunity. For example, were IBM's stock to decline five points to about $75 per share, the value in the short call would lose the same number of points in intrinsic value. So that 19-point call would decline to 14, and could be closed for a fast $500 profit.

The analysis you undergo in deciding which LEAPS calls to select involves proximity of striking price to current market value. The right decision has to be based on time until expiration, your actual basis in stock, and your willingness to have stock called away.

You face an entirely different set of problems when your basis in stock is higher than current market value. Assuming that you continue to believe that the stock is a worthwhile "hold" for long-term price appreciation, you can approach the problem in one of several ways:

1. *Hold and wait for price to rebound.* As long as the stock is a good value, you may need to wait out a price decline before going into a covered call strategy. However, if the attributes of the stock have changed, you may do better selling shares and looking for better growth prospects.
2. *Use short puts to reduce your basis, making short calls more viable.* By selling puts on the stock, you expose yourself to the potential acquisition of more shares in that stock. This accomplishes two things. First, the premium you receive from selling puts reduces your basis in stock. Second, by acquiring stock at a level below your original basis, the average cost of the combined position will be lower as well, possibly putting the covered call strategy in reach.

> **Strategy # 64 – Paper loss reduction with price averaging**   When your basis in stock is greater than current market value, acquire more shares-assuming you continue to believe in the stock's long-term growth prospects-to reduce average basis price.

3. *Acquire more shares through direct purchase.* Lower your basis in stock by averaging the price-a smart move only if you continue to believe that the price decline is temporary. By acquiring more shares, you reduce the overall basis, so that covered call writing becomes practical.

> **Strategy # 65 – Paper loss reduction with short put contingent purchase**   When your basis in stock is greater than current market value, enter a contingent purchase through short puts, in which case exercise would reduce average price; put premium would further reduce your basis.

In all positions involving covered calls, perform your comparative analysis by calculating the net return in each of three possible outcomes:

1. *Return if exercised.* If your short LEAPS call is exercised, what will your net return be? To calculate this outcome, be sure to include the difference between original cost and striking price (capital gain); dividend income; and call premium.

2. *Return if unchanged.* When the stock's price never moves into the money, the call will expire worthless. In this case, the return can be calculated by dividing the premium you received by your investment in the stock. Under this approach, you treat the stock investment as the asset used to generate LEAPS premium income. Because the call has expired, you are free to sell another LEAPS call right away, increasing the income even further.

3. *Return if closed.* If the premium of the short LEAPS call declines substantially due to decline in time value, intrinsic value, or both, it can be closed through a purchase transaction. The net difference between sale and purchase is your profit. Divide that profit by the purchase price of stock to determine the return on the transaction.

To make these various returns comparable, they should always be annualized. Because a LEAPS position can last from a matter of a day or two, up to 36 months, it would not be accurate to compare very short-term returns to much longer-term returns. For example, a 20% return over three months would calculate out to an 80% annualized return. And a 20% return over 36 months would calculate out to 6.67% annualized.

Example: You sold a LEAPS covered call and received a premium of 9. Seven months later, the call had declined to 7 and you sold, realizing a profit of 2. Without adjustment, this is a 22.22% return. To annualize:

1. Calculate the unadjusted return:
$$2 \div 9 = 22.22\%$$
2. Divide return by number of months held:
$$22.22\% \div 7 = 3.17\%$$
3. Multiply result by 12 (months) to arrive at annualized return:
$$3.17\% \times 12 = 38.04\%$$

The formula for annualizing can be applied to holding periods of less than a full year as well as to those longer than a year. Follow these steps:

1. Calculate the straight return using one of the three methods above (return if exercised, unchanged, or closed).
2. Divide the net return by the number of months the short position was open (round to the closest month).
3. Multiply the result in step 2 by 12 to arrive at the annualized return.

Example: You sold a covered LEAPS call and were paid 17. After 16 months, its value had declined to 12, and you sold, taking a profit of 5. The return was 29.41%. To annualize:

1. Calculate the unadjusted return:
$$5 \div 17 = 29.41\%$$
2. Divide return by number of months held:
$$29.41\% \div 16 = 1.84\%$$
3. Multiply result by 12 (months) to arrive at annualized return:
$$1.84\% \times 12 = 22.08\%$$

In those cases where your return takes place in a matter of hours or days, the annualized return calculation will not be especially revealing. Because you will not be able to create very short-term profits consistently, it is inaccurate to include periods under one month; so treat periods under one month as a factor of '1' in the month calculation. So the minimum calculated holding period will always be assumed to be one month, even if you sell a LEAPS call at 10 A.M. and close the position one hour later, doubling your money.

Risks of uncovered calls

If you do not own 100 shares of the underlying stock, you can also sell uncovered calls. While the covered call is viewed as the most conservative of all option strategies, the uncovered call is the highest-risk strategy. In theory, the stock's market price can rise indefinitely, so your market risk is unlimited when you sell uncovered calls.

One way to analyze the risks associated with uncovered calls is to calculate the safety zone. For example, returning to IBM for the moment, the current price is $80.40. The 29-month LEAPS 90 is priced at $9.30 and the LEAPS 100 is at $6.10. The safety zone for the 90 LEAPS call would top out at the price of $99.30 per share, or 18.9 points higher than current market price. As long as the stock's market price remained below the striking price of $90, there would be no risk of exercise; even above that level, as long as the price of stock remained below $99.30, there would be no risk of loss even if the LEAPS call were exercised (due to premium income of $9.30 you received upon sale of the LEAPS call). These calculations do not include trading costs.

> **Strategy # 66 – Uncovered call sale with acceptable safety zones**   Sell out-of-the-money calls to manage short risk, keeping an eye on the range between current price and safety zone top.

The safety zone for the 100 LEAPS call is even more reassuring. By adding premium to the difference between current market price and striking price, we arrive at a level of 25.7 points (Striking price of 100 less 80.40, plus 6.10 premium). So as long as IBM's price remains at or below $100 per share, there is no risk of exercise; and as long as the stock's price remains at or below $106.10 per share, you would not lose in the event of exercise.

The safety zone for both of these examples is summarized in Figure 8.3

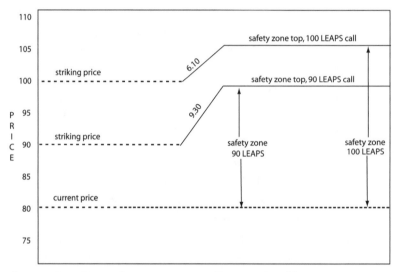

Figure 8.3 ■ Safety zones, uncovered calls

In taking the approach that the greater the safety zone, the more viable the uncovered call, we cannot overlook the very real risks involved with the strategy. Clearly, selling out of the money LEAPS calls is less risky than selling in-the-money ones; however, in the example given, your exposure could extend as long as 29 months. The same features that make several long strategies appealing only augment the risk factors when you go short. So uncovered calls-even when the risks appear manageable on paper-are not for everyone. Most investors tend more toward the conservative approach; and when using covered calls, the outcomes are not only conservative; the yields tend to be handsome as well. Uncovered call writers do not need to spend capital to acquire shares; but in exchange, they expose themselves to potentially greater losses because of the unlimited risk involved. Your ability to write uncovered LEAPS will be further inhibited by the brokerage where your trades are placed. You will be required to keep cash or securities on hand to protect the trading house in the event that your short call is exercised. Thus, you cannot write unlimited calls because the capital you have available will act as a limiting factor.

As with all short strategies, you can also roll up and forward to avoid exercise in the event the stock's market value begins to climb. In some cases, this may only serve to mitigate your eventual loss; in others, it can help to move from an in-the-money threat to an out-of-the-money safety zone. If you can do the exchange and still achieve a credit, then you further help yourself. The extra cash extends your safety zone by the amount received plus the additional points gained.

> **Strategy # 67 – Roll forward and up** *Exchange the current short position for one with later expiration and higher striking price, to remove the in-the-money exposure and replace it with an out-of-the-money position.*

Even if you can only afford to roll forward without adding striking price points in the short LEAPS position, the extended time may further help to reduce the risk of exercise. While exercise can occur at any time during the life of the short LEAPS, it is more likely closer to expiration.

The problem with the rolling technique is that you continue to extend exposure time, thus adding risk in exchange for immediate avoidance of exercise. In cases where the prospect for substantial loss arises, you may limit your loss by offsetting the short position with a long one on the same stock. Of course, this means giving up profits; however, when faced with the chance of losing far more due to rising stock prices, cutting those losses could be the smartest strategy available. You may buy a LEAPS call for five points above the short LEAPS call's striking price, for example. This limits your potential loss to the cost of the long call, plus the five-point difference, and minus the original premium you received for the short position. If time value has deteriorated, this position could be a relatively low-cost solution.

> **Strategy # 68 – Minimized exercise risk**   *If exercise appears a likely outcome for your uncovered LEAPS call, limit your loss by entering a long call position five points higher than the striking price of the short option.*

Example: You sold an uncovered LEAPS call on Microsoft January 2006 January 25, and received a premium of 5.60. Today the stock's value has risen to 30 and you are concerned that if the price continues upward, your short call will be exercised. You buy a Microsoft 30 call, which has a current premium of 2.25. Your net position now is 3.35 to your credit (premium received of 5.60 less premium paid of 2.25). In the event of exercise of the 25 LEAPS, you will only lose $275 (five-point difference between 25 and 30 LEAPS striking prices, minus $225 net credit).

The ratio write covered call and multiple contracts sales

The covered call strategy is fairly straightforward as long as you own 100 shares of stock for each call you sell. When you begin employing ratio writes, the whole question becomes far more complicated-and interesting.

The ratio write is a way to spread risk without having to cover calls on a 1 to 1 basis. For example, if you own 400 shares of stock and sell five calls, you could view this as four covered calls plus one uncovered call; but because not every in-the-money call is exercised, the risk is spread on a ratio write of 5 to 4-five calls sold against 400 shares of stock.

The implications of the ratio write are worth studying. For example, let's say you own 400 shares of IBM stock and current value is $80.40 per share. You sell five calls expiring in 29 months, with striking price of 90. Each call yields 9.30, so you receive total premium of $4,650 for selling the five calls. The immediate return (based on today's market value and not on your actual purchase price) is increased because you wrote five LEAPS calls against 400 shares of stock. In this example, the return would be 14.5%:

$$\frac{\$4,650}{\$32,160} = 14.5\%$$

A straight 1 to 1 return would be 11.6%, based on selling one call per 100 shares of stock. So the ratio write increases your yields while resulting in mitigated risks. In this example, the risk of the 5 to 4 ratio write is minimal not only because of the ratio itself, but also because the position is 10 points out of the money-remember, using LEAPS calls for coverage, you are likely to receive much higher premiums even for such positions because of the time until expiration.

The relative risk would be greater in a 3 to 2 ratio write, of course, because the ratio includes less overall coverage, only 66.7%. In the 5 to 4, you have 80% overall coverage. So while return is increased nearly three points (not to mention an additional $930) the relative risk is not that great. As long as time value declines over the coming months, the ratio write can be eliminated simply by a closing purchase of one of the five short LEAPS calls.

> **Strategy # 69 – Ratio write to increase covered call returns**   Enter high-percentage ratio writes-such as 80% coverage in a 5 to 4 situation-to augment return without increasing risks; employ this strategy for out-of-the-money short calls.

The ratio write is one strategy that is effective for making the most of the covered call when you own multiples of 100-share lots. A second method worth considering is planning for a roll-forward and up, in anticipation that the stock price will actually exceed striking price. When you are confident that the stock price is on the rise, why sell covered calls? There are two reasons. First, if you are mistaken and the price remains the same or falls, selling LEAPS calls discounts your basis and helps recover your paper loss. Second, even if the stock does rise, you can retain profits by rolling forward and up. This is most profitable when you own more than 100 shares and can increase your position with the roll.

> **Strategy # 70 – Timing LEAPS short calls for net credit rolls**   *Avoid exercise by rolling forward and up and at the same time increasing the number of calls written.*

Example: You own 500 shares of IBM and you want to write covered calls. Today's price is 80.40 per share and you write three LEAPS 90 calls expiring in 29 months, receiving 9.30 per contract. A few months later, the stock's price rises to 95. The 90 calls now are valued at 10.50. You want to avoid exercise of your three short LEAPS calls. You enter a closing buy transaction for the three, creating a loss of 1.20 per call (total $360). At the same time, you open *five* short calls expiring three months later at 100. Each is valued at 11.40. This yields $5,700 ($1,140 for five contracts). So the trade consists of spending $3,150 ($1,050 for the original three LEAPS calls) and receiving $5,700, a net credit of $2,550 (receipt of $5,700, payment of $3,150).

In this example, you not only create a net credit by increasing the number of calls; you also add 10 points in striking price, moving your exposure from exercise of 90 up to exercise of 100. Thus, you convert intrinsic value of five points per contract, to 100% time value. This outcome is illustrated in Figure 8.4.

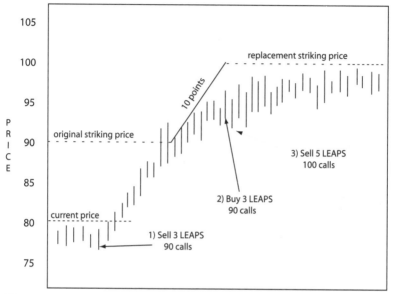

Figure 8.4 ■ **Creating net credits in short LEAPS rolls**

Covered calls as a contingent sale strategy

The covered call is the most basic form of contingent sale. As long as you own the 100 shares and know that the short call can be exercised, you also have to be willing to relinquish those shares if that occurs. Thus, anyone who enters into a covered call position is accepting the fact that their shares might be called away.

Another angle on the covered call involves the use of a straddle-the sale of both a call and a put at the same striking price and with the same expiration date. If you do not own 100 shares, a short straddle would be considered as very high-risk. However, if the call portion of that straddle is covered by 100 shares of stock, the short straddle makes far more sense. First of all, a short straddle creates a broad safety zone using long-term LEAPS, in which time value is fairly high for at-the-money contracts. Second, either side of the position can be rolled to avoid exercise. You would roll the call forward and up if the stock's price rises; and you would roll the put forward and down for the same reason. And either side (or both sides) can be closed if and when time value falls out of the total premium, creating the opportunity to gain simply from lost time value.

> **Strategy # 71 – Short straddle expansion**   *Sell a covered call and a put on the same expiration and striking price to create a short straddle.*

Remember, the short straddle is half covered; and the put side of the position is a form of contingent purchase (if exercised, you would acquire 100 shares at the striking price, even if the current market value were lower). So in order to justify this strategy, you need to believe that the current price is reasonable-so that upon exercise of the put, you would be glad to acquire 100 shares at that price-and that the safety zone created by the total receipt was high enough to justify the straddle itself.

Example: IBM is currently selling 80.40 and you own 100 shares. You want to enter into a covered call but you realize that a short straddle will increase premium income. The 29-month 80 call is valued at $13.50 and the 29-month 80 put is at 10.80. By selling one of each, you will receive a total of $2,430, or 30.2% of the stock's current market value. (This is based on current value and not on your actual purchase price; so actual return could be far higher if you acquired the stock for less.)

In this example, the substantial return also provides you with a 24-point safety zone on either side of the striking price of 80. So even if the stock were to move 24 points (in either direction) and one of the options were exercised, you would break even on the straddle. In the case of an upside price movement, the call is covered; in the case of a downward price movement, you would acquire shares at 80, but their value would be discounted 24 points to $56 per share; so the downside protection is substantial in this strategy. In practice, it is certain that no matter how the stock's value changes, one or both options will lose value and could be closed at a profit. If the stock remains within the 24-point range, the call could be closed (if the stock is down 24 points) or the put could be closed (if the stock is up within 24 points) at a profit in either case. The call is covered, so you are prepared for exercise; the put cannot be covered, so you would acquire another 100 shares at $80 per share upon exercise of the put. Either side of the transaction-or both sides-can be rolled to avoid exercise as well.

The strategy, with the safety zone, is illustrated in Figure 8.5.

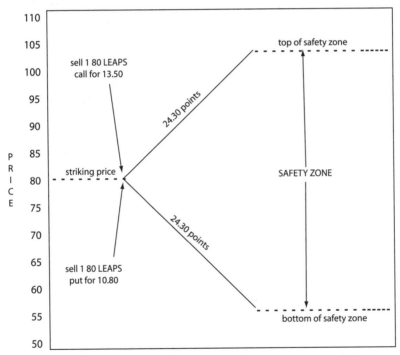

Figure 8.5 ■ Using the short straddle to expand the covered call strategy

The important distinction to recall about the straddle that includes a covered call on one side is the relative risk. If the straddle were uncovered on both sides, the call would represent a very high risk exposure; but because 100 shares are owned for coverage, market risk is limited to the downside uncovered put, less the safety zone. In the example provided, more than 24 points of safety zone were provided by entering a 29-month straddle. While that is a long period of time to remain at risk, remember a final important point: It is all time value. So in the best of all possible outcomes, the stock would move very little and both sides of the straddle could be closed at a good profit. While you have to be prepared for the unexpected or for the worst case, the short straddle as an extension of a long-term covered call provides significant returns—30.2% in the example given. If the basis in stock was originally lower, the return would be higher. For example, if you had bought IBM stock at 55 and entered the straddle illustrated above, return on that straddle would be 44.2% ($2,430 premium, divided by $5,500). For the relatively small risk exposure involved, that is an incredible return.

That potential for double-digit returns accompanied with little risk is what is so appealing with covered call strategies. Remembering that we need to position the striking price to automatically create a profit if and when the call is exercised, you can program the basic strategy to produce profits under any scenario: if exercised, if expired, or if closed. The major benefits to covered call strategies are:

1. Time value works for you, not against you.
2. The strategy can be repeated indefinitely, creating income into the future.
3. Premium income provides you with downside protection for your original stock investment.
4. You can avoid exercise by closing and replacing short positions.

5. As long as your stock was purchased below current market price, and you select striking prices out of the money, you eliminate virtually all risk. You will profit no matter what the outcome.

The elegance of the basic covered call strategy cannot be ignored; but there is more to the strategy as well. Expanding on the initial strategy, the next chapter examines the nature of the long-term opportunities using LEAPS in a variety of ways.

Chapter 9

The Long-Term Covering:
Your investment cash cow

The many possible methods for using LEAPS covered calls open up profit opportunities as well as different forms of risk. Properly managed, covered calls produce double-digit returns while retaining their conservative character-the best of both worlds.

In the usual analysis of risk, we have to accept the premise that high risk and high yield go together, and that the association is inescapable. However, in the case of LEAPS covered calls, this is not so. Because the strategy can be designed so that any possible outcome is desirable, the covered call is the exception to the rule. This applies when:

1. Any outcome would be profitable due to your actual basis in the underlying stock.
2. The stock's market price does not suffer a catastrophic drop in price.
3. You stay with a proven strategy and avoid the temptation to expand into higher risks.

Each of these three points is worth elaboration. Establishing a *profitable* strategy is easiest, of course, when the current market price of the stock is higher than your basis; this expands the possibilities and broadens your potential profit margin. In such situations, stock ownership serves a dual purpose: as a viable long-term growth investment, and as a cash cow for the short-term production of short LEAPS premium income. Expanding on this, as long as you continue to view the current price as attractive, you can sell short puts as a method of contingent purchase, further improving immediate income while contingently increasing your holdings as well.

If and when the stock suffers a large price drop, the tendency among the market as a whole is to want to sell and cut losses. But at such times, real profit opportunities can be made by remaining cool and making rational decisions. In the options market, large point change-up or down-produces many opportunities. Chances are, a well-selected stock is going to suffer unexpected price drops when the market as a whole falls. If the fundamentals remain strong, the stock is going to rebound. When a well-selected stock's value falls, it is likely to be a temporary change, and the stock will return to its established trading range in most cases. In those instances where you simply pick the wrong stock-whether you employ LEAPS options or not-the possibility of a market loss is ever-present.

The third point-avoiding the temptation to stray from a proven strategy-may be the greatest danger for options traders. Temptation should be avoided because strategies work well when they are followed, including bail-out goals, contingency plans, and execution points. Strategies work poorly when they are ignored or abandoned because a change in market conditions raises what looks like a quick opportunity-ignoring the fact that it is accompanied by unacceptable risks. So self-discipline is a most important attribute worth developing and practicing, especially when you are using strategies known to produce double-digit yields with relatively low risk.

LEAPS used to augment covered call income

The most basic approach to covered call writing is to select an out-of-the-money contract with maximum time value, write it against 100 shares, and simply hold until expiration. While this is a simple and acceptable method, it will not necessarily yield the greatest level of profits. The problem with holding such a call for up to 36 months is that it limits the yield; by selecting time values and then trading out of positions at the right time, you can literally turn 100 shares of stock into a big source for cash flow-and at the same time avoid exercise most of the time to preserve the long-term investment *and* your ability to continue producing profits.

Example: You purchased 100 shares of IBM at $55 per share; today the stock's market price is $80.40. You sell a 29-month LEAPS 90 call and receive a premium of 9.30, a 16.9% yield based on your purchase price of $55 per share. A few months later, the stock's value remains out of the money and the LEAPS call's value has declined to 4.60. You enter a closing purchase transaction and replace it with a later-expiring LEAPS call. You pay $460 to close out the original call but you receive $1,015. By repeating the process every five to six months, trading on time value, the total outcome over 29 months is:

Month	LEAPS sale	LEAPS purchase	Net proceeds
1	$ 930		$ 930
7	1,015	$ 460	555
13	855	330	525
19	1,100	410	690
24	840	580	260
29		315	(315)
Totals	$4,740	$2,095	$2,645

The strategy shown above is also illustrated in Figure 9.1. In this example, the strategy is shown during a 29-month period in which the stock's value rises, and subsequent calls are replaced with higher striking price contracts, to avoid exercise. Note that in the process, you also "buy" an additional 10 points of striking price with the roll up.

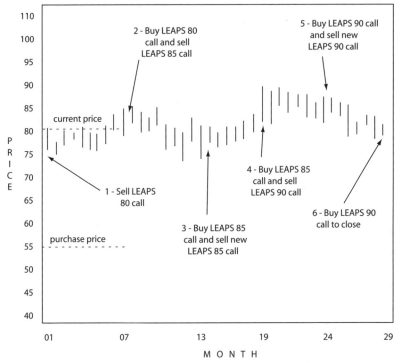

Figure 9.1 ■ **The covered LEAPS progressive LEAPS write series**

This overall outcome, based on original purchase price of $55 per share, represents a 48.1% return. At the same time, when the 29-month period has ended, you still own the 100 shares. Each LEAPS call in the example was closed as soon as time value began to evaporate, and was replaced with a later-expiring LEAPS call containing greater time value. The standard here was to continually select out-of-the-money calls with maximum time value; increase the striking price level to avoid exercise when necessary; and maximize the net return.

> **Strategy # 72 – Progressive covered LEAPS writes**
> *Seek high-time value, out-of-the-money short positions to cover and then close and replace continually, increasing striking price as required to avoid exercise.*

The multiple-part exercise for this strategy demonstrates that outcomes with double-digit returns can and do occur. The power of the covered call strategy is that, with well-selected stocks, LEAPS covered call income can be quite substantial, especially in terms of the yield based on your original basis in the stock.

We have not identified striking prices, and for a good reason: It does not really matter what striking prices are used, as long as you can select short positions that are out of the money at the time the LEAPS calls are sold that also produce premium income sufficient to justify the exposure. The distance and premium combined provide the all-important price cushion, creating flexibility in both time value and price flexibility. Even if the stock's value rises during the time you are short the LEAPS call, the time value will decline. Time value is not going to be responsive to stock price movement. So as long as the stock's price remains in that safety zone below striking price, you can enjoy the steadily declining time value. Closing of these positions should be timed with two factors in mind: the value of the premium relative to the original sales price, and the proximity to the striking price.

You want to maximize profit in the position, so the more decline in time value, the better. At the same time, this strategy works best when you remain below striking price; so it is smarter to take a relatively modest profit when market price approaches striking price, and replace the position with a new short LEAPS call with later expiration and higher striking price-the standard roll forward and up. This enables you to continue the strategy indefinitely without having shares exercised.

With the long-term LEAPS, time value will decline more gradually than it would if you were within one year of expiration; but for out-of-the-money LEAPS, you receive maximum premium when you are working with maximum time. So under this strategy, your overall performance is enhanced by using longer-term LEAPS contracts. That does not mean you are committed forever; by continually trading out of the current position and going to the next one, you retain flexibility while increasing income. In the example, you're earning 48% over 29 months, which annualizes out to about 20% per year-not counting dividends and paper profits on the stock. To annualize in this example, we want to reduce the total return over 29 months, to the equivalent 12-month average:

$$\frac{48.1}{29} \times 12 = 19.9\%$$

This example is idealized, of course. We cannot know with certainty how premium values will change over a five- to six-month period, and we cannot know how the stock's price will change either. The point, however, is that if we can retain the out-of-the-money status of the short LEAPS call, such outcomes are practical and realistic. It may take a longer amount of time, and it may happen more quickly, depending on the stock, amount of time value, and price and option volatility.

By using the 100 shares as the vehicle to produce these conservative returns, we literally surf the stock over the waves of potential profit. So the stock serves a dual purpose. It is part of the portfolio of long-term holdings, and it increases cash flow and current income. Given the example above, if the stock were to grow up an average of 7% per year and yield an average 2% dividend, real return over the long term could be 29% or more:

Option return	19.9%
Average growth	7.0
Dividend income	2.0
Total return	28.9%

Of course, this is based on the example, which is hypothetical. If you own multiple blocks of 100 shares, you have even greater flexibility to employ many combinations and roll-out techniques to improve the situation even more. At times when the stock's price does dip, you can put a hold on LEAPS call trades and revert to selling puts. This continues to provide you with current income, along with the potential of picking up stock at depressed prices-riding the downward trend with short puts. While this means you are picking up shares above market value if exercised, you achieve several advantages:

1. You average purchase price.
2. You take advantage of market declines that are temporary for a strong long-term growth stock.
3. You continue to receive current income from short LEAPS options, but using puts in place of calls until the price rebounds.

> **Strategy # 73 – Short put sale with stock price decline**   *When prices are in a downward trend, sell puts. This averages your purchase price, takes advantage of temporary price declines, and continues your current income from LEAPS options.*

This strategy is the exact opposite of the basic covered call. The call strategy works well when prices are gradually rising; to avoid exercise, you roll forward and up and track the call along with the stock price. Even the most successful covered call writer has to wait out periods when the stock price is moving downward. This is where the short put makes sense. Premium from selling the put discounts your basis in the stock, mitigating the price decline; it also enables you to continue earning premium income on LEAPS writes. With the put, you avoid exercise by rolling forward and out when necessary. As prices turn around and begin rising again, you can revert to the covered call strategy.

Flexibility to close, exercise or roll

It is a mistake to view any option strategy as having only one possible outcome. By its very nature, the options market has any number of potential twists and turns. When using covered calls to maximize short-term income, you want to keep the three basic programs in mind: close, exercise, or roll.

The close and replace program. In order to maximize the covered call strategy, we propose an aggressive series of replacement strategies. By opening the short position and then replacing it as soon as it is profitable to do so, you can continually create short-term income while avoiding exercise. If the stock's price remains with a price range so that the same striking price works, then the roll forward is most appropriate. If the stock's price is moving upward, the close of a current option is replaced with a later-expiring, higher striking price contract. If the price of the stock declines, you have several choices:

1. Let the short position continue to run, waiting out the price decline. In this approach, patience pays off, so be willing to hold off and see what will happen next. In a highly volatile market, you may need to ride out the dips without taking any action.

2. Close the short position at a profit and roll forward with the same striking price, so that you increase short-term income and extend your exposure.
3. Close the position and sell a put, with the idea that the price will turn around at some point and you continue short-term income without having to wait. If the stock's price continues its fall, you pick up another 100 shares per put written. When the price does rebound, this serves to increase your base for producing more current income from LEAPS activity.

> **Strategy # 74 – Close and replace tactics**   *When the stock's price declines, shift to one of the three defensive modes of close and replace.*

The exercise program. Another approach to selling covered calls is to accept exercise if and when the position goes in the money. In this situation, you probably are willing to sell the stock and, perhaps, you think it is time to sell. If you no longer wish to hold for the long term, using at-the-money or even in-the-money calls to bring about exercise is an excellent way to achieve the goal. This raises the question of what to do with the proceeds. Upon exercise, you sell the shares of stock, but then need to find another place to invest your funds. This opens up all kinds of possibilities, such as reverting to long LEAPS calls as contingent purchase for a diversified range of stocks.

> **Strategy # 75 – Covered calls to exercise**   *If you want to sell stock, select short LEAPS to (a) maximize premium income, and (b) produce acceptable capital gains.*

The roll program. This is different than the close and replace program. Under close and replace, the whole idea is to generate turnover as often as possible to produce short-term income while avoiding exercise. The roll program is a contingency plan you use when you want to stay short on the covered LEAPS call, and avoid exercise. The short-term income is not the goal; you are more interested in exhausting time value premium to the point that the short call expires or can be sold for next to nothing. Under this approach, you are likely to realize far higher percentage returns, but over a longer period of time. The final outcome may be greater or less than the close and replace. The roll program is appropriate under some situations, especially when you believe that trading on the time value of the current short position will yield more profit than closing and replacing it. For example, if time value is falling very slowly, you will want to wait out the decline for many more months; however, the stock's market price is also inching toward the striking price, so you decide to roll out of the current short position into a higher striking price. If you want to retain the same expiration terms, you might even give up some profit to avoid exercise. If you believe the stock's price will continue to climb, this could be a smart move. As long as the difference in premium value is less than five points, replacing today's striking price with the higher one could be a profitable move. For example, you currently are short on a LEAPS 55 call valued at 8.40. You can roll out of that and sell a LEAPS 60 with the same expiration for 10.50, a difference of 2.10. By doing so, you "buy" five points ($500) in the striking price for a cost of $210.

> **Strategy # 76 – Roll out to exhaust time value**   *In situations where you want to remain covered over an extended period of time to maximize time value profits, roll out only to avoid exercise.*

All three of the programs can be employed or mixed as circumstances require. While self-discipline is an important attribute for every options trader, flexibility and the ability to change tactics quickly is equally valuable. It is typical that investors enter into a covered call position on the assumption that the stock's price will rise or remain about where it is today. Circumstances do not always conform to expectations. So contingency planning or even defensive mode may become more important than the primary plan. Remember, as long as you have selected stocks well, unexpected downward price movement is not cause for alarm; it is probably temporary in nature, especially if following the larger market trend. Strong stocks reward stockholders over time, and short-term change does not destroy an otherwise strong strategy; it may only mean you need to look for alternatives. One of those alternatives may be to wait out the change and see what happens.

The time value strategic advantage

A detailed analysis of time value trends identifies covered call strategies and timing to produce maximum profits. This is based on the premise that the stocks you pick for covered call writing have sound fundamentals and represent worthwhile long-term holds on their own merit. More volatile stocks will tend to offer richer option premiums, primarily due to their volatile nature. So it is a mistake to pick stocks based primarily on the potential for option profits, if in fact the stock itself is not a worthy investment.

Given that caveat, how can you maximize time value in the covered call strategy? We have already shown how using long-term short positions maximizes your flexibility even when selling out-of-the-money LEAPS. By employing the time value of the long-term contract, you can achieve immediate double-digit returns on your stock just from option premium. However, the timing of not only the initial sale, but closing and rolling that position, are crucial to the on-going success in your covered call program.

In a perfect world, we could simply set goals and follow formulas. For example, if you could achieve a 15% return after trading costs, it would be time to enter a closing purchase transaction and get out of a position; and then follow that with a subsequent short position with later expiration and, potentially, a higher striking price. In practice, however, the actual timing of the transition from a current short position to a replacement depends more on the stock's price movement than on anything else.

To avoid exercise altogether, you might need to transact far more frequently than originally planned; if the stock's price moves upward dramatically and in a short time period, you will need to act quickly to ensure that exercise does not occur. (Remember, in all forms of covered call strategies, you have to be willing to accept exercise. Although a strategy calls for avoiding it by buying more premium *and* higher striking prices in a rising price situation, exercise does happen.) For example, let's say you sell an 80 call when the stock's price is at or near 80. That price immediately jumps into the mid-80s range. You may want to quickly close out the original short position and replace it with a rolled-up and rolled-forward 85 call. This avoids exercise while buying more striking price (potential profit if and when exercised). In the alternative, you can simply roll forward, get more premium credit and accept a longer at-risk period, knowing that exercise is more likely close to expiration.

On the other side of the spectrum of possibilities, the stock's market price could remain within a narrow trading range. This means that you can patiently wait out the decline in time value, or replace the existing call on a slower schedule than you originally thought. In these situations, once time value has come out of the premium, you can close at a profit and replace a later-expiring call with a higher striking price. This is the greatest advantage of all. You not only add a price cushion by taking more time value premium in the new short position; you also continue receiving premium income, meaning (a) more flexibility for later rolls even if the stock's price rises, (b) more downside protection due to discounting of your basis in stock, and (c) less likelihood of exercise due to further out-of-the-money striking price.

So there is no absolute formula for the timing of replacement for short LEAPS in the covered call position. As long as the stock's price remains where you would prefer-meaning just below the striking price-you can time your replacement strategy with ease. Stocks rarely act exactly as we would like, however. Once you entered to covered call position, the stock might rise quickly, remain in a narrow trading range, or plunge. Remember, as long as you have selected stocks using accurate fundamental analysis, short-term price change will not affect that company's long-term growth value. However, depending on the direction of price movement, you may need to alter strategies accordingly.

Not only do strategies need adjustment along the way; your timing is just as critical. In Figure 9.1, note that replacement often is made at price spikes. So if you are short on an 85 LEAPS call and the stock spikes up to 84-close to striking price-you can avoid exercise by trading out of the 85 and replacing it with a later-expiring 90 LEAPS call. Since both positions involve time value only (since both are below their respective striking prices) you lose nothing in intrinsic value.

When you are in the money, timing can work to your advantage as well. For example, if you are short on the 85 LEAPS call and the price has risen to 88, that means that three points of the premium are intrinsic value. If the stock then declines to 85 the following day, it is likely that the decline in the 85 call will be more dramatic than it would be for a 90 LEAPS call expiring later. The reason is that with the 85 LEAPS call, a portion of the lost premium is intrinsic value; in the case of the further-out 90 LEAPS call, no intrinsic value is involved, so the option premium value is not as responsive to the stock's price change. In this situation, you have an advantage in rolling out of the 85 and replacing it with the

90. You probably will gain by taking the reduced intrinsic value and replacing it with time value of the higher, later-expiring LEAPS due to the relative premium value changes.

Problems of long-term risk exposure

Given the ability to trade in and out of positions with relative ease, you also need to devise an exit strategy for the covered call position-assuming that you will want to either stop writing the calls and allow the stock to find its new trading range during volatile periods, or simply accept exercise if and when it occurs.

Another possibility is that you will be willing to trade in and out of short covered positions for some period of time, and then exit from the strategy and revert to the status of long-position stockholder. In that case, there are several ways to exit:

> ***Strategy # 77 – Wait out expiration*** *When the stock's price remains below striking price, wait for expiration.*

1. *Wait out expiration.* The easiest way to exit the covered call strategy is to enter the position and take no action. This assumes, of course, that the stock's price remains below striking price for the entire term. This can and does occur and, as long as exercise is not imminent, the strategy makes sense.

> ***Strategy # 78 – Close to exit*** *When premium value is low, or when you want to take advantage of climbing stock prices, close the short position to avoid exercise and risk exposure.*

2. *Buy to close.* There are two conditions in which you would want to enter a closing purchase transaction. First is when time value has declined to a minimal level and you want to get out of the position just to be free of the continued exposure. Second is when the stock's price is

rising and you expect it to continue, so you are willing to take a loss on the LEAPS call in order to maximize the potential capital gain on the stock. You would view the loss as the price you pay to avoid the lost opportunity.

> **Strategy # 79 – Indefinite roll on price support**
> *Wait out the stock's price cycle by rolling forward and up indefinitely; and when the stock price declines, close out the position without replacement.*

3. *Continue rolling until the stock's price falls.* You can avoid exercise indefinitely-as long as you can find higher-striking price, later-expiring LEAPS calls whose premium is equal to or higher than the current value of your short LEAPS call. Eventually, the price cycle will decline and you will be able to wait out expiration, or buy out of the position at a very low cost.

> **Strategy # 80 – Short call conversion to reduce risks**
> *Exit the covered call position by converting to a spread; buy long LEAPS to reduce, eliminate, or offset the short risk exposure.*

4. *Spread against the short position with an affordable long LEAPS call.* You can also cancel or reduce the risk by buying a long LEAPS call that offsets the risk through a horizontal spread (same striking price but later expiration); through a vertical spread (same expiration, higher or lower striking price); or through a diagonal spread (a roll).

There are two aspects to covered call writing that the cautious investor will find difficult to accept. First is the notion that this is a *conservative* strategy, and second is the claim that you can earn consistent double-digit yields with covered calls. Both of these aspects are true. Covered call writing is conservative because it is low-risk. If properly structured, any outcome will be profitable and the only risk not elimi-nated is market risk. (You experience this as a stockholder, but by selling covered calls, you *reduce* market risk due to the discounting feature.) The second aspect-double-digit returns-are impossible to ignore. If, like many option investors, you enter the short strategy and close it as soon as a profit can be realized, it is likely that substantial returns will occur in a period of weeks (sometimes days). Even keeping a short position open longer will produce double-digit returns, because the LEAPS time value is rich to begin with.

Those opposed to options or, stockholders who frown on options as a profitable device, will point out that the risk of exercise cannot be ignored. This is true. If you are not willing to accept exercise as one of several possible outcomes, you should avoid covered calls. However, even that risk can be mitigated and, in many cases, eliminated altogether. The next chapter explains how.

Chapter 10

Avoiding Exercise:
Slim down to stay financially fit

Whether you are using short calls or short puts, you probably will want to avoid exercise. As much as that outcome is acceptable, you might view it as far more desirable (and profitable) to roll out of the short position and trade to a more advantageous striking price. By exchanging time for potential exercise value, you can enhance current income via LEAPS net credits on the roll, and effectively avoid exercise indefinitely.

The process of avoiding exercise has to be a part of the overall short LEAPS strategy. If your ultimate goal is to exercise a long call and buy shares, then offsetting that call with short calls may defeat the larger goal. You can use short calls to recapture the cost of the long call; but you still need to ensure that your original goal-to exercise the long call if the stock's price rises-is not lost to the secondary strategy.

For any LEAPS short position, you have to be prepared for exercise as a possible outcome. Anyone who goes short on a LEAPS call or put needs to be aware of this. The overall strategy should be designed so that exercise is perfectly acceptable. In some cases, it is even desirable.

In the case of a LEAPS short call, you have two choices. An uncovered call has the greatest profit potential, but an extraordinary level of risk; in the event the stock's market price rises substantially, you could experience a large loss. A covered call,

in comparison, is a very conservative strategy. Properly structured (especially in cases where your basis in the stock is far
below striking price), the covered call is as close to risk-free as
possible. You can create double-digit profits with little risk
using covered calls.

In the case of a LEAPS put, you may be required to purchase
100 shares of stock at a price higher than current market value
of the stock. In that regard, exercise is undesirable; however, as
long as you would consider the striking price a good value for
the stock, you may view a price decline below that level to be
temporary. So as long as your assessment is correct, exercise
would not be undesirable. When you further discount your
basis for the amount of premium received upon sell of the put,
it is entirely possible that using short puts-as a form of contingent purchase-is a sensible alternate to buying LEAPS calls. The
money flows in rather than out and, when the striking price is
selected carefully, the decline in stock value may be offset by
time value premium profits.

Rolling forward

The roll-out achieves the desired result of avoiding exercise,
or at least delaying it. There are three methods to the roll:

1. A roll forward only-which has the effect of deferring
   exercise date.
2. A roll forward and up-used when you are short LEAPS
   calls.
3. A roll forward and down-used when you are short
   LEAPS puts.

In all three techniques, the intention is to create a net
credit in the exchange while also improving your position
regarding ultimate exercise. As a part of the strategy, we
would expect that a stock's price will reverse direction after
the roll so that (a) the threat of exercise is removed, or (b)
the current short position can be closed at a profit.

Strategy # 81 – Timed stock price cycle roll-out
Roll to avoid exercise, and then close the short position when the stock's price moves out of the money

Example: You own 100 shares of stock and you sold a covered call with a striking price of 65. The stock has since moved to 67 and you wish to avoid exercise; you roll forward three months at the same striking price, creating a net credit through replacement. A month later, the stock's price falls to 61 and you enter a closing purchase transaction.

Example: You sold a 30 LEAPS put on a stock whose current price is 33. Since then the stock's price has fallen to 28. You buy the put and roll forward to a later 30 put, creating a net credit. The stock's price rebounds to 35; you close out the short put at a profit.

Both of these examples are illustrated in Figure 10.1.

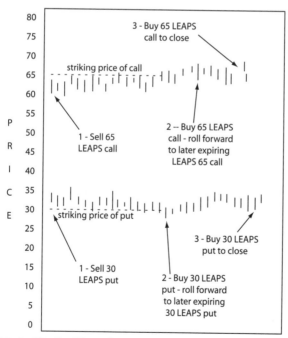

Figure 10.1 ■ **Rolling forward to avoid exercise**

In these examples, note that the roll forward occurs when the stock moves in the money. At that time, exercise is possible even if there remains many months until expiration. Rolling forward to a later expiring option at the same striking price does not remove the threat of expiration; however, by moving to the later expiration date, it does reduce the probability.

Rolling forward and up

When you write calls-whether covered or uncovered-the roll forward and up is a sensible strategy for avoiding exercise. When the stock approaches the at-the-money position, it is easy for it to continue upward; so the possibility of exercise becomes immediate. For uncovered call sellers, this is a potentially dangerous situation; if the stock were to jump 12 points and the LEAPS call were exercised, the uncovered LEAPS call writer would lose $1,200, for example.

For covered call writers, there is less urgency. Exercise is an acceptable outcome and if you do your homework prior to entering the strategy, you have already calculated the return in the case of no change, exercise, and expiration. However, even though exercise is acceptable in the properly designed covered call strategy, it may remain profitable and desirable to perpetually roll forward and up.

> *Strategy # 82 – Roll forward and up to increase profits.* *Avoid exercise while adding striking price points by rolling forward and up*

Example: You own 100 shares of stock with a basis of 35; when the stock was trading at 51, you sold a 28-month LEAPS 55 call and received 13 ($1,300). Today the stock is selling at 56. You close the original LEAPS call, paying 8 and replace it with a later-expiring 60 call, for which you receive 10. The difference, $200, is a net credit.

In this example, if exercise were to occur, you would keep the $1,300 received for selling the LEAPS call, and would also realize a capital gain on the stock of $2,000. That is an overall return on your investment of 60%. Even so, you recognize that the roll forward and up can be achieved with a net credit, while also buying you an extra five points in striking price. If that later LEAPS call were to be exercised later, you would earn a total $3,500 ($2,500 on stock plus a total of $1,500 in call premium, a 63.6% return overall.

One advantage of rolling forward and up is obvious: in buying additional striking price points, you also increase your gain in the event of exercise. At the same time, though, you are trading intrinsic value for time value, a significant point that cannot be overlooked. By doing so, you increase the chances that the stock will remain out of the money; that value will decline in the LEAPS call over time; and that you will be able to either close at a profit or allow the option to expire worthless. By trading out of the position with the roll forward and up, you increase your chances of avoiding exercise, so that the strategy can be repeated in the future.

Because time value is so much greater in LEAPS than in short-term traditional listed options, it is a realistic goal to earn *more* than 100% return on your stock by repetitive covered call writing. For example, if your basis in stock is 55 per share, and you can receive an average of $1,300 each time you sell a covered call, you could recapture the entire $5,500 investment by repeating the strategy just over four times. This assumes that you allow the LEAPS call to expire worthless in each case. More realistically, you could trade in covered calls, selling maximum time value and then closing out positions when time value has declined; this strategy works in place of the roll forward and up, as long as the stock remains out of the money.

> **Strategy # 83 – Covered call trade to recapture stock investment.** *Trade a series of covered calls and close at a profit to recapture stock investment basis over time*

This approach is the default position as long as the stock remains out of the money; once it extends to and above the striking price, you need to use the roll to avoid exercise. But consider the potential outcome when using covered calls to replace your initial investment. Assuming that on average, you can receive $1,300 per LEAPS short call, and that you can close the position in an average time of five months at $400, you would earn a net of $900 every five months. Returning to the previous example using a basis of 55 per share, the time required to completely replace your purchase price is about two years:

Month	Opening Sale	Closing Purchase
1	$1,300	$ 400
6	1,300	400
11	1,300	400
16	1,300	400
21	1,300	400
26	1,300	400
Total	$7,800	$2,400
Net	$5,400	

In the example, you recovered $5,400 on a $5,500 investment in 26 months, a 98.2% overall return that annualizes out to 45.3%. This type of return is not unrealistic as long as the stock remains at or below striking price and continues to show depreciated time value at the same rate.

Rolling forward and down

An opposite strategy is applied when you write LEAPS puts. Because a put cannot be covered in the same way as a call, the comparison between covered and uncovered does not apply. It is possible to "cover" the put by going long on one contract and then writing a series of lower-striking price, earlier-expiration puts to offset. However, a more realistic strategy is to sell puts as a form of contingent purchase, and then avoid exercise by rolling forward and down.

> **Strategy # 84 – Roll forward and down to increase profits**   Roll out of put positions when stock falls in the money, to avoid exercise and subtract striking price points

The short put strategy, discussed in past chapters, allows you to buy stock at a price you consider reasonable, discounted by the premium you are paid when you sell the LEAPS put. So for example, if you would consider $45 a reasonable price to pay for stock, and you sell a 50 LEAPS put receiving a premium of 5, then your discounted basis-in the event of exercise-would be $45 per share.

Even if you would accept exercise under those conditions, you may also consider the contingent purchase to be more advantageous if stock could be purchased at a lower rate and, at the same time, if put premium could be increased.

Example: You sold a LEAPS 50 put at a time that the underlying stock was selling for $54 per share, receiving a premium of 5. Since then, the stock's price has slipped down to $47. To avoid exercise, you enter a closing purchase transaction and pay a premium of 3, and roll forward and down to sell a later-expiring LEAPS 45 put. You are paid a premium of 4, so that you get a net credit of $100. More important, however, is the reduction in cost of five points of striking price in the event of expiration. Even though you considered the original striking price to be a reasonable exercise level, the roll forward and down reduces the contingent cost of stock by five points.

In situations where you roll forward and down (or even forward and up in the case of covered calls), it could even make sense to accept a net debit. If buying the extra five points of striking price is worthwhile, in your opinion, then the trade could make sense.

> **Strategy # 85 – Roll with a net debit** *Accept a loss on the LEAPS option replacement, in exchange for a more advantageous striking price level*

Example: You sold a LEAPS 50 put and since then the stock has fallen. To roll forward and down today, you would have to pay 3 to close the short put, but you would receive only 2 for the later-expiring LEAPS put five points lower in striking price. The net debit is $100.

In this case, you decide to pay the $100 net difference in order to trade out of the original striking price for a lower one. If the short put were to be exercised, you would be required to pay $500 less for the stock. This strategy makes sense when you determine that the downward trend in the stock is going to continue in the next few months; but when you continue to believe that this is a temporary trend and, ultimately, the stock's price will rebound. When you need to adjust your estimation of the stock's trading range due to timing, you face the prospect of accepting exercise with the change of a deep discount to market price; or mitigating that effect by buying into five points less purchase price with a roll forward and down.

Tracking net profit or loss

It is all too easy to concentrate on strategies-especially when rolling out of one position and into another-to the extent that you lose sight of the larger goal. While it is desirable to avoid exercise in many of the contingent purchase strategies, for example, it is not worth it if by avoiding exercise you fail to meet your acquisition goal.

Example: You buy 10 LEAPS calls on a single stock as a form of basic contingent purchase. Your primary goal is to buy shares of stock and then write covered calls; you use the LEAPS approach rather than putting a large sum of capital at risk, knowing that your goal will work only if the stock's market value rises. As with all forms of contingent purchase, if the stock's value does not perform as expected, you do not have to exercise the calls.

To offset the cost of the long calls, you begin writing a series of higher-striking price, shorter expiring calls against the position. This secondary goal is designed to recapture the cost of the long position. Assuming that the stock's price will rise, you write only three calls at the next higher striking price and an additional three calls above that level, holding the remaining four position in reserve in case they are needed for a later roll forward and up.

This strategy is a familiar one. The flexibility of working with multiple LEAPS calls is a great advantage when creating the spread with short against long. However, consider the problems this creates in a situation where the stock's market price continues rising. If the stock's value goes to the point that rolling is no longer possible without losses, you could end up fully committed with 10 short calls against the long positions, and having all of them exercised.

In that situation, you might break even or make a small profit, but your primary goal-acquiring shares of stock below market value-would not be possible. If all of your short LEAPS positions are ultimately exercised, then you have defeated your primary goal by covering all of your long calls. As an alternative, you may purchase a multiple of long positions with the idea of splitting them. Given the above example of

10 long LEAPS calls, you could enter a strategy in which you want to acquire 500 shares if the stock rises; and will spread against the remaining five contracts with short positions.

> **Strategy # 86 – Dual-purpose long position calls**
> *Split multiple-contract long positions between short call spreads and holds for contingent purchase*

In this strategy, you have a lot of flexibility. For example, if you used a five-five approach with 10 long LEAPS, you could begin by writing two short calls against the long; if the stock rises, you roll forward and up exchanging the two for five at a higher striking price. You are free to later trade these forward and up again if necessary.

If the stock does not rise, you can write the remaining three short calls and wait to see what happens, allowing the original two short positions to expire. This leaves five long positions in reserve in case the stock rises in later months. (Remember, with up to 36 months to go, a lot can happen in the stock's market price.)

If the stock does eventually rise but you are able to avoid exercise on the five short positions, you could exercise five of the remaining LEAPS long calls and convert the short calls to covered calls. In this case, you would have a lower basis in the long calls than the striking price of the corresponding short calls; and you would still have five long calls available to either exercise or use for future short spreads.

> **Strategy # 87 – Conversion, short spread calls to covered calls** *Convert short calls written against long LEAPS calls, to covered calls upon exercise of the long contracts*

With the long life of the LEAPS contracts, you can use the long positions in many ways. Flexibility is increased when you use multiple contracts; the above example demonstrates this.

By splitting a 10-contract long position into two parts-a spread strategy with the potential for covered call conversion-you keep your choices open. If the stock's price is disappointing, you can abandon the original strategy and go short on all 10 contracts in an attempt to recapture all or part of your original LEAPS investment; you can combine the short call spread with short puts to maximize premium income and continue the contingent purchase plan through the short straddle. This approach works only if you consider the call/put striking price a respectable price for the stock; and as long as the call expires higher and later than the original long position.

Example: You buy LEAPS calls at 40 and months later, the underlying stock remains within a few points of $40 per share, currently at 44. You were hoping the stock would move upward, but so far you are disappointed. You have sold three 45 calls against the long position, but have decided that the original strategy isn't working. You convert to a straddle approach, selling three 45 puts. This increases your premium income, recapturing some of your original investment in the LEAPS long calls. You consider $45 per share a good price for the stock, also recognizing that either position-LEAPS short calls or short puts-can be rolled to avoid exercise if necessary. If the stock's price rises, you can roll out of the calls and exchange the three positions for five later-expiring, higher striking price contracts. If the stock's price declines, you can buy the puts to close and replace them with three later-expiring puts at the same striking price or at a lower striking price.

> ### Strategy # 88 – Conversion, contingent purchase to short straddle
> When the contingent purchase plan is not working, recapture some or all of the long investment by converting to the short straddle position; avoid exercise through rolling on either side

In the above example, you retain a lot of flexibility. Returning to the example of 10 long positions, you have entered a straddle on three contracts. You will recall that the short straddle risk is considered minimal when two factors are present: first, you consider the striking price a reasonable one for acquiring stock, and second, the call is covered. In the original example of the short straddle, coverage consisted of owning 100 shares. In this example, the short call is "covered" through the spread against the long LEAPS positions.

Using multiple contracts allows you maximum flexibility to earn a profit, avoid exercise, and recapture all or part of your investment if the original contingent purchase plan appears to be failing. Because you have a long time to go until expiration, you also enjoy the flexibility to revert to defensive strategies and wait out the decline in time value.

No matter what strategies you employ while using short positions to offset long position costs, keep track of the potential consequences. With a primary goal in mind-contingent purchase, for example-you want to ensure that you don't get carried away with ever-growing rolls. Making a small amount of profit upon final exercise is not worth the effort if you lose the opportunity to execute a contingent purchase strategy-especially when the stock has appreciated greatly since the first step, buying the long LEAPS calls.

Exercise acceptance

When is exercise acceptable or even encouraged? One possible approach to short position planning is to view exercise as the best outcome possible-if it does occur.

At first glance, this seems contrary to the option trader's best interests. Clearly, exercise indicates that a movement in the stock has placed the short option seller in an unfavorable position. An exercised call means being required to sell stock below current market value; and an exercised put means being required to buy shares of stock above current market value.

The desirability of exercise is part of a programmed approach, specifically under two circumstances:

1. When a covered call has been written deep in the money to force a profitable capital gain accompanied by rich option premium.
2. When short LEAPS puts are used to acquire stock, recognizing an in-the-money move as temporary; and when the striking price is viewed as a favorable basis in stock (when discounted for the put premium earned).

In the first instance, you sell a call against 100 shares hoping that exercise does occur. However, if the stock declines in value before exercise takes place, the call would lose point-for-point intrinsic value, and the position could be closed profitably. So while the primary strategy may be to force exercise at a profit, a secondary strategy would be to achieve short-term profits in the short call; once closed, you would be free to repeat the strategy.

> **Strategy # 89 – Forced exercise with deep in-the-money short LEAPS calls.**   *Write deep in-the-money calls to force exercise or, in the alternative, to earn short-term profits on declining value in intrinsic value of the call*

When the stock's value moves, the in-the-money call tracks the movement. In the case of falling prices, profits in the short call offset the paper loss in the stock. So by closing the position, you *take* the profits in the call but continue holding onto the stock.

In the event of exercise, you combine profits in the LEAPS call premium with a capital gain in the stock.

Example: You bought IBM at $65 per share and today the stock is worth $80. The 55 LEAPS call expiring in 29 months is worth 24 today. By selling the call, you immediately receive the premium of $2,400, a 43.6% return on your original basis in the stock. If the LEAPS call is exercised, your total profit would be $3,400 ($2,400 on the option plus $1,000 on the stock); that would be a return of 61.8%. Encouraging exercise at this level would be profitable beyond most stock investors' expectations. (The example of IBM's price and LEAPS premium values are all based on actual values as of August, 2003.)

This example shows how the extreme in-the-money strategy would work. However, one variation would be to seek out a LEAPS call not quite as deep in the money. For example, given the current value of $80 per share, you could sell a 70 contract and receive a premium of 19. The $1,900 represents a return of 34.5% on the basis of $55 per share you paid for the stock. If this is exercised, you still gain the $3,400 as in the previous example; however, given the fact that the stock is only 10 points in the money, there is the possibility that its value could decline out of the money, meaning that the rich intrinsic 10-point value would disappear, with eventual decline in the 9-point time value as well.

In this variation, although exercise remains desirable, it would be possible to defer it while earning respectable profits via option premium and potentially be able to augment income, offsetting temporary price drops in the stock.

> **Strategy # 90 – Sale of in-the-money calls for exercise or contingent downside offset.** *Modify the forced-exercise strategy, using moderate-level in-the-money calls; in the event of a price decline in the stock, close the short position for profits offsetting paper losses in the stock*

The desirability of exercise continues to be the primary objective, but only as long as the stock holds or surpasses its current market value. Once that market value begins to subside, the forced exercise-while it may still occur-can be replaced with the more immediate opportunity for short-term gains on LEAPS intrinsic value loss.

Reverting to speculative gains on short calls is a worthy replacement strategy when the opportunity presents itself. Given the likelihood that decline in the stock's value is temporary in nature, you can defer the forced exercise outcome until the stock rises once again-perhaps even increasing the total profit by using higher striking prices at or near the top of a swing from downward to upward price range. The risk to this, of course, is that the stock might be entering into a long-term downward spiral rather than the more common price range variations; recognizing the different trends occurs all too often after it is too late. With this problem in mind, you can combine the forced exercise strategy with a reversion to covered call profits *with* insurance.

Example: Your basis in stock is $55 per share and the stock is now worth $80. You sell a 70 LEAPS call with 29 months remaining until expiration, with the idea of forcing exercise. You receive 19 in call premium. Your plan is to wait out exercise or, if the stock's market value declines, to close out the short call at a profit, wait for the stock to rebound, and then re-enter the strategy. Recognizing the possibility that the stock could continue to fall, you also buy a five-month LEAPS 70 put, paying 1.80.

In this example, you receive a net of $1,720 ($1,900 less $180) for the position; but it is risk-free for the next five months. The short LEAPS call runs for 29 months, thus offering greater time value along with its 10 points of intrinsic value; but the put, because it has only five months to expiration and is 10 points out of the money, is a relative bargain.

By entering this strategy, you buy five months of complete protection below the $70-per-share level. If the stock were to fall below that level between now and the expiration of the LEAPS put, you would gain intrinsic value in the put that would match your stock loss point for point. This strategy is sensible as long as you intend to make a decision regarding the short call within the five months. If the put is about to expire, you may (a) exercise it to offset losses in the stock, (b) close out the short call position to avoid exercise, or (c) close both positions and sell stock before further losses occur.

> **Strategy # 91 – Sale of in-the-money calls for exercise or contingent downside offset, with added long put for insurance.** *Enter a forced-exercise strategy with the ability to close the short call for profit; and buy a long put to provide added protection against stock price decline*

By combining the in-the-money short call with the out-of-the-money long put, you retain a profitable credit in the premium but you also cover the contingency for decline in the stock's value. The forced exercise strategy in its original form is designed to ensure profits when your stock has gained market value since acquisition, while also providing downside protection in case the market value falls before exercise can occur. Assuming that you share these concerns upon entering such a strategy, buying a long put also makes sense.

The net credit is possible in this example because, while the in-the-money short LEAPS call has 29 months remaining before expiration, the out-of-the-money long LEAPS put has only five months remaining. So in order for such a strategy to work, you need to plan for a decision within five months. If the stock remains at or below the 80 level (in the example given) the time value may have declined by then enough to justify closing the position; if the stock's value has declined between 70 and 80, then you will also have lower intrinsic value. In either case, closing the short LEAPS call would be profitable; and you continue to hold the long LEAPS put for downside protection, even if you re-enter the forced exercise strategy. However, because the time remaining on the long put is closer than it will be on the short LEAPS call, you will need to either (a) accept the downside protection in the call premium as adequate or (b) replace the expiring put with another, aiming for shorter expiration to hold down the cost. The second alternative represents a repeat of the first strategy, and can be continued indefinitely until exercise does occur or until you decide to close the short positions or wait out expiration, and then sell the appreciated stock-or revert to another LEAPS covered call strategy.

The decision to accept exercise or to continue avoiding it has many potential avenues. It is important to always track potential profits and to keep the original strategies in mind. Avoiding exercise as a strategy should not replace the primary goal if that could also mean losing the advantage you originally sought in entering a LEAPS strategy.

That advantage probably included the use of LEAPS in a contingent purchase plan. This allows you to utilize capital to control 100 shares of stock at today's price, and to decide when or if to buy shares later through exercise. While the idea makes sense on the surface, it is equally important to ensure that you employ LEAPS for stocks that are suitable for your portfolio. If you want long-term, strong growth candidates, for example, you would not want to pick a highly volatile, poorly-capitalized stock. The next chapter puts the important LEAPS strategies in context, providing you with guidelines for picking the best stocks.

Chapter 11

Picking the Right Stock:
Profitable strategies for smart investing

The conservative nature of covered call writing depends on one crucial aspect: that you select stocks well. As every investor knows, that is easy in hindsight but far more difficult in advance. This is why the concept of contingent purchase is so valuable; as a starting point, a low-risk way into a long position is through the use of contingent purchase, leveraging capital with LEAPS long calls or short puts as an alternative to placing larger sums of capital at risk.

Because any form of analysis is uncertain, investors make mistakes picking stocks. Even using the traditional fundamental and technical indicators, it is most difficult to pin down the actual *likelihood* that a specific stock's price is going to rise rather than fall. This is where the LEAPS contingent purchase becomes most valuable. You could, for example, use $10,000 to buy 100 shares of two $50 stocks or of 4 $25 stocks. However, your money doesn't go very far under this approach. As an alternative, you can purchase 10 LEAPS calls worth $1,000 each for the same money.

Given the premise that contingent purchase is a smart approach to acquiring stocks, we next turn to the question of which stocks to use. This question applies whether you simply buy shares or use LEAPS contingent purchase strategies. The mistake made all too often is to pick those stocks whose options are rich. The problem with this approach is that it ignores the reasons for rich LEAPS premium. Beyond the interaction between time and intrinsic value, the more volatile stocks (usually defined by price deviation) are likely to exhibit higher premium as well. That higher premium is a reflection of market risk. So if you pick stocks based solely on the richest option premium levels, you are also selecting the highest-risk stocks. While rich premiums are desirable for covered call writing, there needs to be a balance between premium levels and risk levels.

Reducing risk of stock ownership

The first observation concerning covered call writing is that the selection of stock can be made on a sort of "discounted" basis. Because you plan to write calls against stock, each instance of premium income also discounts your basis in the stock. So covered call writing is a form of discounting the risk of owning stock. Of course, this does not mean that it makes sense to invest in stocks without being concerned about whether their market price rises or falls. In the ideal situation, you want the stock to rise regularly over time, with a few qualifications:

1. Ideally, the stock's price should rise to the striking price, but not beyond. This ensures that time value will evaporate, but without risk of exercise.
2. In the event that the stock goes in the money, you will want to roll forward and up, buying more time value while avoiding exercise. Thus, subsequent price increases in the stock would ideally repeat the "ideal" price movement up to the next striking price increment.
3. At a point where price pauses momentarily, you want to be able to close out the short LEAPS call through

purchase or expiration, planning to repeat the strategy once the stock's price begins to move again.

4. The very best and most flexible situation involves writing covered calls against appreciated stock. This means that you can afford exercise with wider profit margins, and that the downside protection you achieve through writing covered calls may even make exercise more acceptable and even desirable.

The use of contingent purchase through long-position LEAPS calls helps achieve all of these ideal goals, especially the last one. If your LEAPS call appreciates in value enough that you decide to exercise it, you will then own stock below current market value. If the ultimate goal is stock ownership, then exercise would be more desirable than selling the LEAPS call at a profit. The exercise of your long LEAPS call and acquisition of shares of stock can then be followed by the second phase, writing covered calls against shares of stock.

The only inhibiting factor against contingent purchase using long LEAPS calls is the requirement that you have to pay a premium. This cost may offset the entire discount benefit. For example, if you pay 10 for the LEAPS call but exercise it when current market value is only 10 points above your striking price, then you have not achieved a net advantage. The discount between current market value and striking price is offset by the cost of the LEAPS call. This is where the conversion strategy becomes sensible. If you then turn around and sell a call against the 100 shares, you literally offset the offset. The premium you receive for writing the call may equal or even surpass the original cost of the long call.

> **Strategy # 92 – Long LEAPS cost offset using covered calls.**   *Exercise long LEAPS to purchase shares, and then write covered calls to recapture the original LEAPS premium cost*

Example: You entered into a contingent purchase, paying 8 for a single LEAPS call when the stock was at the money. Eight months later, the stock rose 10 points and you exercised the call, purchasing 100 shares for 10 points below market value. Given the cost of the LEAPS call, you are only ahead two points (10 points in market value minus 8 points for the LEAPS purchase). However, you immediately sell a LEAPS covered call and receive a premium of 11. This takes your net discount position up to 13 points, justifying the overall strategy.

Clearly, a contingent purchase providing a margin of only two points will not justify the risks of the long position in the LEAPS call. This is especially true if you purchase many calls, hoping that those that do appreciate will justify the losses in the rest. For that idea to work out, you will need to do better than a two-point discount on exercised LEAPS calls. In previous chapters, you saw how to mitigate the cost of the long position with carefully-selected short calls written against the long position, with higher striking prices and shorter expirations. This is a wise strategy for reducing the net cost of the LEAPS, and it works as long as the stock holds its value or increases in value. In those cases where the stock's value falls, exercise is out of the question and you may lose the premium investment. However, to make the decision worthwhile in total, you will need to convert the strategy and write covered calls against stock you acquire by way of exercising the LEAPS long calls.

So you reduce the risk of stock ownership by the careful selection of stocks, but also through good management of the LEAPS as well. This has two parts. First is the offset of long LEAPS call costs by writing shorter-term, higher striking price calls; second is converting from contingent purchase to covered calls.

Remembering that the covered call has to be viewed as a form of contingent sale, the two-part conversion strategy can also be looked at as a flip. You move from contingent purchase to contingent sale upon exercise. As long as you are able to achieve a net discount higher than the overall cost of contingent purchase, the strategy will succeed. For example, if you purchase 10 LEAPS calls on different underlying stocks, and the total cost is $10,000, you will need to calculate how many of those need to be turned around profitably. You can write LEAPS calls against any or all of them to reduce costs; you can then convert all exercised situations into covered calls.

The contingent purchase strategy works with the covered call as a second phase. However, even with this type of management-ensuring that the overall discounted basis in acquired stock exceeds the cost of the original investment in contingent purchase-your chances of success will be far greater if you apply common sense rules for selecting the right stocks as a first step. Using LEAPS through contingent purchase is a risk-reduction strategy, but it does not serve as a substitute for smart stock selection.

Guidelines for stock selection

How do you pick strong growth stocks? The answer, of course, depends largely on your goals in buying stocks to begin with. If you intend to select long-term growth stocks, whether through direct purchase or with contingent purchase via LEAPS contracts, then a good rule of thumb is:

Pick stocks on the merit of their fundamental strength, regardless of how potentially profitable LEAPS strategies may appear.

Applying this simple logic is always a smart approach. However, if you want to use stocks strictly to speculate, then you probably would be more attracted to higher risk strategies, such as going short on stock or selling puts and risking being required to buy shares above market value. So clearly, the purpose you bring to the decision will define what makes sense.

In selecting stocks on the assumption that you seek strong growth candidates, some general guidelines are worth review. These include:

1. *Pick stocks on the merits and strengths of the fundamentals, without regard to the level of option premium.* This is the most critical rule for every option investor. Many people have entered into a market strategy involving the selection of stocks with the highest option premium. When overall markets fall, those stocks tend to outpace the overall rate of decline, so it is all too easy to end up with a portfolio of losing stocks. In these cases, the investor has an unfortunate choice: wait for the stock's price to rebound or sell and cut losses. In either case, the intended on-going covered call strategy cannot be used profitably. As long as striking prices would be lower than the discounted original basis, it would be ill-advised to attempt to offset significant market losses with covered calls.

For some investors, the use of covered calls in a discounted basis could work, but the risks contradict the whole purpose of covered call LEAPS positions-to maximize income while reducing risk. You can use LEAPS covered calls with the intention of riding the stock price upward through a series of rolls forward and up; but if the stock rebounds quickly, this strategy could lead to exercise with a net loss.

> **Strategy # 93 – Sale of covered calls with depressed stock values.**   *Sell covered calls when stock prices are lower than original discounted basis, with the intention of rolling forward and up to avoid exercise*

This strategy has to be viewed as high-risk. It may be far preferable to simply wait out a market rebound, and wait until it becomes possible to write LEAPS calls that, if exercised, will produce a net profit in stock and LEAPS.

Another variation makes more sense when stock prices are discounted: reverting to selling puts as an alternative form. While covered calls are contingent sales of stock and thus high-risk when striking price is lower than net basis, the sale of puts is the opposite, a type of contingent purchase. The short put offers two examples when stock prices are lower than your basis. First, you receive premium, reducing the gap between market value and current value. Second, if the put is exercised and 100 shares are put to you, your overall cost of stock is reduced. It will still be higher than current market value, but the averaging effect moves the overall position closer to the point where covered call writing will again be possible.

> **Strategy # 94 – Sale of puts when stock value is depressed.**   *Sell puts to narrow the gap between original basis and current value; and upon exercise, further reduce the average original price paid for stock*

Example: You bought 100 shares of stock at $45 per share and sold a LEAPS call for 6, reducing your net basis to $39 per share. However, the stock's price has fallen to $34 per share and the original short call expired. You now own stock with a net basis five points higher than current market value. You sell a put with a 35 striking price and receive 4. This reduces the gap between discounted basis and current value to only one point. If the put is exercised, you will be required to buy 100 shares at $35 per share. That would change your net basis yet again:

100 shares at 45 =	$4,500
sold one call =	− 600
sold one put =	− 400
100 shares at 35 =	3,500
Total net invested	$7,000

This situation raises some interesting possibilities. Although the shares were originally purchased at $45 per share, the combination of three elements-a short call, a short put, and an exercise of the short put-brought the overall basis down to $35. With 200 shares now in your portfolio, you are free to write calls. As long as the *net* you receive for selling calls is adequate to offset current value, this could return you to a net paper profit. For example, if you were able to sell calls with striking prices of 35 and receive premium for the two calls of five points, you would further reduce your net basis to $30 per share. The example is summarized in Figure 11.1.

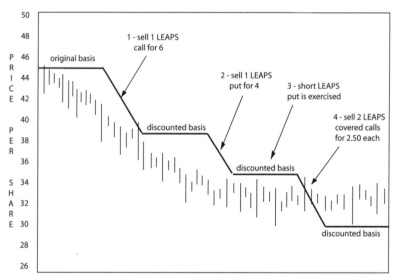

Figure 11.1 ■ Discounting basis as a stock value falls

2. *Apply sensible fundamental tests.* Every investor who believes in the fundamental approach has a series of favorite trends; some combine stock-based and option-based trends when their acquisition strategy incorporates covered call writing. For the purpose of stock selection, the fundamental tests should make

sense. For example, you may track sales and earnings, dividends trends, PE ratio, and other well-known fundamentals. In order to further evaluate the underlying strength of the corporation, also consider its merger and acquisition activities, especially if mergers diversify the operating units and ultimately, growth in sales. Also watch capitalization ratios. The bond ratio is a very important fundamental test, in which long-term debt is expressed as a percentage of total capitalization (long-term debt plus shareholders' equity). If the portion of long-term debt remains the same or declines over time, that is a positive indicator. But if the bond ratio begins to rise, that is a sign of weakening growth. As the corporation commits itself to ever-growing debt service and interest expense, there will be less profit left over to fund operations and to continue paying dividends.

Each investor should pick a short list of fundamental tests that provide meaningful comparative data for stock selection. Decisions about whether to buy stock and, once purchased, whether to continue holding it, should be based on a continual study of those fundamental tests to (a) ensure that positive trends are continuing or (b) discover turn-around points which may indicate that it is time to sell.

3. *Add appropriate technical tests to judge price volatility.* The PE ratio is a combination of fundamental (earnings) and technical (price) information. This may be one of the reasons for its popularity. Other technical data are worth following as well. Specifically, tracking the trading range and looking for emerging patterns, may indicate when prices are going to begin moving. As a trading range broadens, that could signal higher volatility and potential profits or losses, as well as the possibility of richer option premium. Also track the support and resistance levels of stocks to make your

own informed judgments about trading range and
market risk.

4. *Watch market-wide trends and industry cycles to time your
decisions, especially when you will be using contingent
purchase strategies.* Don't limit your selection of stocks
to only fundamental and technical tests. Also keep an
eye on the big picture, including market-wide trends as
expressed through popular indexes such as the Dow
Jones, S&P 500, and NASDAQ. Also be aware of how
specific industry sectors act in different economic cycles.
Stocks that are interest-sensitive, such as utilities or real
estate sectors, may tend to exhibit increased price
weakness when interest rates begin to rise, for example.

5. *Recognize mistakes when they become apparent, and be
willing to cut losses.* In the game of chess, experienced
players know that when they make a mistake, the best
tactic is to retreat and take up a defensive position. In
comparison, the inexperienced player tends to go on
the attack to compensate for the error, hoping to create
a similar error for the opponent. The same observation
applies in the market. If you purchase shares of stock or
take up an option position and you later conclude that
you were mistaken, close those positions out and take
the loss; learn from the experience; and make more
informed decisions next time. The relatively small cost
of a loss you cut is a valuable progression, because the
experience itself makes you a smarter investor.

Revised fundamental analysis-core earnings

The traditional approach to fundamental analysis has always
been based on some general assumptions. These include a
belief that the results of operations being reported are complete and accurate. For the purpose of identifying likely
long-term growth stocks, this assumption may be wrong. In
many cases, in fact, the reported numbers are quite inaccu-

rate, but they are allowed under GAAP (Generally Accepted Accounting Principles).

In 2002, Standard & Poors' began adjusting reported results among companies in its S&P500 based on a concept of "core earnings." The adjustment excludes profit or loss from discontinued operations, so-called extraordinary (non-recurring) items, profit or loss from the sale of capital assets, restructuring charges, and estimated income from invest-ment of pension assets. One of the largest adjustments is the addition of employee stock option expense. None of these adjustments were required under GAAP rules prior to 2002, and since then several large corporations have begun voluntarily making some of the adjustments on their own. However, it may take many years for the slow-moving GAAP system to make changes requiring core earnings adjust-ments.[1]

How significant are these adjustments? Many corpora-tions would have reported more than one billion dollars in lower earnings if core earnings adjustments were required, based on reported 2001 fiscal year results.[2] By 2002, adjust-ments for core earnings were even bigger.[3]

The major contributing items in most instances are pro-jected pension earnings and employee stock option expenses. Pension earnings are excluded and stock option expenses added to make core earnings adjustments. These

Notes:

[1] "Core Earnings: a better measure," CFOweb, July 13, 2002

[2] *Ibid.*, negative adjustments based on core earnings according to S&P were Dupont (decrease of $4.2 billion); IBM ($2.8); Microsoft ($2.2); General Electric ($2.2); Verizon ($1.8); Motorola ($1.5); Cisco ($1.5); AOL Time Warner ($1.2); SBC Communications ($1.2); and Boeing ($1.1).

[3] "2002 S&P Core Earnings," BusinessWeek online, March, 2002: DuPont (decrease of $5.4 billion); IBM ($5.3); General Motors ($4.1); General Electric ($3.9); Ford ($3.1); SBC Communications ($2.7); Boeing ($2.4 billion); Citigroup ($2.2); Proctor & Gamble ($1.3); Exxon Mobil ($1.0); and Lockheed Martin ($1.0).

adjustments do not indicate that the corporations on the lists have done anything wrong; however, core earnings adjustments often significantly reduce earnings per share and affect other fundamental indicators as well. In many instances, the adjustments would replace a reported net profit with a net loss.

The premise behind making core earnings adjustments is that when investors are looking for long-term growth candidates, they should restrict their search. They should review operations for each company on the basis of core earnings, since non-recurring income and excluded expense distort any forecast. S&P has begun using its core earnings calculations to rate corporate bonds, a decision that may affect several corporations that depend on long-term debt capitalization as part of its growth strategy. Certainly, a reduction in credit rating should cause investors to take a second look at those corporations.

The most obvious fundamental tests are based on the revenue and earnings reported by the corporation. So in any review, investors are not able to make like-kind comparisons between companies if their core earnings adjustments are dissimilar. A corporation granting relatively large stock options to its employees and not expensing those options may be presenting a profitability picture that is quite unrealistic. A competing company whose stock options are being expensed would have a disadvantage in the comparison, even though their disclosures were more accurate. For example, General Electric and Wal-Mart, among others, have announced that they have begun reporting stock option expenses and have restated past years results. If competing corporations have not made the same adjustment, is it realistic to downgrade GE and Wal-Mart because their numbers do not look as good? Clearly, making core earnings adjustments is the only accurate way to select stocks with the long term in mind.

Until the GAAP system catches up with the adjustments being made by S&P, investors are going to have on-going problems comparing stocks. Fortunately, public companies have websites and the adjustments can be found with a little digging. By checking footnotes to the financial statements, the significant core earnings adjustments can be located. Responsible corporate management will take the lead in making those adjustments voluntarily; but when making comparisons between companies, investors have to remember that not every public company is voluntarily changing their numbers for core earnings adjustments.

For LEAPS investors, the question of how to perform fundamental analysis is a potentially troubling one. The relative richness of LEAPS premiums can include distortions for inaccurate reporting of earnings-an inaccuracy allowed under current GAAP rules, but nonetheless, still inaccurate. For the option speculator, this inaccuracy can be a great advantage. Knowing that earnings for a particular company are inflated, one could take advantage of the extra time value when shorting LEAPS, and increase profits. However, for those interested in the contingent purchase of stocks, the underlying interest is going to be in picking long-term winners. To the extent that earnings are inflated, buying LEAPS calls would require paying inflated time value premium, and potentially the ultimate purchase of stock based on over-blown earnings as well.

Price volatility and technical indicators

In the selection of stocks, investors using fundamentals can benefit by also monitoring certain technical indicators. The technical tests, oriented toward price, can help to compare price volatility. These indicators include studies of trading range including support and resistance.

The trading range can quantify price volatility. For example, a relatively narrow trading range established over many months indicates low price volatility. Ignoring for the moment a stock's tendency to follow overall market trends, the specific trading range itself is quite revealing. In situations where prices spike far above or below trading range and then return to previously established levels, those spikes should be excluded from the price volatility study. In most situations of price spikes, the causes are easily identifiable. They may be part of a market-wide movement in index levels, a political event or occurrence, or rumors about a company that proved to be false. The test of how to interpret a spike is found in the question of whether or not price levels return to the previously established trading range.

During periods of change in a stock's trading range, the breadth of that range may also change. When the range returns to previously established range levels, that is yet another sign of stability. Those stocks whose trading range breadth is consistent over many years-given temporary spikes during uncertain times, as well as breadth adjustments during periods of growth, for example-the long-term volatility of a stock can be defined by the trends seen in breadth of trading range.

Another technical indicator that can be used to judge a stock's price volatility is the strength of support and resistance. Price support is the low price level of the trading range, and resistance is the upper level. Some stocks have fairly weak support and resistance, so that the trading range is less certain and prices often violate support and resistance levels. Other stocks are quite solid in terms of trading range, and any breakout above resistance or below support would signal the beginning of a price movement. As support and resistance levels are "tested"-meaning prices fall to support or rise to resistance-without a successful breakout, that may also signal the beginning of a price movement in the opposite direction.

To some technicians, these indicators are hard and fast rules; to others, they serve only as general tendencies and cannot be depended upon to make monetary decisions. For most investors seriously looking for long-term growth stocks, short-term price trends cannot be used as part of the buy-hold-sell equation; but the degree of price volatility can serve as one of many tests in determining the level of market risk for stocks.

LEAPS investors pursuing a course of contingent purchase using either long calls or short puts, will also want to quantify market risk. The level of price volatility directly affects time value premium. This points out a potential disadvantage as well as a potential advantage to the LEAPS investor.

Example: You are considering using available capital to purchase a number of LEAPS calls in several stocks. Some are surprisingly expensive. A further study reveals that the stocks with higher time value premium (measured as a percentage of stock value in like-kind expiration terms) have greater price volatility. The obvious reason for richer premium is the higher market risk for those stocks.

In this situation, there is a sensible solution-assuming that you believe that the proposed striking price would be a good price to pay for stock. This assumption lies at the heart of all contingent purchase strategies: The striking price must be considered a reasonable price to pay for stock, in the event you decide to exercise the LEAPS call. Following that logic to the next step, what do you do in the situation where higher price volatility also means richer premium levels? Rather than buying LEAPS calls, you can sell LEAPS puts. This enables you to take advantage of the higher premium levels (assuming the rich premium levels are experienced in puts as well as in calls).

> **Strategy # 95 – Short contingent purchase as a solution to high-volatility situations**   *Sell LEAPS puts instead of buying LEAPS calls when greater price volatility has created higher time value on both sides*

Example: You review several stocks with the idea of buying LEAPS calls, as part of your contingent purchase plan. You have narrowed your list down to six stocks. You want to purchase LEAPS calls with striking prices two to three points above current market value, and you have decided to use 30-month expirations in each case. In five cases, the LEAPS premium is at about 10 percent of the stock's current market value; in one case, the premium is closer to 13%. In examining the recent trading in that stock, you notice greater than average price volatility. You believe the stock is a worthwhile long-term investment and you would be happy to acquire shares at the striking price if you decided to exercise a LEAPS call. However, given the cost of the call, you also examine the LEAPS puts at the same striking price. They are higher than average as well. You decide to use the alternative approach, selling a LEAPS put, as your contingent purchase plan in that instance.

Another version, fundamental volatility

Investors understand "market risk" in terms of price volatility. Invariably, the connection between risk and price is inescapable. However, this is also inconsistent for those who believe that stock selection should be based on fundamental trends. Both the Dow Theory and Random Walk agree that short-term price is not a dependable indicator; but it is often used as the primary means for timing of market decisions.

An alternative is the study of fundamentals as the most dependable measurement of market risk. So rather than monitoring price volatility which, by its very nature, is short-term and not reliable as an indicator for long-term strength, investors may study and compare fundamental volatility. This may be defined as the tendency toward (or away from) consistency in what is reported. The definition of fundamental volatility may include several components, including:

1. Core earnings adjustments to make true comparisons between stocks and within one company from one year to another.
2. The trend in revenue growth, with detailed examination of growth within units of the company as well as on a consolidated basis.
3. Consistency in gross margin and net return-here, investors seek well controlled gross margins and steady net earnings *rates* of return. It is not realistic to expect the net return to grow each year, because each type of business has a realistic range of likely outcome. It is enough that a company control the rate of return, and consistency is a strength.
4. Additional consistency in the balance between long-term debt and total capitalization (long-term debt plus shareholders' equity). Investors seek control in this area to ensure that profits will not increasingly be used to pay interest, with less available for future growth, working capital and dividends.

The level of fundamental volatility often defines likely future growth, especially if core earnings adjustments are made before any analysis begins. When a company reports steady growth in sales with adequate working capital, controlled debt capitalization, and strictly controlled gross margin and net profit, then fundamental volatility will be low. In the long-term, this is a positive sign for investors and can serve as the true test of market risk.

Keep in mind that the real market risk for long-term investing is found not in price volatility this month, but in the consistency of fundamental growth over recent years and growth that is likely to occur in the future. It is imperative to pay attention to valid technical tests as supplements to the tried-and-true fundamental analyses. The most important consideration for all LEAPS strategies is that, as long as the ultimate goal is to own shares of stock, the fundamentals have to play a central role in your selection of stock; it is a mistake to pick LEAPS based on premium levels, even though tempting. Remember, the application of fundamental and technical tests help identify safe stocks versus more volatile ones. A trap in options investing is that the higher-risk stocks tend to have richer premium levels and greater volatility, so they may be more attractive, especially if you are going to go short.

In addition to making good use of traditional fundamental and technical tests, adjust your conclusions with an analysis of core earnings, to ensure that the financial numbers you are using are reasonable for judging long-term growth. Make adjustments for comparative purposes. The exercise is worthwhile, especially if you are able to identify overvalued situations earlier than other investors and options traders. Finally, be keenly aware of fundamental volatility as a symptom of underlying causes; and identify methods for equating the value of a LEAPS strategy with degrees of fundamental volatility.

With the emphasis on contingent purchase of sale, it is also easy to overlook the fact that options can be used for a broad range of advantages. Notable among these is insuring long equity positions when (a) you are concerned about potential price drops and loss of paper profits you have today, and (b) you would still like to hold shares as long-term investments and not have to be concerned with timing temporary market price swings. The next section summarizes the many strategies that LEAPS can be employed for protecting profits and reducing risk.

Part IV

Variations: Expanding your profit potential

Chapter 12

Downside Protection:
Techniques for insuring your profits

Every investor has to keep an eye on market value of equity positions. As long as you own stock or plan to own stock in the future, the central concern is going to be whether that stock's value will rise or fall. Most investors understand that they cannot build long-term wealth in LEAPS contracts alone; they need to develop a foundation of equity. While LEAPS contracts can provide a degree of safety in entering positions-as well as discounting the basis over time-most investors will eventually want to buy and hold shares. When that happens, LEAPS provide a secondary type of benefit-protection of paper profits.

A typical pattern experienced by stock investors is that, even with the best-timed purchase, prices run up and tend to go too high too fast. So you are faced with a choice: either ride out the market exaggerations of value, and accept corrections, or take profits and attempt to time the market. If you take profits, the idea is to buy back into the stock when prices fall. But every experienced investor knows how difficult it is to time this correctly each time. You will eventually lose opportunities by moving too soon, or by waiting too long. The solution: use LEAPS to protect paper profits.

The basic plan-insuring long or short positions

Even investors who intend to hold stock for the long term are going to be tempted to take paper profits when they are available. For example, if you bought stock three months ago, expecting prices to inch upward a few points per month, and the price suddenly jumps by 50%, you will be tempted to cash in and take those profits right away. This is especially true if you believe that the price jump is unrealistic, and a correction is likely to follow.

The danger in taking profits is that your timing will rarely be perfect. If the stock does not correct but continues heading upward, a premature sale is lost opportunity. While taking profits ensures you realize them, if you intend to hold stock for long-term investment value, taking immediate paper profits is contrary to your broader goal.

The solution: buy LEAPS puts, one per 100 shares, to protect paper profits. Select LEAPS puts so that the striking price is at a point below current market value, but not deep out of the money. If stock prices do fall below striking price, the LEAPS put will increase in value dollar for dollar with the drop in equity value.

> **Strategy # 96 – LEAPS puts as insurance when stock prices run up.** Buy LEAPS puts to protect paper profits when stock prices run above what you consider realistic levels

A potential problem in buying LEAPS puts involves the interaction between time value and intrinsic value. It is possible that increasing intrinsic value will be offset by declining time value, so that it will not be possible to exercise the put to recapture lost equity in the stock. For example, let's say that your stock has run up to $57 per share, and you buy a LEAPS put with a striking price of 55. You pay a premium of 7, all time value. In the following months, the stock's value declines to $49 per share. But as expiration date approaches, time value has begun to evaporate and the put is currently worth only 9. You could sell and take a profit of $200; but the stock has fallen 6 points below exercise price. In this situation, the insurance did not provide value adequate to protect your position. Time value worked against you.

There are several solutions. These include:

1. *Sell calls instead of buying puts.* The problem with buying options to hedge any stock position involves time value. Going long on options is invariably a disadvantage because, even if the stock moves in the direction you are protecting against, time value decline is going to offset intrinsic value growth. So as an alternative, you can use covered calls, recognizing that the premium you receive works as a discount against lost equity value in the stock.

2. *Buy puts deep out of the money puts to reduce the cost.* You can reduce the market risk in the long position of the LEAPS put by buying deep out of the money contracts. For example, instead of picking the closest striking price, go down 5 or 10 points and buy at bargain levels. In this way, you can consider the insurance to be against catastrophic losses-declines in the stock's price below the put's striking price-while you accept the more immediate 5 to 10-point risk.

3. *Buy puts with shorter expiration.* It also makes sense in some conditions to buy relatively short-term puts as insurance. You may select short-term LEAPS or even traditional listed options to serve this purpose. If you believe the current price run-up is temporary and likely to correct in the near future, you might only need short-term insurance, so it is not necessary to pay for a lot of time value.

4. *Offset the cost of the long LEAPS put by selling other puts.* Finally, you can employ the previously introduced idea

of selling puts against the long LEAPS position, a form of "covering" the long position which reduces its cost. As long as the short position expires sooner and has a lower striking price, the risk is minimal. In the event of a large decline in stock value, an exercised short position will be offset by your long LEAPS put. However, in using this strategy, you potentially give up the insurance value of using long LEAPS puts. So the covered put approach is worthwhile only if you believe the market risk is found in the range below the long striking price but above the short striking price.

Example: Your stock has run up in value to $57 per share. You believe that the "right" market value is between $50 and $55, and you expect a correction. If you are right, then it makes sense to enter into a covered put. A long 55 put provides downside protection for the stock down to the $50 level. Below that, the offsetting puts apply; if the short 50 put were exercised, your long 55 put reduces your market risk. As long as the stock's market value remains at or above $50 per share, you are not at risk of exercise.

Modified insurance to reduce costs

Using LEAPS puts for insurance may provide more than the obvious benefit, that of protecting your long position in stock. On a practical level, however, this only works if the stock's value falls substantially below the LEAPS put's striking price. The offset between time value and intrinsic value is going to work against you, unless the fall in value occurs rapidly.

By selling subsequent puts with lower striking price and shorter expiration you offset the cost of the long LEAPS put. So the long insurance position's cost can be reduced in the same way that the long call position is discounted in the basic contingent purchase plan. As long as the stock's value stays within a fairly narrow trading range, you can sell a series of LEAPS puts and, possibly, recapture the entire long put insurance premium.

Example: You own stock with an original basis of $45 per share. Recently, it has risen to $57 and you want to use a LEAPS put to insure paper profits. You buy a 55 put and pay 7. The stock remains between $50 and $60 per share over a period of months and, during that same period of time, you sell a series of LEAPS puts with 50 striking prices. By doing so, you eventually earn back the original $700 invested in the long put.

> **Strategy # 97 – Offset of long puts with short puts.**
> *Combine limited-range insurance using LEAPS puts, with short LEAPS to recapture initial insurance cost*

Being aware of the limited range of protection-that area below the long LEAPS put and the short LEAPS put striking prices-makes the strategy sensible. You have to be willing to accept the risk that the stock's price may fall below the short position striking price, meaning that the relatively limited insurance protection will be lost. In that outcome, you lose the insurance benefit and the short LEAPS put would be exercised against your long LEAPS put.

One solution to this is to employ a ratio of long to short puts. For example, you could buy two LEAPS puts per 100 shares of stock, and then undertake the writing of LEAPS puts with lower striking prices. You could, for example, write only one put at a time, meaning that you would have one offset of long to short positions, and one remaining put for insurance.

> **Strategy # 98 – Increased number of puts for insurance offset.** *Buy more than one put per 100 shares of stock, and reduce the cost by selling LEAPS puts, leaving one put for 100 shares for insurance protection*

The strategy does not necessarily make sense when dealing with 100 shares of stock, two long puts, and one short put. However, when larger multiples are involved, the ratio approach could be very feasible.

Example: You own 400 shares of stock, and you want to insure a paper profit. The basic strategy would call for the purchase of 4 LEAPS puts. However, you purchase 7 LEAPS puts and then sell 3 puts against that position. The short LEAPS have lower striking prices and shorter expiration. Your overall plan calls for offsetting the long position costs with short position premium.

This approach makes even more sense when striking prices and expirations are staggered on both long and short sides. For example, you can buy LEAPS puts at two or three declining striking price levels, offsetting them with short LEAPS positions that produce maximum premium. In the previous example, you could employ this strategy by buying two LEAPS puts at 55 and at 50; and by selling 4 50 puts expiring three months earlier.

Over time, as time value premium disappears from the short positions, you will be able to recapture part of the cost of the long LEAPS positions. If you sell shorter-term LEAPS puts, you can go through a repetitive writing strategy and recover even more premium. Applying the same strategy as demonstrated for LEAPS contingent purchase shown in previous chapters, you may be able to recapture the entire cost of the long LEAPS puts. If the stock's value begins to decline, you can also roll forward and down to avoid exercise of the short position.

Insuring short stock positions

You can use insurance with the same effectiveness when you are short on stock. Instead of buying puts, you would buy calls. In the event that the stock's value rises, the call positions protect your short stock losses.

As with the long position in stock, the use of calls for insurance against short stock positions will be limited. The cost of the premium is likely to consist of 100% time value. So as the intrinsic value of the call increases over time, declining time value premium will offset it. This situation is a chronic problem for anyone going long in LEAPS contracts. The same strategies can be employed to offset this problem. These include selling calls against the long LEAPS call position. A sold call should have shorter expiration and higher time value. If you employ a one-to-one offset in the LEAPS calls, you risk losing the insurance protection if the shorted stock rises above the short call offset position. So using a ratio of long to short calls may be required to eliminate this risk altogether.

You can also offset long and short calls and roll forward and up to avoid exercise in the event the stock's price rises. Considering the risks of going short on stock-compared to the varied uses of LEAPS contracts for either contingent purchase or contingent sale-it may not make sense to short stock at all. If you believe the stock's price is likely to fall and you want to take advantage of that situation, you can employ combinations of LEAPS calls or puts to create the same potential advantage you achieve shorting stock-but without the rather significant risks of shorting stock. If you time the decision poorly and stock rises, you eventually have to take a loss or offset that loss using options; but you can use the LEAPS position to control 100 shares up to three years. For example, you could buy LEAPS puts believing that the stock's value is going to fall. The cost of investing in the long put position can be offset by selling shorter-term, lower-striking price puts-the "covered" LEAPS position.

Using the long-and-short offset in puts provides you the same opportunity as shorting stock, with the potential to recover your costs through going short against the long positions. So while the opportunity range is limited (between striking prices of the long and short LEAPS puts) that range can be extended by rolling forward and down with the short positions. If you use a ratio approach, you can also augment your income. For example, if you purchase five LEAPS puts and then offset that cost with six short LEAPS, you increase premium income on the short positions, with a 5-to-6 coverage. Another way to look at this is a 5-to-5 covered LEAPS put position plus a single contingent purchase at the lowest striking price.

> **Strategy # 99 – Combination of covered puts and contingent purchase.** *Offset long LEAPS puts investment with a higher number of short LEAPS puts, creating a limited contingent purchase position*

Example: You have been watching a stock trading in the mid-40 range. It recently rose to $57 per share. You believe the stock is likely to retreat back to its previous trading range. So you buy five LEAPS puts with striking prices of 55 and 50. You believe that the fair market price for this stock is between $40 and $45 per share. So at the same time, you sell six LEAPS puts with shorter expiration terms; three have striking prices of 50 and three have striking prices of 45.

In the example above, five of the six short puts offset the long LEAPS put positions. They "cover" the long positions because they will expire sooner. So in the event of exercise, you would satisfy each put with the long positions you currently hold. At the same time, the sixth LEAPS put serves as a contingent purchase at a price you consider fair.

The ratio could even be increased so that the number of short LEAPS puts would be more than the six-to-five in the example. If you are willing to have 300 shares put to you at the striking price, you could sell eight LEAPS puts against the five long positions. The "worst case" would then be that you pick up 300 shares upon exercise of the puts.

Even though you would consider the striking price a reasonable market price, you could still avoid exercise by rolling forward and down-reducing your contingent cost upon exercise while also increasing premium income.

You will also want to consider how to manage insurance when the stock's price continues to rise over time. For example, if you buy a LEAPS put in the belief that the stock's value is inflated and is going to correct in the near future, but the price continues to rise, you can adopt the wait-and-see strategy. Or you can buy additional puts to protect ever-growing paper profits. The problem with this approach is the same as with any other timing question. If the stock's value continues to rise, it will be increasingly difficult to offset put investments with short positions. As the stock's market value rises, the corresponding value of puts will decline. So in order to buy subsequent put contracts, you will need to believe that the price is inflated.

> **Strategy # 100 – Purchase of additional LEAPS puts when stock continues to rise.**   *Buy additional puts when the stock's market value rises, to protect higher paper profits*

You may view the purchase of additional puts for insurance as a worthwhile investment, as long as you continue to believe that the stock's price is unreasonably high. Because LEAPS contracts have a life up to 36 months, you can afford to wait out even an extended period of inflated stock prices. You could be wrong, but you have more time to be right. And offsetting the cost of the LEAPS puts with related short positions remains one way to mitigate the cost of the long LEAPS put.

In considering whether or not it makes sense to invest in puts for insurance, whether entering the strategy only once or using a series of puts, you need to consider several important issues:

1. *The strategy is different if you actually own stock.* If you are watching stock and see an opportunity to speculate in LEAPS puts, that is one way to proceed. The strategy is far different if you own shares and want to protect paper profits, in which case you will have much more at stake. Buying LEAPS puts to protect paper profits on long stock positions (and then possibly offset with short put positions as well) will be more of a vested interest, since those paper profits will be very real to you.

2. *The cost of the long LEAPS put has to be evaluated in comparison to the potential loss of paper profits.* If you simply want to purchase LEAPS puts to protect paper profits, and you are not interested in offsetting short LEAPS positions, you have to evaluate whether the cost is justified. The premium cost of the LEAPS put should be compared to the potential lost paper profits, and a decision made on that basis. Depending on the proximity of striking price of the put to current market value of the stock, and the length of time you select for the insurance put, the cost-versus-benefit outcome could vary considerably. By using relatively short-term puts for the insurance strategy, you can reduce time value substantially. However, that also reduces your insurance protection period. So ultimately, the decision to buy a LEAPS put is going to depend on richness of the premium, selection of striking price and expiration, and the amount of paper profit you want to protect.

3. *The alternative of using covered calls should be examined as well.* The covered call-or writing a series of covered calls over time-provides you with two benefits. First, because you sell the call, the money flows to you instead of away from you. The spread can be significant. If the put is currently worth 7 but the call with the same striking price can be sold for 8, that is a 15-point spread,

or a difference of $1,500. So rather than buying a LEAPS put, you could sell a LEAPS call and achieve a substantial benefit from the spread.

> **Strategy # 101 – Short calls used for insurance in place of long puts.**   *Sell calls to provide limited insurance of long stock positions, instead of long puts*

The significant spread between purchasing a LEAPS put, and selling a LEAPS call, cannot be overlooked. In the example above, the net difference of 15 points-not at all an unlikely situation-provides you with considerable cost-benefit leeway. In other words, if you want insurance, but you don't want to spend $700 to buy a put, the alternative of selling a call and receiving $800 in premium gives you a more desirable alternative. While the covered call may result in exercise in the event the stock rises and the call is exercised, remember that this strategy is being considered at a time when you believe the stock's market price is inflated. You can avoid exercise of the covered call by trading forward and up; but if your timing is correct, you will be able to offset a loss of paper profits in the stock by closing the covered call position.

Because you will be in a short position, a decline in the stock's value will result in *reduced* intrinsic value as well as in reduced time value. The paper profits will have gone, but these will be offset by the profit in the short call. You can simply keep the short LEAPS call open until expiration, or you can close it and take the profit. The advantage of the short call over the long put is twofold: Not only does the money flow to you, but the strategy can be repeated over and over indefinitely, as long as the current position expires or is closed before the next position is opened. Each time you sell a covered call, the premium reduces your basis in the stock, which is the best outcome to protect yourself against future price declines.

Cyclical market price trends should not affect your long-term strategy for stock ownership. If you pick stocks with growth potential, you will accumulate wealth over time. LEAPS can be used to insure against short-term paper losses or to preserve momentary paper profits along the way. Using the short call discounts your basis, and if you use this approach many times, you can create an income stream without giving up the investment.

Whether you insure long positions with a long put or a short call, the purpose of insurance is to provide downside protection. To an extent, writing covered LEAPS calls provides a perpetual form of insurance; but in practice, we also want to insure today's position in stock and not just the original investment value. The traditional listed option was useful for very short-term insurance; but it was expensive and expiration was an ever-present problem. The LEAPS option solves this problem with the exceptionally long life of each contract. Because we know that a lot can happen in three years, being able to insure an equity position for that long a term is comforting.

Insuring your equity position with the use of LEAPS options is one of many alternative strategic applications available. You may also consider using index options to speculate on broader market trends. The next chapter explores index options as an additional potential strategic approach.

Chapter 13

Strategic Expansion:
Thinking outside the box

The single-stock LEAPS option is a powerful device that you can use to round out your portfolio, leverage capital, and protect existing equity positions. If you want to speculate using LEAPS, the long-term nature of the LEAPS contract opens new possibilities; these have not always been practical with the more traditional listed option.

The higher time value that you derive from working with contracts lasting up to three years further provides opportunities for covered call writing or for offsetting LEAPS positions to mitigate the cost of taking long positions. While we have emphasized the concepts of contingent purchase or sale using LEAPS, you may design your portfolio to include LEAPS more selectively. For example, you might view the longer-term life of a LEAPS option as a practical device for speculation in options.

Beyond the single-stock LEAPS options discussed in previous chapters, are other alternatives that have emerged as relatively new. These include index options and stock futures. The potential use of these as alternatives to traditional listed options or LEAPS options, or using them in conjunction with them, is yet another way you can expand on the ideas presented here.

The index LEAPS

The index is a grouping of stocks that are related in some way. Among the best known are indexes such as NASDAQ, the S&P 500, or the Dow Jones Industrial Averages. Several other indexes exist of course, and LEAPS index options are expanding rapidly. Just as more and more LEAPS are available on individual stocks as the popularity of LEAPS grows, the same is likely to occur using index options.

The idea of leveraging into a related group of stocks has appeal to many Investors. If you consider a particular index to be more predictable than individual stocks, then trading in index LEAPS-either calls or puts-can provide an interesting alternative to individual stock LEAPS, and can also provide yet another method for diversifying your capital.

Some important differences will be found between index LEAPS contracts and individual stock LEAPS contracts. Stock LEAPS relate to 100 shares of stock per contract, so settlement for exercised LEAPS options takes place in shares of stock. An exercised call requires the seller to deliver 100 shares at the striking price; and an exercised put requires the seller to accept 100 shares of stock at the striking price. In the case of index LEAPS, settlement is always done in cash. So if you enter a position in a LEAPS index option, you cannot use that option to buy or sell shares of stock at the fixed striking price; the use of index LEAPS is to seek profits in the purchase and sale of the contract itself.

Trading hours in stock LEAPS usually correspond with market hours. Markets are open until 4 p.m. Eastern time on each trading day. Some index options also settle at the same time; however, some settle based on the opening prices of the index components on expiration Friday; these are known as A.M.-settlement options. They do not trade on expiration day; the last trading day for A.M.-settlement index LEAPS is the previous day, the Thursday before expiration. If you intend to time closing a position at a profit, you need to determine the trading hours upon expiration to avoid an expensive mistake.

Most option investors are accustomed to being able to exercise or close options whenever they wish, between the time a position is opened up to expiration. This rule-allowing early exercise-refers to what are called "American style" options. Many index options, however, are traded using the "European-style" rules. Under that system, positions cannot be closed or sold before expiration. The advantage to European-style options is achieved when you employ spreads and straddles, in which one side of the transaction is protected by the other. If early exercise occurs in one-half of the position, as occurs with American-style options, that can ruin the overall strategy; or you have to use rolling techniques to avoid exercise. With European-style options, the entire position is protected from exercise until expiration. The major disadvantage is that, when you open a position and later decide it was a mistake, you cannot cut your losses by getting out early.

Index option strategies

The first and most obvious index LEAPS strategy is buying calls. For those interested in an index-wide investment, it is impractical to buy shares of each and every component; so the index LEAPS presents a sensible alternative. Because capital in the LEAPS is spread among all of the index components, the index will usually be less volatile than the individual stocks, so in that respect, the index option may contain lower market risk.

> **Strategy # 102 – Reduced market risk with index LEAPS.** *Use index LEAPS' lower volatility to reduce exposure, especially in uncovered short positions*

As with individual stock LEAPS, buying calls or puts on index LEAPS is going to involve a combination of time value and intrinsic value. Buyers are at a disadvantage because time value evaporates as expiration approaches. It is not enough for the index to move to offset lost time value; it needs to move enough points in the desired direction to (a) offset lost time value and (b) create profits in intrinsic value. Given the observation that index LEAPS are likely to be less volatile than the individual components, the index LEAPS buyer may be at a greater disadvantage than the individual stock LEAPS buyer.

You can "cover" the long LEAPS position by writing offsetting options against them. In the case of calls, you can sell higher-striking price, shorter-expiration term calls; in the case of puts, covering the long position will involve selling lower-striking price, shorter-expiration contracts. However, if the underlying premise of buying any options involves contingent purchase (in the case of buying calls or selling puts) or contingent sale (through selling calls or buying puts), you also need to recognize that the index option is not appropriate. Because settlement always takes place in cash, the index LEAPS is purely speculative. It can be used to hedge against portfolio positions, so that you will offset portfolio losses if the market falls. (For example, if you own many long positions in stocks, you may buy an index put; if the index falls, you profit from the put, which may offset losses in your individual stocks.)

> **Strategy # 103 – Index LEAPS for portfolio-wide insurance.** *Use index LEAPS to insure portfolios or mutual fund holdings when your portfolio or fund follows index movements closely*

The strategy of using index LEAPS to offset potential portfolio losses is questionable, given the more focused use you can make of individual stock LEAPS calls and puts. However, some investors prefer the speculative nature of index LEAPS.

You can also sell index LEAPS contracts, or combine a purchase and a sale to create one of many forms of combinations.

By combining the purchase and sale of index LEAPS positions, you may be able to create minimum-risk scenarios, or even to speculate boldly, accepting higher risks and gaining the chance for more profitable gains. Some investors employ index LEAPS as insurance when they have capital invested in mutual funds. If the fund tends to follow market directions as measured by a specific index, an index LEAPS put can provide downside protection in the event of a price drop. If the fund's value were to mimic the market, then the index LEAPS put investment makes sense. However, as with all long position insurance strategies, you will need to balance the cost against the term of protection. The longer the life of the option, the more you will pay for the insurance feature found in the put.

> **Strategy # 104 – Combinations with index LEAPS to reduce risk.** *Use straddles or spreads to profit from index LEAPS positions*

If you sell calls against the index for the same reason, you risk loss if that index rises. While the short position does not involve the same time value-related risks in index speculation, it does involve greater initial risk. Not knowing how high the index could rise, shorting it with a long-term short call could be dangerous. At the same time, you have less flexibility to offset the short position; index LEAPS settle in cash, not in stock. So you cannot cover a short position other than through offsetting long positions in the same index. This limitation reduces flexibility in the index LEAPS. Given your ability to utilize individual stock LEAPS contracts in numerous ways, including early exercise if desirable, will be more comforting for most investors.

One difficulty in using index LEAPS to insure your portfolio is in the selection of the best product. Your portfolio is going to include many dissimilar stocks and, if you own shares of a mutual fund, it will also have its own mix. So the likely price movement in your portfolio or in your mutual fund is not always going to be a close mix to any one index LEAPS. It is unlikely that your portfolio is designed to track movement in the S&P 500 or the DJIA, for example. So if you are going to use index LEAPS for portfolio insurance, you will need to find a close match. Compared to individual stock LEAPS, in which you have an exact match, you cannot achieve a precise form of insurance for most portfolio situations. So we have to accept the idea that insurance employing index LEAPS is going to be imperfect.

If you are concerned about the need for insurance, you may prefer to consider buying puts or selling covered calls on the individual stocks; buying puts; or if you think prices have run up beyond reasonable values, take the profits by selling stock. If you consider today's price a reasonable one, you can also sell a call and a put at the same striking price. This constitutes the combination of a contingent sale (with the short call) *and* a contingent purchase (with the short put). You have the ability to roll forward to avoid exercise in either position; you also create a form of insurance with the combined time value premium from selling both of these positions at the same time.

The strategy involving individual LEAPS provides a more focused form of insurance, and one that provides you with greater flexibility at the same time. The problem with index LEAPS contracts is that you cannot exercise them as a buyer, or even accept exercise as a seller; settlement is always in cash, so unlike the equity-minded investor using LEAPS for contingent portfolio changes, the index LEAPS investor is limited to a purely speculative position.

For the speculator, the index LEAPS contract may be a perfect vehicle. However, if you intend to use LEAPS options as part of a long-term strategy to build equity in your portfolio while creating cash flow as well, then it is best to stay with individual stock LEAPS and to avoid index LEAPS.

Because you cannot use equity positions to satisfy exercise of an index LEAPS short position, all short positions in index LEAPS are uncovered. (If you offset short positions with related long positions, you can limit these risks; however, you cannot create a regular stream of income using index LEAPS as you can with covered calls.) The great advantage to covered call writers owning stock is that the risk is minimal. Covered call writing on stock is, in fact, quite a conservative position, often creating double-digit returns. In previous chapters, we have demonstrated how time value works for the seller and against the buyer. The risk of the uncovered LEAPS short position-unlimited without owning stock-is substantial. The risk of the covered LEAPS short position is so small, and returns large enough, to make it one of the best strategies that can be used by equity investors. Now reviewing the same question with index LEAPS-going short and depending on ever-diminishing time value to create profits-you cannot escape the same risk as that faced by the uncovered call seller. In theory, the index could rise indefinitely by expiration date, so that your potential loss would be quite high.

These important considerations point out that the decision to use individual stock LEAPS or index LEAPS is a matter of risk tolerance. The index option is purely speculative and cannot be covered with long equity positions. Combinations can be created to offset risks, but those same strategies also limit potential gains. If you consider yourself a more conservative investor and you are interested in strengthening the growth and cash flow in your portfolio, the index LEAPS comes with severe limitations, and those cannot be overlooked.

LEAPS for long-term speculation

The speculator may use either individual stocks LEAPS or index LEAPS. The great advantage of either LEAPS venue over traditional options, is all a matter of time. Because you have far more time in the life of a LEAPS contract, speculation does not have to be limited to trading within a short period of time, as has been the case traditionally. Speculation has always been associated with day trading or, in an expanded version, with in-and-out strategies.

It is even fair to define traditional speculation as being as short-term as possible. Speculators want to get as much profit as quickly as they can, with the greatest leverage. When it comes to LEAPS contracts, that is not necessarily the best way to proceed, nor the most profitable.

Many of the strategies introduced and explained in previous chapters demonstrate how you can profit from LEAPS without holding an equity position. While emphasis has been on the concepts of contingent purchase and sale of securities, and on using LEAPS to maximize income while owning stock, the speculator can use the same ideas to maximize speculative income. For example, the simple contingent purchase makes a lot of sense for the speculator. The chronic problem associated with buying calls has been the struggle against declining time value. If you have to spend $700 to buy a single contract, you will need 7 points in the money just to break even. So buying options to speculate has always been high-risk.

In the case of the LEAPS contract, you can reduce or eliminate the risk while still holding the speculative potential for future gains. If you purchase a long-term LEAPS call, you have exposure to potential gains. That can translate to exercise at a lower price than current market value or, for most speculators, the chance to sell the call at a profit. The declining time value can be offset, often completely, by selling higher-striking price, earlier-expiration calls against the long position. This puts the idea of speculation on an entirely different plane.

> **Strategy # 105 – Offset long and short LEAPS calls for speculative upside gains.** Use the contingent purchase method employing long call and short positions, but for speculative gains with little or no net cost

Example: You purchase a call for 7, all time value. You have 34 months until expiration. During that time, you can sell higher-striking price, earlier-expiring calls and receive income upon sale. If you can accumulate 7 points or more in premium from selling a series of calls against your long-term long position, you recapture the entire investment. This is possible by letting short calls expire worthless, or trading out of positions at a profit and replacing them over the term of the long LEAPS call. By going through this exercise, you have long-term opportunity with little or no cost; and you are able to speculate without the risks usually associated with speculation. You can engage in the "covered" LEAPS strategy endlessly, limited only by available capital and, if applicable, limitations imposed on you by your brokerage firm.

The same strategy is applicable using puts. You purchase one LEAPS put with a relatively long term until expiration. You then sell a series of lower-striking price, earlier-expiring puts, eventually recapturing all or most of your long put investment. While earlier chapters demonstrated how these strategies could be used as part of a contingent purchase strategy, they work equally well if your strategy is to speculate only.

> **Strategy # 106 – Offset long and short LEAPS puts for speculative downside gains.** Use the contingent purchase method employing long put and short positions, but for speculative gains with little or no net cost

Can LEAPS speculators earn high profits? Using the covered LEAPS strategy for either calls or puts limits your potential income, since the main activity during the holding period involves recapturing the initial investment. The problem with offsetting short positions is that, if and when the underlying stock begins to move, you may end up needing to use the long position to satisfy either the short call or the short put upon exercise. The speculator looks for a specific type of opportunity, one in which the short position can be rolled to avoid exercise and eventually expires, and then the long position can be sold at a profit.

The covered LEAPS strategy has limitations. Lacking the component of contingent purchase or contingent sale, the simple speculation in LEAPS requires luck and timing as well as skill. Profits will be marginal in some cases; ideally, the goal in the covered position should be to recapture all or most of the investment cost, leaving a period in the later months when the investment will pay off. For example, if you buy a 32-month call for 7 and are able to recapture 6 points by selling calls over a 24-month period, you then face the possibility that the long call will become more profitable. With 8 months remaining until expiration, the net cost would be only $100 (7 points original purchase, minus 6 points gained from sales). This is where the speculator can make significant profits-when the net cost is low enough so that risk is close to nothing, but the potential for gain continues for several more months. In this case, it would be wise to cease writing short positions against the long LEAPS once investment has been recaptured, and wait out the stock's price movement.

The same idea applies using puts. If you are able to recapture your initial long investment and end up with a zero-cost basis, you can stop writing puts against the long position, and you end up with several months' opportunity period. If the underlying stock falls, the put gains in value and can be sold at a profit before expiration.

A third variation may involve a long straddle. You buy a call and a put with the same striking price and expiration. Normally, the cost of a long straddle-given the time value problem-makes it very difficult to realize a profit, unless the stock moves substantially. For example, if your LEAPS call and put together cost 15 points, you need that stock to move either up or down 15 points to break even, *before* you will realize a profit. However, you can follow the initial entry into the long position with a series of short sales, of both calls and puts. Whichever direction the stock moves during the holding period, you can roll forward and up (with calls) or forward and down (with puts) to avoid exercise, if necessary. If the stock trades within the out-of-the-money range (between striking prices of long and short positions on either side) then the short positions can be closed at a lower price, creating a profit, and then replaced with new short positions. They can also be allowed to expire worthless.

> **Strategy # 107 – The long straddle for no-cost speculative profits.** *Buy both call and put and then offset the cost by writing short calls above and short puts below, so that net cost is at or near zero; then wait for price movement in the stock in either direction for speculative profits*

Speculators enjoy as much flexibility using LEAPS options as those more interested in contingent purchase or sale, or those who simply want to use LEAPS to improve yield on their stock positions (covered call writers). The requirement in most situations is to stop offsetting long positions at a point that the initial cost is recovered, so that the potential for later gains can be realized without limitation. As long as short positions are open, speculators cannot realize gains from long positions. The purpose in writing options against the long positions is to reduce the net cost, making future speculative profits feasible.

Whether you employ index LEAPS contracts or individual stock LEAPS to speculate, the possibilities are interesting. It all depends on your risk tolerance and an understanding of how the market works. Using index LEAPS requires that you first know the rules and can distinguish the risks between individual and index contracts. As a LEAPS trader, you need to master terminology, trading rules, and strategies. Among the important strategies we have not yet brought up, is the all-important one of tax planning. By timing your trades, you can have a degree of control over when and how your LEAPS profits or losses are reported. This is the topic of the next chapter.

Chapter 14

Tax Planning:
Keeping it simple

The U.S. tax code is a complex and ever-changing document. Even the most basic tax return is subject to complications as soon as you begin to invest, even if you simply buy shares in a mutual fund or invest in a few stocks. When you evolve beyond and start buying and selling options, those complications are considerable-but not insurmountable.

As a smart rule of thumb, any investor who is confused by the rules or uncertain about tax questions, should hire a qualified tax expert to help. You can master the basics and figure out how to time your trades for the most part; but it also makes sense to review the tax rules periodically so that you will know what to expect when the forms are filled out.

Income taxes and LEAPS

LEAPS investors, like everyone else, need to plan ahead for their taxes. Federal tax rules apply to option investing with some important variations from the more traditional capital gains rules. Complicating this even further, state tax regulations vary and have to be researched individually.

Options gains and losses are treated as capital gains. So even when your option covers a stock position and is ultimately exercised, treatment of the stock trade and the option trade will be handled differently than if you simply sold the stock. Here is a brief summary of the federal tax rules:

1. *Buying options.* The determination of whether a profit or loss in a long position is short-term or long-term is decided by the holding period, the same as it is for straight stock purchase and sale.
2. *Expired short options.* If you hold a short option until it expires, the gain is treated as taxable in the year of expiration; however, it is always a short-term gain no matter how long the holding period.
3. *Writing covered calls.* The most complex rules apply to treatment of both stock capital gains or losses and treatment of options, when you use covered calls. A so-called "qualified covered write" is one written at-the-money or out-of-the-money. When you write such a call, it does not affect the holding period of the stock. Writing an unqualified covered call (one that is in-the-money) resets the stock's holding period to zero months; this presents a possible disadvantage for stockholders who have owned stock for less than the one-year period required to create a long-term gain. For example, if you have owned stock for 8 months, you normally have 4 months to go before a sale would be treated under long-term rules. Writing an unqualified option in that situation begins the clock running from zero for purposes of the stock's status. So if the call is exercised within one year from the time the unqualified call was written, the gain on stock would be treated as short-term. The definition of "qualified" is further defined based on the stock price and holding period. It is complex enough that you may need to consult with a professional tax expert. Before deciding on a specific LEAPS strategy, tax consequences should be kept in mind.

4. *Index option taxation.* The "rule" for treatment of U.S. stock index options is referred to as "mark to market." Combined gains and losses are netted together and the net difference is treated as 60% long-term and 40% short-term gain or loss. This includes contracts that are open at the end of the year; so the tax treatment is calculated as though you had closed the open position based on year-end price, and then repurchased at the same price (which becomes the basis for the following year's calculation).

5. *Year-end sale of stock.* You can sell stock at a loss position before the end of your tax year and claim the loss. However, you cannot purchase the stock or an equivalent position (such as an option) within 30 days of the sell-that means 30 days before or after the sell. If you do so, it negates the write-off of the stock loss. So, for example, if you want to sell 100 shares of stock at year-end to take a loss, but you want to repurchase shares after the new year, you have to wait at least 30 days or you cannot claim the loss. If you purchase a call within 30 days (either before or after) the sale of stock, that also washes the write-off. So year-end strategies have to be undertaken with an awareness of the limitations on timing, but both repurchase of stock and for the use of options. The only way around this rule would be to purchase a LEAPS call more than 30 days before you sell stock; and then wait at least 30 days after the sale to either exercise the call or repurchase the stock. If the stock were to rise in the first month of the new year, owning the LEAPS call would preserve your basis at the striking price.

6. *Exercise in hedged positions.* You may view offset long and short positions as protecting you against unexpected losses upon exercise. An exercised short position is simply satisfied with the offsetting long

position. However, there may also be tax ramifications. The exercise itself could create a constructive capital gain, and a taxable transaction. If your profits are marginal, they could be offset by the tax liability created by exercise.

In all matters regarding the tax planning and tax avoidance strategies for LEAPS, you should consult with an expert and incorporate the tax issues into your overall strategies.

LEAPS in qualified tax deferred accounts

Are you allowed to use LEAPS in portfolio strategies for your tax-deferred retirement accounts? Most brokers do allow you to use covered calls, or the purchase of puts for insurance. The majority accept LEAPS as well as shorter-term traditional listed options. Your broker may also require you to get special permission before LEAPS activity will be allowed in your tax-deferred account.

The more speculative types of option activities-buying calls or puts on speculation or creating hedges-will not be allowed in most cases. So if you want to use LEAPS, determine ahead of time what rules apply. Select a broker whose retirement account rules provide you with the highest possible level of flexibility and convenience.

As with your non-retirement account, every brokerage firm is required to pre-qualify you to trade in LEAPS. You will need to fill out paperwork in which you state that you understand the risks of LEAPS investing; the broker will send you a copy of the required prospectus, the OCC's "Characteristics and Risks of Standardized Options." Finally, the broker is required to allow you to trade options only after determining that you have the experience and knowledge of risks associated with the options market.

Tax strategies for LEAPS transactions

The 30-day year end rule prevents you from being able to claim a loss in one year and immediately reversing it in the next. If you sell and then re-purchase stock, for example, within 30 days, there is no tax benefit in the transaction.

You can use LEAPS options to dispose of stock but continue to control shares, and still comply with the law. Here is a strategy you can employ:

> ### Strategy # 108 – LEAPS call year-end purchase.
> *Buy one call per 100 shares at least 30 days before selling stock*

The 30-day wash rule applies, so this strategy has to be timed to observe that rule. Given the circumstances-in which you want to claim a loss this year but you do not want to permanently lose control of the stock-using the LEAPS call is a good solution. It creates a legitimate tax loss this year while replacing ownership with a variation of contingent purchase.

Example: You own 100 shares in a company that has lost $2,000 since purchase. You would like to take the loss this year; but you also want to remain invested, in the belief that the stock's value is going to rise in the future. Your original purchase price was $70 per share and the stock is currently worth $50. You have five weeks until the end of the year. On November 20, you buy one LEAPS 60 call and pay $800; the contract has 14 months until expiration. On December 26, you sell the 100 shares of stock and take the loss.

In this example, the LEAPS call is purchased more than 30 days before the stock is sold, so you have not violated the wash rule. Once the shares of stock have been sold, you have to wait at least 30 days before you can repurchase. If you buy the shares before the 30 days, you would not be allowed to claim the capital loss. So you cannot take any action until January 26 at the earliest.

By owning the LEAPS call, you continue to *control* 100 shares without owning it. And because you have observed the 30-day rule both before and after the sale, you are entitled to claim the loss on stock this year. If the stock were to soar in January, you would be in a position to benefit because you own a LEAPS call; so selling the stock and waiting 30 days does not place you at risk of missing the opportunity. If the stock remains in the same trading range or falls, you do not have to exercise the call (you have replaced outright ownership with contingent ownership).

What about the $800 you paid to buy the LEAPS call? Given that you have created a tax loss of $2,000 in the current year, you need to assess this cost on an after-tax basis. So if your effective tax rate (including federal *and* state rates) is 40% or higher, the cost of the LEAPS call is offset by tax savings. However, now that you own the call, you have a number of choices. You have 14 months until expiration (based on the example), so you could employ a covered LEAPS strategy to offset a portion of your cost. If the stock's value rises, you could ultimately exercise the call and return to your previous equity position (or revert to a covered call strategy using LEAPS calls).

In this example, we picked an option with 14 months because it will not have an excessive amount of time value premium, and also will not be likely to decline in time value over the next two months to a great degree. In other words, there is enough time remaining before expiration to minimize the deterioration of time value, but not so much time left that the premium is excessively high.

LEAPS options are not available on all stocks, so this strategy might not work well in every case. A similar move can be employed using traditional listed options with six to eight months to go until expiration. As long as you remember the 30-day rule (which applies both before and after the date you sell stock) you will be able to claim a legitimate deduction; continue to control 100 shares of stock; and decide later how to mitigate the cost of buying the call.

Taxes and short-term speculation

The tax rules for covered and hedged options are quite complex. Some tax reformers have suggested reforming the rules to create special tax rules relating to LEAPS trading. For example, the use of LEAPS options to provide downside protection while also limiting potential gains could be treated as a constructive sale of the stock. While this may or may not ever happen, as a LEAPS investor, you need to keep an eye on developing tax news and consult with your tax adviser to track any changes in these rules.

If a particular strategy-such as a collar, in which you buy a put and sell a call at the same time-were treated as a constructive receipt, you would be taxed as though you sold stock, even if you did not actually execute a sale. The intent of such a change would be to prevent investors from using the tax laws to claim losses while continuing to control shares, and from deferring taxes on gains to future years. A constructive sale would require, by definition, that you (a) have reduced or mitigated the downside risk and (b) at the same time, have limited future potential gains. A collar meets this definition. However, an argument could be made that by taxing LEAPS strategies, the entire matter is complicated beyond reason.

Until the rules have been changed, there is no point in worrying about how future LEAPS speculation may be affected. The speculator-especially one who does not own stock but limits activity to buying and selling contracts-is able to exert control over the *timing* of taxes. As a buyer, the speculator depends on option premium levels rising so that contracts can be sold at a profit. Given the ever-looming threat of time value decline, the buyer does not have great control over the timing; profits have to be taken if and when they become available. When it comes to claiming losses, though, LEAPS speculators have the same control that stockholders enjoy. You can decide to sell and take a loss before the end of the year if you need and want the loss in this year's tax return. However, if losses to date already exceed the maximum you are allowed to claim, it makes more sense to defer selling the LEAPS option until next year. The decision could be a matter of waiting a few days, from December 29 until January 3, for example.

When speculators open short positions, they have the same amount of flexibility. For example, if you sold a put a few months ago and it has declined in value, you can sell before the end of the year and report the gain; or you can defer the decision until January and put off the tax liability to the next year. The gain will be treated as a short-term gain, so there is no advantage to holding off closing a position in the hope of creating a more favorable long-term capital gain tax rate. The timing can be determined solely based on when you need to report a loss, or when you want to recognize a profit.

In all matters regarding taxes, the foremost consideration should be to follow a wise investment or speculation plan. It makes no sense to miss opportunities because the timing is poor for tax purposes. There is also no advantage in claiming a loss for tax purposes, even in the highest tax brackets. Even if your combined federal and state rate is 48%, your after-tax loss is still 52% of your investment. A profit-even with the requirement to pay taxes-is *always* preferable to a loss. So the investment consideration should always prevail in any strategy. As long as you are able to also accomplish a tax advantage, or defer a liability without additional risk, it makes sense to time your transactions with taxes in mind.

The point that investment decisions should always prevail may serve as part of a basic investing philosophy. Some additional ideas along these lines are offered in the next, and final chapter.

Chapter 15

Higher Profit Potential:
LEAPS in the big picture

If you have ever watched any of the popular financial television shows, you have probably noticed that they are scripted along a common format: They begin with a discussion of the fundamentals; followed by a few stock recommendations from guest experts; ending with a panel of talking heads trying to guess where "the Dow" will go in the next six months.

What is wrong with this picture? Although all of the experts profess that they believe in the fundamentals, the highlight of the show is prediction about the Dow Industrials, the best-known technical indicator. Even making specific recommendations for stock picks is questionable, because the reasons are not always provided. A viewer has no way to know whether the reasons for recommending a particular stock are sound or not.

This basic problem concerning investing affects every option trader; however, the problem that you face in picking option strategies is twofold. First, you have to pick appropriate stocks, given risk elements, growth potential, and capital limitations. Second, you have to decide which strategy is best for you. Not every strategy is going to achieve your goals. And it may easily occur that while you are in the middle of executing one strategy, market forces may compel you to switch to another.

Can you use LEAPS in combination with traditional investing methods? Or do you need to take a new look at the underlying premise of how to pick stocks, build wealth, and manage market risks? Given the history of the market from the mid-1990s until today, it makes sense to question traditional assumptions. The market has gone through the day trading craze, survived the Enron scandal, and experienced a turnaround from a robust economy to a weakened one. The combination of scandals and cyclical change made the decade one of the most difficult in stock market history. Even the time-honored audited financial statement is now viewed with cynicism and suspicion, following the Arthur Andersen scandal. As a LEAPS investor, you cannot afford to go along with the majority in your approach to the market. You need to ignore the common, but often wrong beliefs, and face the market with a new point of view.

Traditional versus creative investing

How do you need to alter your strategies and your point of view about the market? Option investors need to act as contrarians in every respect, be able to anticipate market movements in either direction, and position themselves to maximize profits. This requires analysis of possible outcomes, acceptance of limited risks, and a thorough understanding of what causes values to rise and fall-not only in option contracts, but also in stocks.

The traditional method of investing has been to buy shares of stock in companies that are well known, trusted, and dependable; to hold those shares for the long term to create slow but steady growth; and to expand a portfolio through diversified direct investment, or with a combination of directly owned stocks, money market instruments, and shares of mutual funds.

There is nothing wrong with the traditional approach, as long as the market continues to move in the desired direction. We know now that many of the most respected mutual funds invested heavily in stocks like Enron and WorldCom, to the detriment of their shareholders. Why didn't the professional managers of those funds recognize the emerging problems? The traditional approach works well when the market is strong and healthy; but when the economy goes through its downward cycle, the traditional approach leaves much to be desired.

This is where you as a LEAPS investor can out-perform the average investor. Many strategies introduced in this book-contingent purchase and covered call writing using time value-rich contracts, for example-are excellent strategies for weak or uncertain markets. Because you can employ either LEAPS calls or puts in your strategies for a variety of reasons, you can take advantage of market movement in either direction. Some strategies even work best when the stock's price is not moving at all. Furthermore, you can design strategies not only to profit from time value decline or changes in intrinsic premium value; you can also protect stock positions by using LEAPS for insurance. So for the LEAPS investor, the strategic possibilities are varied and can be applied in many different situations.

Most stockholders have a fairly limited view of the market, and their strategic possibilities are quite limited. Those who buy stock and wait for its value to rise-without adding any option strategies into the mix-can only wait out a decline and hope a stock's value rebounds. They may average down, buying more shares to reduce average cost, and that is about the only strategy available to the traditional stock investor. Timing of purchase and sale, diversification among different stocks, and dollar cost averaging are the primary strategies for long-position stockholders. In fact, with a limited exposure to the market, dollar cost averaging is considered to be a sophisticated strategy. Anyone who has studied the many potential uses of LEAPS knows that the alternatives to dollar cost averaging are far better.

By the same argument, a bearish stock investor with better than average sophistication would traditionally sell stock short. Considering the risks involved as well as the costs, why not use LEAPS long puts (or short calls, or a combination of the two) to achieve the same outcome? It simply makes more sense to leverage capital and reduce exposure to risk, using LEAPS in place of the more traditional methods.

Even the purchase of shares, a traditional investing method, is too risky in a volatile market. The various forms of contingent purchase reduce investment exposure and risk, while allowing you to leverage your capital. Because LEAPS survive up to three years, many strategies are available that listed option investors cannot apply in a practical many, simply due to lack of adequate time. Going long in a contingent purchase plan, the luxury of time enables you to reduce or even eliminate the investment cost by writing short contracts against the long call or put position.

LEAPS investors have the opportunity to take a more creative approach to investing. The long-term goals may be identical to those of traditional investors. You want to accumulate wealth, expand capital value, reduce market risk, and protect profits. All of those goals can be reached using strategically timed LEAPS calls and puts. You can use contingent purchase and sale strategies, insurance, covered positions to reduce cost, and the very profitable covered call strategy, all to augment cash flow and income, while discounting basis and protecting paper profits. Because time value in LEAPS calls is richer than in the shorter-term listed option, covered call writing with LEAPS can be highly profitable. The combined short straddle is one of the most profitable LEAPS strategies. If you own 100 shares of stock that has appreciated in value, the simultaneous sale of a covered call and a put-at the same striking price and with the same expiration date-is a powerful way to profit in the LEAPS market. We demonstrated in previous chapters how the combined covered call and naked put, essentially a contingent sale (covered call) *and* contingent purchase (uncovered put) work together to produce a substantial return on the stock. Well positioned short straddles can return 30% or more on your original investment; and depending on the direction the stock moves after the short position is opened, you can roll forward and up (for the3 call) or forward and down (for the put) to avoid exercise while continuing to create net credits.

A variation of this idea is to create a 5-point spread. The covered call can be written five points above current value of the stock; and the uncovered put can be written five points below. Then the same exercise avoidance strategies can be used depending on the direction the stock moves. While premium income is lower with the spread than when using the straddle, it is far easier to avoid exercise due to the overall 10-point spread between striking prices of the two LEAPS positions.

The spread can also be created after another position has already been opened. For example, an initial covered call and be expanded into a spread if the lower put's premium becomes rich after the initial position has been opened.

So the LEAPS investor is not limited to the traditional buy-and-wait strategy well known to the stockholder. At the same time, the LEAPS investor does not have to limit market activity to pure speculation. The reputation of options is that they are high-risk and speculative only, and a serious investor will not be interested in exposing their capital to the options market. As we have demonstrated with the dozens of strategies you can employ, LEAPS investing can be used to create an advantage over traditional methods; to insure paper profits; and to create a steady stream of cash flow. All of this is possible while also pursuing the same long-term equity goals that most investors share.

New strategies to address new problems

The opportunities presented with the use of LEAPS go well beyond mere speculation. Using LEAPS on individual stocks provides the means to protect equity positions, create short-term income, leverage capital and, on a larger scale, to take an entirely new approach to investing.

Your goal is to identify ways to create growth and income, while keeping risks to a minimum. Knowing that opportunity and risk are unavoidably associated with one another, it is impossible to produce consistently high yields without an associated risk. The solution is to identify *acceptable* forms of risk; with LEAPS, you can create short-term income with acceptable risks.

Example: The LEAPS covered call is exceptionally appealing because time value is far higher than it can ever be with shorter-term listed options. So writing long-term covered calls against long stock positions provides downside protection by reducing your basis in stock; you continue to receive dividends; you are paid cash for selling calls; and you can trade forward and up to avoid exercise, delay exercise, or "buy" additional striking price points. So what are the risks?

The primary risk to covered calls is lost opportunity risk. In those cases where the underlying stock's value rises quickly and far above striking price, you may experience exercise before you even have the chance to roll out of the position and replace it. Whenever you enter a covered call position, the possibility of exercise has to be accepted. So the lost opportunity is the profit you could have earned if you had not sold the call; or by waiting, the profits you could have protected by selling a higher striking price LEAPS call.

Option traders dealing with covered calls accept lost opportunity risk, recognizing that they can produce consistent double-digit returns with virtually no other additional risks. So the lost opportunity risk is acceptable. In those few instances where a sudden price run-up causes exercise, the LEAPS writer accepts the double-digit return consisting of capital gains on stock, dividend income, and call premium, in exchange for losing the potential future returns from higher stock market prices.

So LEAPS traders learn to adopt a different approach to investing-one in which contingent purchase and sale take the place of actual purchase and sale. As a LEAPS trader, you recognize the advantage of creating scenarios in which one of several outcomes are possible, but all are desirable. Covered calls produce returns if the LEAPS call expires worthless; if it is exercised; if you roll forward and up; or if you end up buying to close at a lower price than the original sale price. The contingent sale involved with covered call writing is desirable, because in the event of exercise, you will profit as long as your original basis is lower than the striking price.

The same different point of view applies to the various forms of contingent purchase. Whether you employ long LEAPS calls or short LEAPS puts, the various strategies enable you to expose yourself to the potential for purchase of shares at what you consider a reasonable price. With LEAPS calls, you have to pay for the right to control 100 shares; with LEAPS puts, you receive money and give up the control to someone else. In either case, the very idea of *contingent* purchase is a different approach to the market. Given the uncertainty and volatility of the market as a whole since the new millennium, LEAPS contingent purchase appears a more reasonable strategy than the commitment of a large block of capital-even in the event that a stock's value falls. How many investors would have experienced smaller losses buying LEAPS calls on Enron rather than buying hundreds of shares?

In the more uncertain modern stock market, in which potential for fast profits and fast losses is a reality, investors need to protect their capital in new ways. Because that uncertainty extends by necessity beyond the forces of market supply and demand or economic strength, investors have to be wary of a complex series of forces at work. These include individual executives in publicly listed companies, passive regulators, so-called "independent" auditing firms, and Wall Street analysts. The expensive lessons of the Enron age make LEAPS a viable alternative to the traditional idea of buying stock, and holding it for the long term.

Of course, even with thorough fundamental analysis and a leverage contingent purchase strategy in play, it remains possible to end up invested in companies whose stock does not perform well. Every experienced investor accepts market risk as a reality, and recognizes that no level of analysis is going to be thorough enough to ensure success. So even the astute LEAPS investor needs to diversify among stocks and industries, and to sell to cut losses when circumstances change unexpectedly. The sound investing philosophy of accepting but minimizing losses while seeking to beat the averages by making smart choices based on sound judgment, continues to apply.

LEAPS investors, as contrarians, need to constantly evaluate the possible outcomes in both LEAPS and equity positions. The use of LEAPS to hedge other positions-whether to create income (as with LEAPS covered call writing) or to protect paper profits (via the purchase of LEAPS puts), the process of trading in LEAPS requires a higher level of monitoring that that required for traditional long-position equity investors. Because you deal so much with timing of decisions, you have to be prepared to take advantage of momentary changes in value of LEAPS contracts. If a stock's movement takes the short LEAPS call or put in the money, you may need to roll out of the position immediately to avoid exercise; or you may evaluate the potential and decide to take no action. In either case, you should be able to monitor your positions each day to ensure that the decisions are yours and not thrust upon you by someone else.

Dealing with the new forms of risk

LEAPS investors generally understand the well-known forms of market risk. However, like all investors, you now have to deal with new forms of risk that are derived from a new market environment. With the scandals and huge market losses associated with the Enron years, you now face the risks of conflict of interest on the part of accounting firms, Wall Street analysts, and corporate executives.

These new risks may be at least partially eliminated by new, tough laws and by stricter exchange rules. In 2002, the Sarbanes-Oxley Act was passed, providing both civil and criminal penalties for executives; new rules governing accounting firms and analysts; and providing a large increase in the SEC budget. For those investors who lost money, these changes come too late; however, they are designed to prevent future abuses. The degree to which this new law actually has that effect, remains to be seen.

How, then, should LEAPS traders deal with the new risks? Some suggestions:

1. *Accounting risk:* The Arthur Andersen story shows how fragile the whole system was, and how little the problem was recognized until it was too late. Investors had always relied completely on the independence of the outside audit, and on the reputation of the accounting industry. That has all changed.

Today, you can reduce the new accounting risk by studying how corporations deal with their accounting firms. Those firms continue to operate with their previous conflicts of interest, providing audit and non-audit services for the same clients. The new law has been largely ineffective in preventing that conflict, and the accounting industry has not taken a lead in changing their own environment. So investors have to look to corporate leadership. Those listed companies who voluntarily use different firms for audit and non-audit work-a simple solution-impose reform on the accounting industry while demonstrating that they want to avoid the accounting conflicts that have caused so many problems in the past. In the selection of stocks for potential LEAPS activity, identify those corporations that exhibit leadership and exceptional corporate governance by separating the various functions for which they hire outside accounting firms.

2. *Corporate executive risk:* Many of the problems experienced in the Enron age involved individual executives. Clearly, the incentive compensation plans provided to some executives were too tempting to resist. As long as those forms of compensation-bonuses and stock options-were based on profitability and maintenance of the stock's market value, the executives had motivation to falsify or exaggerate the books. So in evaluating companies for possible LEAPS activity, examine disclosure about executive compensation. Seek companies whose compensation packages do not provide incentives that could harm stockholders.

3. *Analyst risk:* Most LEAPS traders should be performing their own, independent analysis or utilizing the services of a professional subscription service. Both ValueLine and S&P provide such basic services, and some analytical subscriptions or firms go beyond the basic fundamental and technical analysis of stocks and options. Whether you use a private analytical service or a subscription such as ValueLine or S&P, you should not depend on advice from analysts working in one of the Wall Street firms. Specifically, you should avoid any analyst whose firm also provides investment banking

services. Even though some efforts have been made to remove conflicts of interest, at least in appearance, two points should be kept in mind. First, the Wall Street firms do not necessarily want to comply any more than they are forced to. Second, you should not require the services of a Wall Street firm. As a LEAPS investor, you are better served working alone or using a more objective subscription service.

Beyond these new forms of risk, you continue to face the better understood risks that every investor has to deal with: market risk (price); diversification risk; liquidity risk; and economic risk. While these risks are unavoidable, the entire purpose of using LEAPS is to mitigate or eliminate much of the risk element. For example, using LEAPS puts for insurance offsets the traditional risk of losing paper profits. And any LEAPS strategy that produces short-term income also discounts your long position basis, further reducing investment risk.

By using limited capital to enter into contingent purchase strategies by buying LEAPS calls, you leverage capital while also diversifying your contingent holdings. You will be most interested in pursuing stocks that rise in value after you purchase a LEAPS call, of course. The overall strategic approach to buying stocks-while reducing basis as well-is a sensible way to move capital into the market while managing risk. The basic plan that incorporates the use of LEAPS can be summarizes in the following steps, the details of which were explained in detail in previous chapters:

1. *The contingent purchase long or short position:* The overall approach begins with the purchase of a LEAPS call or the sale of a LEAPS put. Either of these represent a contingent purchase. The difference involves the direction of the flow of cash and control over the decision to exercise.

2. *The offset of cost with "covered" LEAPS calls.* If you employ the long call contingent purchase strategy, you can reduce the initial investment cost by selling shorter-expiring, higher-striking price calls against the long LEAPS call. As long as you are able to roll forward and up, this strategy works to recapture long premium; in the event of exercise, the initial strategy is replaced with the offset between long and short calls.

3. *Exercise of the long call to acquire stock below market value.* The contingent purchase using long LEAPS calls may have several possible outcomes. The most desirable is the ultimate exercise of the call to acquire 100 shares of stock below current market value. The difference between basis and current market value protects your position. If market value were to fall after exercise, your basis will remain below market value to the extent of the offset.

4. *Conversion to a covered call strategy.* Once you have purchased shares of stock, you are free to convert from contingent purchase to contingent sale. By selling covered calls, you produce short-term income-potentially a high percentage of your basis in the stock due to time value premium-and through rolling techniques, you can avoid or defer exercise.

5. *Expansion to the short spread contingent purchase/sale.* To produce maximum income, you can combine contingent sale with contingent purchase. By selling a covered call *and* an uncovered put, it is possible to produce immediate double-digit income based on your initial net purchase price of stock. Either the short call or the short put can later be rolled forward and up (for the call) or down (for the put) to avoid exercise and buy more striking price points. By rolling forward, it is also reasonable to offset costs or even increase net income through LEAPS trading.

So by combining a series of strategies-contingent purchase, exercise of long calls, contingent sale, accepting exercise of short puts, rolling forward to avoid exercise, and combining contingent purchase and sale in a short spread or short straddle-you will be able to exert greater control over your portfolio. There are two phases to this control.

1. *Control before purchase of stock.* The entire concept of contingent purchase is based on the premise that it makes more sense to control stock than to risk capital buying shares. If the stock performs well, a contingent purchase can be converted to an actual purchase.
2. *Control after purchase of stock.* Once you own stock, you naturally hope that its market value will grow over a period of years. You protect your initial basis in stock as well as any paper profits through several LEAPS strategies. These include contingent sale achieved with covered call writing involving LEAPS calls; contingent purchase of additional shares using long LEAPS puts; buying LEAPS puts to provide insurance of long-position paper profits; and combinations of strategies to reduce risk while recapturing cash invested.

As part of an overall strategy, you may view any premium income from the sale of LEAPS as a reduction of your basis in the stock. In fact, tracking your LEAPS activity should involve the calculation of profits and losses under one of two methods. First is return when you do not own shares of stock; for example, you may purchase a LEAPS call for 7 and six months later sell it for a net of 9. Your profit in this example is $200, or 28.6% (annualized out to 57.2% based on a six-month holding period).

Second is a calculation of return on stock investment; this should always be based on your initial purchase price. The discount you achieve by selling covered calls should be tracked as a percentage of original cost of the stock. In this way, subsequent profits or losses will be based on the same initial cost, rather than distorted by ever-changing basis in stock.

The critical need for fundamental analysis

A final important reminder: even with the advantages you gain from using LEAPS, you cannot afford to ignore the importance of fundamental analysis. Even though LEAPS enable you to make strategic use of contingent purchase of stocks, the selection itself should be based on sound principles. The value investing concept has to be based on sustainable growth, strong competitive stance, working capital and capitalization trends, and effectiveness of corporate governance. If we have learned anything from the Enron scandal, it is that analysis and investigation are the keys to successful investing.

Many option investors, especially those interesting in covered call writing, are attracted to stocks whose LEAPS calls have the richest premium. So a very popular way to enter the market is to purchase shares and sell calls at the same time. However, if the reason for buying shares was to profit from selling covered calls, an important question was left out: Why is the call premium on this stock richer than most others? In applying fundamental analysis to the question, you might discover that there are reasons for the unusual relationship between market price of stock and its related LEAPS calls.

For a variety of reasons, it may be that the stock's market price is inflated as well. This means that a correction is likely. So you could lose equity value that more than offsets the call premium you received. Many inexperienced option investors applying the approach have ended up with a portfolio full of stocks whose current market value is below their original basis. Even though LEAPS strategies enable you to protect your positions, it only works if the stocks you select are strong to begin with, based on a study of the fundamental trends. Even when using contingent purchase, you should limit your exposure to stocks you consider to be strong, as a basic premise and as a starting point.

LEAPS do not answer every question, and they are not a fix-all for the depressed portfolio. For example, it makes no sense to sell a covered call as a "repair strategy" when your stock's original basis is higher than the striking price. That programs in a loss in the event of exercise. That loss may be discounted by the call premium, but what is the point of programming in a loss. In this situation, you may consider selling the stock and putting your losses. The only alternative that makes sense is found in which the premium you would receive from selling a covered call will offset the difference between current value and original basis.

Example: You bought 100 shares of stock at $41 and today that stock is selling for $35 per share. A 30-month LEAPS call is currently valued at 8. By selling that call, you will effectively reduce your initial investment basis from $41 per share down to $33, two points below striking price. In the event of exercise, you would recover your original investment (before considering the trading costs involved). While this strategy requires you to tie up capital for 30 months, it may be preferable to simply holding the stock indefinitely and hoping for a rebound. In subsequent months, the call may be closed at a profit, rolled forward and up, or held until expiration. This approach is one way to offset paper losses, but it is not as desirable as having to protect a paper profit.

By careful selection of stock, you minimize the risk of paper losses. You can never eliminate it entirely; you can only beat the averages by applying sound principles for picking stocks. That should include a study of the fundamentals of the stock, and not merely the selection of the richest option premiums available. To combine profit potential with wisdom, you need to constantly evaluate risk in its many forms, and select risks that you believe are reasonable. Every investor should know that market risk is unavoidable. Stocks may fall in price, and even the most detailed analysis cannot avoid this from occurring at times. Lost opportunity risk is usually acceptable to LEAPS investors, because you know that the income you earn from selling covered calls is likely to be greater overall than the occasional lost profit.

In the broad view, using LEAPS to protect paper profits, contingent purchase in place of outright capital commit-ment, and covered call writing to create income and reduce basis, all make sense as tools for managing your portfolio. As a sensible series of strategies, it is wise to keep one eye on risk while continuing to seek out advantages using LEAPS calls and puts. No matter how the market in a particular stock changes, there is an appropriate LEAPS strategy to avoid loss while enhancing profit.

Glossary

American-style LEAPS   a LEAPS contract that can be exercised prior to expiration at any time.

annualized yield   the yield that is earned if an investment is held for exactly one year, computed by (a) dividing the holding period by the number of months held, and (b) multiplying the result by 12.

at the money   condition when the underlying stock's current market value is at the striking price of the LEAPS option.

bear spread   a spread designed to produce profits if and when the underlying stock's market value falls.

bull spread   a spread designed to produce profits if and when the underlying stock's market value rises.

call   a LEAPS option providing the buyer with the right to purchase 100 shares of the underlying stock at the fixed striking price, by or before expiration date.

closing purchase transaction   a transaction to buy a LEAPS contract, that closes a previously sold short position.

closing sale transaction   a transaction to sell a LEAPS contract, that closes a previously purchased long position.

combination   any simultaneous trade in options with non-identical terms and on the same underlying stock.

contingent purchase   a strategy in which a LEAPS call is purchased or a LEAPS put is sold, in which exercise would result in the acquisition of 100 shares of the underlying stock.

contingent sale   a strategy in which a LEAPS call is sold or a LEAPS put is purchased, in which exercise would result in the sale of 100 shares of the underlying stock.

contract   a single LEAPS option, providing the buyer and obligating the seller to buy (call) or to sell (put) 100 shares of the underlying stock.

covered call   a LEAPS call sold when the seller also owns 100 shares of the underlying stock. The stock provides cover in the event of exercise.

deep in or **out**   a condition in which the underlying stock's current market value is more than five points from the LEAPS option's striking price. For calls, when the stock is five or more points above striking price, the condition is deep in; when the stock's market value is five or more points below striking price of the LEAPS call, it is deep out. The condition is reversed for LEAPS puts (when the stock is lower than striking price, the condition is deep in; when the stock is higher than the LEAPS put's striking price, it is deep out).

dollar cost averaging   a technique for acquiring shares of stock in increments. As a stock's market price falls, average basis will always be higher than current market value; as the stock rises, average basis will always be lower than current market value. DCA may be applied using a specific number of shares or a fixed dollar value.

downside protection   a benefit to using LEAPS that protects paper profits. The two most popular methods are selling covered calls (which discounts the basis) or buying LEAPS puts, which insures paper profits in the event the underlying stock's market value declines below the put's striking price.

European-style option   a LEAPS option that cannot be exercised early. Exercise is permitted only during a period immediate4ly before expiration, usually the Thursday before a Friday expiration date or the expiration date itself. This rule applies to many index LEAPS.

exercise   a LEAPS buyer's decision to call 100 shares from the buyer at the fixed striking price, or to put 100 shares to the seller at the fixed striking price.

hedge   any strategy involving the use of LEAPS contracts to protect, offset, or reduce the risk in another position. The second position may involve other LEAPS or long or short stock holdings.

in the money   a condition in which the current market value of stock is higher than a LEAPS call's striking price, or lower than a LEAPS put's striking price.

intrinsic value   the portion of a LEAPS premium represented by the number of points the stock is in the money. For example, a 30 LEAPS call worth 5 points when the stock is at $32 per share consists of two points intrinsic value and three points time value. A 40 LEAPS put worth 7 points when the stock is at $24 per share consists of six points intrinsic value and one point time value.

LEAPS   Long-term Equity AnticiPation Securities, option contracts with expiration terms up to three years.

leverage   the use of capital to control greater values. For example, a $10,000 investment may be used to purchased 200 shares of a $50 stock; or leveraged to control 10 LEAPS contracts vclued at $1,000 each.

long position   an open position initiated by the purchase of stock or a LEAPS contract.

opening purchase transaction   an opening transaction (a 'buy') involving the purchase of stock or a LEAPS contract.

opening sale transaction   an opening transaction (a 'sell') involving the sale of stock or a LEAPS contract.

option   a contract providing the buyer the right to buy 100 shares of a specific underlying stock (a call) or to sell 100 shares (a put); and obligating the seller to sell 100 shares (a call) or to accept 100 shares (a put) in the event of exercise, and at a fixed striking price per share.

out of the money   a condition in which the current market value of stock is lower than the striking price of a LEAPS call, or higher than the striking price of a LEAPS put.

premium   the dollar value received by a seller or paid by a purchase of a LEAPS option. Premium values are expressed in numeric form; for example, a premium of 3 means the current premium is worth $300.00.

put   a LEAPS option providing the buyer with the right to sell 100 shares of the underlying stock at the fixed striking price, by or before expiration date.

ratio write   selling LEAPS calls in a ratio other than one contract per 100 shares. The ratio may be less than 1 to 1 or more than 1 to 1, depending on the purpose for employing the ratio write.

return if exercised   the overall return in a LEAPS covered call strategy, that will be realized if and when the buyer exercised the short call. The return includes capital gains on stock, dividend income, and LEAPS premium received.

return if unchanged   the overall return in a LEAPS covered call strategy, that will be realized if the short call expires worthless. The return should be expressed as a percentage of the option premium to the basis in stock.

rolling   a technique employed by LEAPS writers to avoid or defer exercise. Rolling forward at the same striking price produces a new credit to the seller, because additional time value will be received for the later-expiring position. A call writer may also roll forward and up, deferring the expiration and extending the striking price upward to reposition stock out of the money. A put writer may roll forward and down to extend expiration and to reposition stock out of the money.

short position   an open position initiated by the sale of stock or a LEAPS contract.

spread   a strategy in which LEAPS options are purchased and sold on the same underlying stock. The two sides will contain different striking prices, different expiration dates, or both.

straddle   a strategy in which LEAPS options are purchased and sold on the same underlying stock, involving the same number of calls and puts with the same striking price and expiration dates.

striking price   the contractual fixed price at which any LEAPS option may be exercised, regardless of the market value of the stock at the time of exercise.

terms   the conditions and characteristics unique to a LEAPS option. These are striking price, expiration month and year, type of contract (call or put) and the underlying stock.

time value   the portion of option premium related specifically to time, above any intrinsic value. For example, if the underlying stock is at $32 per share and a 30 call is worth 35, it contains three points of time value and two points of intrinsic value. Any 30 puts on the same stock would consist entirely of time value; because those LEAPS puts are out of the money, there is no intrinsic value in the premium.

uncovered option   also called a naked option, a short position not covered by stock.

underlying stock   the stock unique to each LEAPS option.

writer   alternate term for a seller of a LEAPS option.

Index of Strategies

Alphabetical Listing of Strategies

General Index

Michael C. Thomsett is author of 60 books for investors
and business managers. His best-selling "Getting Started in
Options" (John Wiley & Sons) has sold over 180,000 copies.
Thomsett has also written books with Dearborn, Amacom,
and many other publishers; and has worked on many
projects with Marketplace Books, Inc. He lives in Port
Townsend, Washington.